CROSSROADS
OF
DEATH

CROSSROADS OF DEATH

THE STORY OF
THE MALMÉDY MASSACRE
AND TRIAL

JAMES J. WEINGARTNER

UNIVERSITY OF
CALIFORNIA PRESS
Berkeley
Los Angeles
London

University of California Press
Berkeley and Los Angeles, California

University of California Press, Ltd.
London, England

Copyright © 1979 by
The Regents of the University of California

ISBN 0-520-03623-9
Library of Congress Catalog Card Number: 77-91771
Printed in the United States of America

1 2 3 4 5 6 7 8 9

For those who suffered

CONTENTS

Note on Names   ix

Acknowledgments   xi

Introduction   1

   I. THE WAY OF THE WAFFEN-SS   4

  II. LIVES FOR THE FÜHRER   20

 III. DASH FOR THE MEUSE   41

 IV. MANHUNT   65

  V. JUSTICE AT DACHAU—PRELIMINARIES AND PROSECUTION   95

 VI. JUSTICE AT DACHAU—DEFENSE AND JUDGMENT   121

 VII. CONFLICT AND CONTROVERSY   166

VIII. McCARTHY AND FREEDOM   196

 IX. HINDSIGHT AND HISTORY   239

Bibliography   265

Index   267

Maps

1. Kampfgruppe Peiper's Operational Area,
   December 16-24, 1944   48

2. The Baugnez Crossroads   52

Plates   (following page 146)

NOTE ON NAMES

The murder of Jochen Peiper in the summer of 1976 has made the author acutely conscious of the continued sensitivity of the issues addressed in this book. Pseudonyms have therefore been used in instances where the revelation of actual names might result in harm or needless distress for surviving participants or their families. The use of pseudonyms is limited to lesser figures in the Malmédy affair and in no way impedes the understanding of these events. Pseudonyms will be marked with an asterisk when introduced in the text.

ACKNOWLEDGMENTS

Much of whatever merit this book possesses is due to the efforts of a multitude of individuals who in many ways assisted the author. The family of the late Willis M. Everett, Jr. made available personal papers, which were invaluable to the completion of the study, and proved most gracious hosts. Col. Burton F. Ellis gave generously of his time and knowledge of the Malmédy case. Ambassador John Eisenhower, Gen. Hal McCown, Atty. Benjamin Narvid, and Dr. William R. Perl rendered valuable assistance. Robert Wolfe, John Mendelsohn, and others of the staff of the Modern Military Branch, U.S. National Archives, as well as the staff of the Federal Record Center, Suitland, Maryland, functioned with efficiency in identifying vital research materials. Important documents were supplied by the Berlin Document Center and the Wisconsin State Historical Society, as well as the Franklin D. Roosevelt and Harry S. Truman libraries. Relevant film footage was viewed with the assistance of Dominick J. Sparaco of the U.S. Army Film Depository, Tobyhanna, Pennsylvania. Diane Clements produced maps on short notice, and Alan Chazanow provided copies of published materials which were difficult for me to secure. Alain Hénon and Susan Welling of the University of California Press offered much-appreciated editorial advice and encouragement.

Special note must be made of the information supplied to the author by the late Jochen Peiper. Peiper was distrustful of strangers, but with the help of Willis M. Everett III a lengthy correspondence was established which evolved into plans for a personal interview. Shortly before the interview was to take place, Peiper was murdered in a night attack on his home. Nothing could fully substitute for a face-to-face meeting with this remarkable man, but the author remembers with gratitude the aid of Dr. Ernst Klink of the Militärgeschichtliches Forschungsamt in Freiburg im Breisgau who expressed himself as a scholar and as a friend of Jochen Peiper.

Thanks are also due the Graduate School of Southern Illinois University at Edwardsville for having named the author University Research Scholar for 1974-1975. The freedom and financial resources that accompanied this honor greatly facilitated the completion of the study.

Finally, all other supportive efforts are far overshadowed by those of the author's wife who typed, criticized, encouraged, and corrected over a period of many months to the great benefit of the final product. So brief a statement does not do justice to her role, but she knows that I know.

Gratitude is owed to many for their parts in the making of the present book, but responsibility for factual errors and interpretive flaws is the author's alone.

INTRODUCTION

"There is nothing that any of us can recall in recorded history that approaches the unwarranted type of mass slaughter that occurred at Malmédy. . . ."[1] So spoke a United States senator notable neither for his honesty nor his erudition. He was referring to the killing of over seventy American prisoners of war at a road junction a few kilometers southeast of the Belgian town of Malmédy by troops of the German First SS Panzer Division during World War II's "Battle of the Bulge." The incident had come to be known as the "Malmédy Massacre" and had entered the consciousness of the American people as an example of Axis barbarity alongside the bombing of Pearl Harbor and the Bataan "death march." In the context of a war that saw tens of thousands of civilians killed and mutilated in single bombing raids and millions slaughtered in extermination camps, the Malmédy Massacre would appear to have been a wicked act of very modest proportions. But it took place at a time that was militarily crucial for the U.S. Army. American forces were falling back before the German onslaught in the Ardennes, a particularly unsettling experience in that the Wehrmacht had been widely believed incapable of a major offensive in the West so late in the war. News of the massacre acted as a stimulant to flagging American resistance, and it was widely circulated. American troops would be less likely to surrender to

1. *Malmedy Massacre Investigation. Hearings Before a Subcommittee of the Committee on Armed Services, United States Senate Pursuant to S. Res. 42*, hereafter MMIH (Washington, 1949), p. 8.

1

an enemy whose willingness to respect the right to life of prisoners of war was highly suspect. On the home front, the atrocity converted discouragement to outrage, the latter, an altogether more desirable sentiment for a people at war.

The apparent perpetrators of the crime were soldiers of the Waffen-SS, the battlefield component of Heinrich Himmler's Schutzstaffel (SS). As reports of the Malmédy Massacre reached the air waves and press, they impinged upon the highly complex debates in progress within the U.S. government concerning guidelines for a great postwar trial of Nazi leaders and organizations. The War Department was uncertain as to whether SS military units should be included in an indictment of the Nazi Schutzstaffel. Malmédy settled the question. The Waffen-SS deserved inclusion.[2]

In spite of the fact, therefore, that the killing of prisoners of war was hardly a novelty and was a crime, moreover, of which the Germans were not uniquely guilty, the Malmédy Massacre assumed an importance that it did not fully deserve. Its propaganda value and its role in justifying an indictment of the Waffen-SS had been linked to the stark horror of the murder scene as described by survivors. American prisoners of war had been assembled in a pasture and deliberately mowed down by machine-gun and small arms fire. Waffen-SS troops had then walked among the bodies shooting and clubbing those who seemed still alive; motorized soldiers passing on the road had repeatedly and laughingly raked the field with fire. Photographs of American Graves Registration personnel gathering the crumpled remains of the murdered GIs were published widely. Although a war crime of limited physical proportions, it was a particularly revolting one and seemed to capture the essence of the Nazi evil. The symbolic significance of the incident could only be enhanced by the fact that not only were the apparent criminals SS men but members of a battlegroup of the First SS Panzer Division ''Leibstandarte SS

2. Bradley F. Smith, *Reaching Judgment at Nuremburg. The Untold Story of How the Nazi War Criminals Were Judged* (New York, 1977), p. 34.

Adolf Hitler," the Führer's "own" and the offshoot of his personal bodyguard. In command of the battlegroup was a young officer who had served as adjutant to the Reichsführer-SS (Commander-in-Chief of the SS) Heinrich Himmler. Hitler and Himmler could not be brought to trial for their horrendous crimes. In some sense, a substitute might be found in the trial of the ostensible perpetrators of the Malmédy Massacre.

Suspects were assembled and a trial conducted by the U.S. Army in the spring and summer of 1946. All defendants were found guilty of major violations of the "laws and usages of war," and over half were sentenced to death. But no Malmédy defendant mounted the scaffold, and by the end of 1956 the last convict had been released as the result of a controversy that reverberated in the halls of Congress and helped start on his climb to national prominence the junior senator from Wisconsin, Joseph McCarthy. Had the U.S. Army in its investigation of the Malmédy Massacre and trial of more than seventy SS men been itself guilty of "Gestapo tactics"? Was the image of the Malmédy incident and its perpetrators as presented in the trial accurate? The recent murder of the leading German defendant in the trial has raised once more these still unanswered questions. Now, in the fourth decade following that bleak December afternoon of 1944, it is time to lay the Malmédy controversy to rest.

I. THE WAY OF THE WAFFEN-SS

The historical significance of the Malmédy Massacre lies partly in the fact that its perpetrators were members of the Nazi SS (Schutzstaffel or, literally, "protection detachment"). The SS has received much attention from writers in the years since 1945, and for good reason. To the sensation-seeker, the SS offers the lure of mystery suggested by its black service uniforms and aura of secret brotherhood, while scenes of the million-fold slaughter of "racial undesirables" in the death camps and shooting grounds of Eastern Europe continue to exert a fascination tolerable only for the inherent abstractness of huge numbers. Scholars explore the labyrinthine corridors of power within the "SS State" the better to understand the nature of Nazi totalitarianism, and they ponder the mechanisms that permitted apparently normal men to murder other human beings in unprecedented numbers.[1]

1. Current bibliography on the SS is vast. The best general histories are Hans Buchheim, et al., *Anatomie des SS-Staates* (Olten and Freiburg im Breisgau, 1965), translated as *The Anatomy of the SS State* (New York, 1968), and Heinz Höhne, *Der Orden unter dem Totenkopf. Die Geschichte der SS* (Gütersloh, 1967), translated as *The Order of the Death's Head. The Story of Hitler's SS* (London, 1969). These have superseded the old standby by Gerald Reitlinger, *The SS: Alibi of a Nation, 1922-1945* (New York, 1957). On Heinrich Himmler and his mental processes, see Bradley F. Smith, *Heinrich Himmler: A Nazi in the Making* (Stanford, 1971), and Josef Ackermann, *Himmler als Ideologe* (Göttingen, 1970). An interesting new perspective is offered by Peter Loewenberg, "The Unsuccessful Adolescence of Heinrich Himmler," *The American Historical Review*, 76 (June 1971). On the SS as secret police, see Shlomo Aronson, *Reinhard Heydrich und die Frühgeschichte von Gestapo und SD* (Stuttgart, 1971). On the Holocaust, Raul Hilberg, *The Destruction of the European Jews* (Chicago, 1967) has not been superseded by Lucy S. Dawidowicz, *The War Against the Jews 1933-1945* (New York, 1975). An effort to

It has long been obvious that the SS was an indispensable component of Nazism as a political movement and as a system of mass control and terror. It is only on a superficial level of functional analysis, however, that the SS can be considered as a single entity, for the tasks which it was assigned and which it arrogated to itself were so variegated that the mature SS was a bewildering conglomeration of numerous subgroups of diverse character, often pursuing mutually contradictory ends. Secret policemen, technocrats, concentration camp administrators, soldiers, spies, and ideologues, all might consider themselves to be in the service of Adolf Hitler and the Nazi movement as SS men but often found themselves propelled by divergent inner dynamics.[2]

Overwhelmingly the largest of these subgroups was the wartime Waffen-SS which by the summer of 1944 numbered over five hundred thousand men.[3] The *Organization Book* of the Nazi Party explained that "the Waffen-SS developed out of the determination to provide the Führer with a select body of long-service troops for the fulfillment of special assignments. . . . It combines with soldierly attitudes a strict spiritual discipline and trains its men as political fighters."[4]

In order to fully appreciate the significance of that definition, it is necessary to examine briefly the prewar origins and development of the Waffen-SS. The SS, prior to Hitler's accession to the German chancellorship, was essentially unarmed. That is not to say that small arms in limited quantities were unavailable to it when needed; but as a relatively small security force within a political movement which had not yet assumed control of the German state and which, in any event, seemed willing to seek it through the electoral process,

---

"psychoanalyze" SS mass-murderer is made in Henry Dicks, *Licensed Mass Murder* (New York, 1972).

2. This is eloquently and sometimes amusingly conveyed by Himmler's correspondence. See *Reichsführer! Briefe an und von Himmler*, ed. Helmut Heiber (Stuttgart, 1968), *passim*.

3. K.-G. Klietmann, *Die Waffen-SS. Eine Dokumentation* (Osnabrück, 1965), pp. 508-10.

4. *Organizationsbuch der NSDAP* (München, 1943), p. 427a.

the SS could neither require nor be permitted armament on a large scale. The situation that developed following Hitler's appointment to the German chancellorship on January 30, 1933, brought with it quite different needs and opportunities. Nazis and Nazi sympathizers quickly took control of the machinery of state, while Party organizations revelled in a new freedom which was not the least of the fruits of victory. Local SS commanders now began to arm detachments of their own men, the better to intimidate remnants of the old order and, by passing them off as auxiliary police, to tap the public purse. These units were designated "political alert units" and constituted a significant component of the growing Nazi terror machine.[5]

Meanwhile, Adolf Hitler, perceiving the need for a personal security force of unshakable loyalty, turned to his bodyguard Sepp Dietrich, who by the spring of 1934 created a thousand-man force dubbed "Leibstandarte SS Adolf Hitler" (literally, "Body Regiment Adolf Hitler").[6] Both the Leibstandarte and the political alert units proved their worth in the purge of the summer of 1934 in which the troublesome leadership of the SA (Sturmabteilungen, "assault detachments") was liquidated and multifarious old scores settled.

Thus, although armed and trained in a fashion approximating orthodox military formations, the armed SS at its inception performed functions purely political in nature, a conclusion that is supported and rendered more ominous by the fact that armed SS men, initially ill distinguished from the Leibstandarte and political alert units, guarded the new and multiplying SS-run concentration camps. In September 1934, an agreement hammered out by Hitler, Himmler, and the army formally legitimized the Leibstandarte and political alert units as components of a new SS-Verfügungstruppe (SS Disposal Troop) which would grow to over ten thousand men by 1938. That agreement envisioned the SS-Verfügungstruppe

5. Höhne, *Orden*, pp. 405-06; Buchheim, et al., *Anatomie*, I, 161-62.
6. See the author's *Hitler's Guard. The Story of the Leibstandarte SS Adolf Hitler, 1933-1945* (Carbondale, 1974), pp. 4-8.

as an instrument for the carrying out of internal political assignments, although its utilization by the army at the front in time of war was also foreseen.[7] Further statements of policy concerning the role of the SS-Verfügungstruppe were to follow but without significantly altering its definition as a political instrument.[8]

Two discrete and, to some extent, contradictory forces operated upon the SS-Verfügungstruppe, giving rise to the ambiguity which still beclouds its image and that of the Waffen-SS which succeeded it. In preparation for roles either as a force protecting the regime against counterrevolution or as Nazi imperial guardsmen fighting against foreign enemies, the SS-Verfügungstruppe required training and equipment of an approximately traditional military character. But as SS men and thus "political fighters," members of the SS-Verfügungstruppe (all of whom had volunteered for the SS) had committed themselves to serve the ideological ends of the regime. All recruits for the SS-Verfügungstruppe had to meet the "racial" standards imposed for active SS membership and were subjected to the ideological training and attitudinal molding deemed necessary by Himmler.[9]

The significance of ideological indoctrination within the SS has been the subject of no little controversy. Veterans of the Verfügungstruppe-Waffen-SS (VT-Waffen-SS) insist that, as far as *their* branch of the SS was concerned, ideological factors were of no importance. Whatever Himmler's ambitions and delusions might have been, they say, and whatever his degree of success in politicizing other echelons of the SS, the VT-Waffen-SS remained an organization of soldiers, extraordinarily brave and resourceful, but, functionally and attitudinally, "soldiers like any others."[10]

The reasons for the vigorous assertion of this position by

7. Klietmann, *Dokumentation*, pp. 15-18.
8. George Stein, *The Waffen SS. Hitler's Elite Guard at War* (Ithaca, 1966), pp. 18-24.
9. Weingartner, *Leibstandarte*, pp. 20-29.
10. The title and theme of Paul Hausser's *Soldaten wie andere auch. Der Weg der Waffen-SS* (Osnabrück, 1966).

former members are various. It is true that the VT-Waffen-SS as a whole never became the body of armed ideologues of Himmler's dreams, although that concession is not tantamount to agreeing that ideology was without significance. Some units, by virtue of the commander's personality and inclination as well as other circumstances, were less open to ideological influence than others; so that individual perceptions based on experience might vary widely. But, above all, veterans of the VT-Waffen-SS deny the significance of ideology in an effort to distance themselves from the horrors of the concentration and extermination camps, where the influence of Nazi ideology seemed obvious, and to implicitly challenge the postwar judgment of the International Military Tribunal which declared the SS, including the VT-Waffen-SS, a criminal organization.[11]

Postwar apologists for the VT-Waffen-SS are, in general, correct in asserting that prewar indoctrination efforts, thick with heavy-handed and dreary dissertations on ancient and medieval Germanic history designed to glorify the Nordic-Germanic "race," pinpoint its enemies, and encourage a return to the healthy peasant life, failed to turn many Verfügungstruppe men into enthusiasts of the rural-racial twaddle so dear to Himmler's heart. This fact, however, is of little value in demonstrating the premise of a fundamental distinction between the VT-Waffen-SS and the remainder of the Schutzstaffel, for the Reichsführer's *politruks* gained few converts from any branch of the organization.[12]

11. *Nazi Conspiracy and Aggression. Opinion and Judgement* (Washington, D.C., 1947), p. 102. It should be noted here that wartime concentration camps were included in the Waffen-SS for administrative purposes and that substantial numbers of camp personnel were transferred to front-line fighting units.

12. See, for example, "Arbeitsbericht des 1. Vierteljahres, 1935," SS-Motorsturm 7/2, March 30, 1935, U.S. National Archives Microfilm Publication, Miscellaneous SS Records: Einwandererzentralstelle, Waffen-SS, and SS-Oberabschnitte, Microcopy No. T-354, Roll 408, Frame 4124350-51 (hereafter cited in the following form: T-354/408/4124350-51); Schulungsleiter, 2. SS-Standarte to Rassereferent, SS-Oberabschnitt Rhein, 16 Heumond (July), 1935, T-354/407/4122573-74 . A veteran officer of the prewar and wartime Leibstandarte has told the author that the prewar Leibstandarte's "Education Leader" was scornfully referred to as "the Priest

Of greater significance in forming the character of the SS and only partly the product of formal indoctrination efforts was the atmosphere of "heroic realism" which came to permeate its ranks. The roots of this attitudinal complex long antedate the foundation of Nazism as a political movement and are partly traceable to Friedrich Nietzsche who stressed that in order to deal successfully with a chaotic universe, man must abandon himself to the "positive" forces of pride, joy, health, sexual love, enmity, and war—in other words, struggle and self-assertion as ends in themselves.[13] The idea of war as a transcendental principle, detached from pragmatic ends and moral limitations, received much impetus in the nihilistic crucible of World War I, especially for many young Germans for whom the humiliation of defeat might be eased by distilling from the war experience the memory of the "good fight" against odds as a higher form of victory. This world view, detached from conventional standards of morality, gave birth to a postwar literary genre and was carried in crude form into the Free Corps, from whose ranks came many of the early cadres of the Nazi SS.[14] The essence of this unprincipled activism was well expressed by the personal recollection of the prewar Leibstandarte as a milieu in which "the heart asked and was answered by other hearts. Sepp Dietrich and his Leibstandarte—that was stirring! The rules of Germanness were not read out; one learned them by leaps from ten-meter towers and by the most severe training on the exercise grounds."[15]

The glorification of struggle, activism, and the overcoming

of Wotan." Sepp Dietrich replaced him on the Leibstandarte's budget with a riding instructor. Jochen Peiper to author, April 9, 1976.

13. Buchheim, et al., *Anatomie*, I, 238; George L. Mosse, *The Culture of Western Europe* (New York, 1961), p. 227.

14. Robert G. L. Waite, *Vanguard of Nazism: The Free Corps Movement in Postwar Germany 1918-1923* (New York, 1969), pp. 23-27; Klemens von Klemperer, *Germany's New Conservatism: Its History and Dilemma in the Twentieth Century* (Princeton, 1957), p. 183.

15. Ernst Günther Krätschmer, *Ritterkreuzträger der Waffen-SS* (Göttingen, 1955), pp. 10-11.

of physical hardship and difficulty constituted a useful attitudinal complex for the SS, whose fundamental purpose was to act as executor of the Führer's will, a force that did not recognize normative limitations. It was rendered even more appropriate when combined with the apotheosizing of *Härte*, best translated as "harshness" or "severity." *Härte*, as an important component of the SS world view, was a logical outgrowth both of the glorification of unprincipled activism and Nazi Social Darwinism, which freely applied the concept of "nature red in tooth and claw" to human society. This was neatly conveyed by the following verse from an SS publication:

> Where unlike meet
> Hatred holds sway.
> Good will does not help.
> Here, God wants no love.[16]

The human implications of this outlook were expressed by Himmler in a wartime speech to high-ranking SS officers: ". . . we must be honorable, decent, loyal and comradely to bearers of our own blood, but to no one else."[17]

By that time, the full significance of *Härte* was to be seen in the extermination camps operated by the SS in Eastern Europe. But *Härte* had obvious applications on the battlefield. A wartime article suggestively entitled *"Du oder ich"* ("You or Me") informed the SS reader that as long as he was fighting for victory, he was also fighting for right and justice. Harshness in combat was "holy" while mercy was intolerable.[18] Should that injunction have been insufficiently specific, the Waffen-SS man was offered further guidance in the form of a letter purportedly written by an SS-Untersturmführer (second lieutenant) of the Waffen-SS shortly before his death. The letter referred pointedly to orders received and

---

16. Oskar Winter, "Gott," *SS-Leitheft* (hereafter LH), Heft 4 (1942), 3ff.
17. Ackermann, *Himmler*, p. 153.
18. "Du oder ich. Gedanken über die Härte im Kampf und den Willen zum Sieg," LH, 7, Folge 10b, 11f.

carried out to shoot a group of Russian prisoners of war, observing that "we have learned to be fearfully harsh when it serves a purpose."[19]

Himmler and his ideological spokesmen projected an image of the wartime SS as a tightly knit brotherhood of ruthless and fanatical combatants for Hitler's "New Order," struggling against its enemies on the plains of Russia, within the vast concentration camp system, on the streets of German cities, and among the populations of occupied Europe and giving those "enemies" the shortest of shrift. "The SS is as hard as steel, a community committed to death, an order of those sworn to the Reich. We chose the difficult way when it was still possible to choose a more comfortable one. We have a right to be hard toward others because we have been hard on ourselves."[20] But statements such as this are less descriptive than they are paradigmatic; they represent the SS as Himmler wished it to be rather than as it actually was, although that is not to deny that the SS of reality shared some characteristics with the ideal.

By the beginning of World War II the SS-Verfügungs-truppe, soon to be renamed "Waffen-SS," had attracted a heterogeneous membership. Nowhere was this clearer than at the highest level of leadership. Sepp Dietrich, commander of Hitler's Leibstandarte, brought a modest level of experience to his position, having served as a noncommissioned officer in the Bavarian Army during World War I and in the Bavarian police and Bund Oberland Free Corps thereafter.[21] Neither a political fanatic nor a sycophant, Dietrich owed his achievement of high rank to an unpolished but instinctive military talent, a willingness to subordinate conscience to Hitler's will, and the genuine respect and affection with which the Führer regarded the rough-hewn Swabian. The Prussian Paul Hausser, peacetime inspector of the SS-Verfügungstruppe

19. "Das Herz mit dem stählernen Ring," LH, 9 (January 1943) 15f.

20. "Unsere Härte," LH, 9 (January 1943), 1-3.

21. Weingartner, *Leibstandarte*, p. 3; Rudolf Lehmann, *Die Leibstandarte* (Osnabrück, 1977), I, 13-14.

and commander of the first of the wartime SS field divisions, combined General Staff experience and general officer's rank in the pre-Hitler army with an apolitical dedication to military efficiency.[22] Felix Steiner, commander of the militarily most proficient of the prewar SS-Verfügungstruppe regiments, SS Standarte "Deutschland," was a veteran of the elite assault units of World War I and saw in the VT-Waffen-SS the opportunity to create a maximally flexible military organization unrestrained by the weight of tradition.[23] Theodor Eicke, a grave embarrassment to postwar apologists for the Waffen-SS, exchanged his "peacetime" career as the psychopathically brutal and, ironically, antimilitaristic head of the SS concentration camp system for a divisional command in the field, to which he brought his prior experience and thousands of camp personnel.[24] Professional police officers such as Karl-Maria Demelhuber and Karl Pfeffer-Wildenbruch brought additional diversity to the highest levels of VT-Waffen-SS field command.[25] So varied were the personalities, backgrounds, and ambitions of individuals at this command level that they could make little contribution to the formation of a homogeneous VT-Waffen-SS character. Dietrich and Steiner, moreover, were notorious for their indifference to political and ideological matters in general and to Himmler's enthusiasms in particular.

It is more likely that valid generalizations can be made concerning the large body of junior officers belonging to the VT-Waffen-SS. Although their backgrounds and ambitions varied too, most of them passed through a unified training program on their way to becoming officers. This is significant because leaders on this level, much more numerous than more senior commanders, were in direct contact with the mass of troops and during World War II provided primary

22. Höhne, *Orden*, p. 411.
23. *Ibid.*, p. 412.
24. Stein, *Waffen SS*, p. 57; Charles W. Sydnor, Jr., *Soldiers of Destruction. The SS Death's Head Division, 1933-1945* (Princeton, 1977), pp. 3-63.
25. Hausser, *Soldaten*, p. 39; Höhne, *Orden*, p. 423.

combat leadership, thus to a substantial degree determining the fighting characteristics of the Waffen-SS.

The basic institutions for the training of VT-Waffen-SS officers were the SS-Junkerschulen (SS cadet schools) of which two, at Bad Tölz and Braunschweig, were established in 1934 and 1935. Not until late in the war were two additional Junkerschulen established, at Klagenfurt in the fall of 1943 and Prague in the summer of 1944.[26] Candidates for these schools were normally selected from recruits who possessed the characteristics (above-average educational level, prior service as officers in the General-SS, personal qualities of leadership, and political dedication) deemed appropriate for officer rank. In the prewar years, successful Junker spent ten months at the Junkerschulen followed by a three-month platoon-leadership course at the SS training installation near the Dachau concentration camp before receiving commissions as SS-Untersturmführer. During the war, cadets combined six months at the Junkerschule with shorter periods of basic training and instruction at special weapons schools and, sometimes, combat experience with field units.[27]

As part of their effort to divorce the VT-Waffen-SS from the remainder of Himmler's black guards, postwar apologists have stressed the purely military character of the SS-Junkerschulen. It is true that military training formed a major part of the curriculum and that that training was based on regulations developed by the German Army. But even in 1944, when tremendous losses at the front, combined with efforts to organize new Waffen-SS divisions, greatly increased the demand for junior officers, almost 20 percent of the curriculum at SS-Junkerschulen was devoted to ideological training, equal to the time spent on the study of tactics. A wartime SS Junker has recalled that among his fellow cadets, the

26. Werner Doerffler-Schuband, *Führer-Nachwuchs der Waffen-SS*. U.S. National Archives Foreign Military Studies Collection, D–178, p. 4.

27. *Ibid.*, pp. 2-3, 5; Hausser, *Soldaten*, p. 46; Speech by Himmler, May 22, 1936. U.S. National Archives Microfilm Publication. Records of the Reich Leader of the SS and Chief of the German Police. T–175/90/2611569-70.

most admired SS figure was not one of the prominent battle-field commanders, such as Sepp Dietrich or Felix Steiner, but Reinhard Heydrich, chief of the Reichssicherheitshauptamt (Reich Security Main Office), which included the Gestapo and SD (Sicherheitsdienst or Security Service), and brutal "Deputy Reich Protector" of Bohemia and Moravia. Heydrich was idolized as the embodiment of *Härte*, and it would seem safe to assume that formal and informal pressures to emulate his practice of that "virtue" were present.[28]

Moreover, the SS-Junkerschulen were not institutions intended by Himmler solely for the training of SS officers destined for military careers, even if one were to concede that service in the VT-Waffen-SS was "purely military," a concession that would not be justified. Thus, many Junker of the "classes" of 1935 and 1936 were posted not to the Verfügungstruppe but to Totenkopf (concentration camp) units and various other bureaus and organs of the "SS State." From a large group of Junker assigned to duty in the spring of 1937, only 27 went to the Verfügungstruppe while 144 were sent to the Order Police.[29] During World War II, it is no doubt true that most, if not all, Junker were assigned to combat units, although precise figures are not available.

In attempting to assess the human products of the SS-Junkerschulen, it is necessary to speak in the broadest of generalities while recognizing the existence of significant differences from individual to individual. In terms of overall military competence—particularly familiarity with the more sophisticated weapons of modern war and associated tactics—prewar Junker did not come up to the standards of junior officers in the German Army. To some extent, they compensated for this shortcoming by superb physical conditioning which permitted a highly active and effective brand of

28. Doerffler-Schuband, *Nachwuchs*, p. 9; Buchheim, et al., *Anatomie*, p. 253.
29. *Dienstaltersliste der Schutzstaffel der NSDAP, Stand vom 1. Dezember, 1936*, pp. 237-43, T-175/204/2674095-98; "Reichsführer-SS, Personalkanzlei, Tageblatt Nr. 180," April 15, 1937, T-175/96/2626140.

personal leadership in the field and which became characteristic of the Waffen-SS.[30] During the war, this "competence gap" narrowed as the result of common army-Waffen-
SS combat experiences and frequent attendance by Waffen-
SS officers at army training establishments; ultimately, the
gap disappeared. What distinguished the younger combat SS
officer from his army counterpart was more frequently a matter of attitude than expertise. Indoctrination efforts both
within and outside the Junkerschulen attempted to inculcate
a fatalistic and passionate enthusiasm for combat which went
well beyond the calculated willingness for self-sacrifice that
must be expected of any soldier. In SS ideological literature,
battle was depicted less as a rational, albeit highly dangerous,
means toward a tangible end than as an ecstatic experience
whose mystical significance was heightened and sanctified by
the death of the participant.[31] We need not assume that all or
even most SS officers approached combat in this spirit, but
indoctrination in this vein undoubtedly had a palpable effect
and may have contributed to the fact that by 1942 almost the
entire first graduating class of Junkerschule Bad Tölz had
been killed.[32] Glorification of death in battle, when combined with the encouragement of *Härte*, went far toward producing the redoubtable adversaries that the Waffen-SS
proved to be.

Although conceived initially as an internal security force,
the VT-Waffen-SS achieved its ultimate definition in practice
as a combat force in World War II. Fighting shoulder-to-
shoulder with the German Army, eventually incorporating
army personnel and receiving conscripts similar to those secured by the army and confronting the same battlefield problems and hazards, the Waffen-SS became progressively more
difficult to distinguish attitudinally and functionally from

30. Stein, *Waffen SS*, pp. 13, 59, 116-17.
31. See, for example, Hans-Henning Festge, "Erlebnis an der Grenze zweier
Welten," LH, 9 (July 1943), 8.
32. Stein, *Waffen SS*, p. 12, n. 28.

the army. But it never lost its separate identity to quite the degree that its postwar spokesmen have asserted. Among the German population, the Waffen-SS had a reputation for ruthlessness which set it apart from the German Army. Bruno Streckenbach of the SD reported to Himmler that many Germans believed the Waffen-SS to be "the most radical troops who, moreover, take no prisoners but, rather, mercilessly annihilate every adversary."[33] Furthermore, by 1943 few young Germans were willing to volunteer for service in the Waffen-SS, partly in the belief that casualties were heavier there than in the army, partly because parents and clergy discouraged them from joining the "godless" SS.[34]

While it is true that SS men were encouraged—and sometimes placed under pressure—to withdraw from the Church, it is not true that the Waffen-SS took no prisoners and "annihilated" the enemy without mercy. Nevertheless, the Waffen-SS was implicated in a disproportionately large number of "excesses" of which the Malmédy Massacre is, perhaps, the best known; criminal acts were much more frequent in the East due to "racial" factors which, in most cases, were not relevant to the West.[35] While the "SS spirit" is a significant factor in these atrocities, failure to probe more deeply would result in an incomplete analysis. It must be remembered that the army, on the whole, was willing to accept the infamous "Commissar Order" which required the liquidation of Red Army political functionaries upon capture.[36] Enormous numbers of Russian prisoners of war for whom the army was responsible died of ill-treatment. The

33. Höhne, *Orden*, p. 404. In a speech to SS-Gruppenführer of November 1938, Himmler declared that, in war, an SS man was never to allow himself to be taken prisoner and would be under no obligation to take prisoners. Ackermann, *Himmler*, p. 125.

34. Höhne, *Orden*, p. 439.

35. On this subject, see Stein, *Waffen SS*, pp. 250-81; Höhne, *Orden*, pp. 435-36. For an important example of an early atrocity in the West, see Sydnor, *Soldiers of Destruction*, pp. 106-07.

36. See Hans-Adolf Jacobsen, "Kommissarbefehl und Massenexekutionen sowjetischer Kriegsgefangener," in Buchheim, et al., *Anatomie*, II, 137-65.

fact that the German Army was implicated in atrocious behavior does nothing, of course, to mitigate the guilt of the Waffen-SS but merely demonstrates that the army, too, albeit to a lesser extent, had become an instrument for the achievement of ideological ends.

Nor should it be considered an exculpation of the Waffen-SS to allude to Russian atrocities. That Stalinism was a force capable of abstracting, dehumanizing, and, ultimately, exterminating huge categories of human beings had already been amply demonstrated in the campaigns to collectivize the Russian peasantry and in the Great Purges.[37] In many instances, Russians treated Germans with savagery which equaled that meted out by Germans to Russians. Members of the Waffen-SS who fell into Russian hands were often handled with particular ferocity.[38] While much of this might be construed as just reprisal for German atrocities, the result was an escalating cycle of brutality and the acquisition of combat habits which Waffen-SS units sometimes found difficult to shed when transferred from East to West.

In some cases, however, it is difficult to distinguish ideologically motivated brutality from the inevitable byproducts of pragmatically directed combat tactics, and here, too, the experience of battle on the Eastern Front was of great importance. This was reflected at SS armored warfare schools, the first of which began to function in 1943. Reacting to the extreme defensive tenacity that the Red Army had demonstrated in the campaigns of 1941 and 1942 and to growing Russian numerical superiority, Waffen-SS tactical doctrine stressed the importance of the greatest possible volume of fire from all weapons, combined with constant movement. "No fire without movement and no movement without fire." The

37. Roy A. Medvedev, *Let History Judge. The Origins and Consequences of Stalinism*, trans. Colleen Taylor (New York, 1972), pp. 97-98, 239.

38. Albert Seaton, *The Russo-German War 1941-45* (New York, 1970), pp. 110-11; *Allierte Kriegsverbrechen und Verbrechen gegen die Menschlichkeit* (Buenos Aires, 1953), pp. 167, 169, 171, 172, 174, 175, 179, 180, 181, 182-83; Höhne, *Orden*, p. 434.

result, in practice, was often a policy of "shooting first and asking questions later." The Russian experience also produced extreme sensitivity to the threat of guerrilla operations. SS instructors, therefore, stressed the necessity of "energetic" measures against guerrilla bands, a generally "dirty" business even when racial and ideological hatreds have not been aroused.[39]

By the end of World War II, the Waffen-SS order of battle listed thirty-eight divisions. Many of these were divisions in name only, and only a relative handful played a significant role on the battlefields of Europe. The elite panzer divisions of the Waffen-SS, however, ultimately seven in number, acquired an almost superhuman reputation for military potency, one that has not been diminished in postwar ruminations by Waffen-SS veterans and which is quite out of proportion to their numbers. The SS panzer divisions were, on the whole, well led and well equipped, had a strong ésprit de corps, went on the offensive with reckless bravery, and stood on the defensive with fierce resolution. Moreover, they were somewhat larger than comparable army divisions and, for that reason if for no other, would have had a disproportionately large impact on the battlefield.[40] In addition, the reputation achieved by the elite Waffen-SS divisions was partly the result of the favor in which they were held by Hitler, which usually resulted in their being found on the most crucial sectors of the front where they had access to the lion's share of attention and glory. Goebbels saw to it that Waffen-SS commanders were highly publicized and engineered an adulatory campaign for Sepp Dietrich which outdid even that accorded Rommel.[41]

39. *Die an der Panzergrenadierschule der Waffen-SS vorhandenen Erfahrungen der Kampfweise des russischen Gegners und ihre Auswertung zur Ausbildung* (anonymous). U.S. National Archives Foreign Military Studies Collection, D–154, pp. 4-5, 7.

40. *Handbook on German Military Forces,* War Department Technical Manual (Washington, D.C., 1945), p. II-8.

41. Milton Shulman, *Defeat in the West* (New York, 1948), p. 104.

As a consequence of their battlefield exploits and the publicity surrounding them, not only were Germans acutely conscious of the Waffen-SS but the Allies were as well. Allied commanders grudgingly recognized the steadfastness and bravery of the Waffen-SS units they faced. To the civilian populations of the Allied nations, the Waffen-SS seemed to blend with the SA and the balance of Himmler's organization and epitomized Nazi brutality and fanaticism. The Waffen-SS troopers who spearheaded Hitler's thrust into the Ardennes in December 1944 were, collectively, neither supermen nor monsters, but both of those images, for which the multifaceted evolution of the VT-Waffen-SS was responsible, would be central to the development of the postwar Malmédy affair.

II. LIVES FOR THE FÜHRER

The seventy-odd men who were brought to trial in the spring of 1946 and subsequently convicted of the Malmédy Massacre and related crimes reflected the broad human spectrum of Waffen-SS membership in the final year of the war. They ranged from the fifty-four-year-old Sepp Dietrich and forty-four-year-old Hermann Priess, veterans of the pre-Nazi German Army and Free Corps and members of the earliest stratum of leadership within the SS-Verfügungstruppe, to the likes of the nineteen-year-old Ernst Haase* and the eighteen-year-old Gerhard Mann,* the former having been drafted into the Waffen-SS in October 1943, the latter donning the SS uniform in August 1944 and seeing combat for the first time in the Ardennes offensive after a bare one month's training. Between these two extremes were the Waffen-SS "core types" such as Jochen Peiper and Johannes Metzger,* men in their late twenties in the waning months of the war, graduates of the SS Junkerschulen, who had spent the entirety of their adult lives in the SS and who had risen to battalion or regimental command by the time of the Ardennes offensive.[1]

The central personality in the complex of events surrounding the Malmédy Massacre was, without question, Joachim

*All names with asterisks are pseudonyms.
1. The biographical data in this chapter has been derived primarily from the holdings of the Berlin Document Center and from the testimony of the defendants at the Malmédy trial. As might be expected, some of the latter tended to be self-serving but can often be checked against the official SS Personnel Office and RuSHA (Rasse und Siedlungshauptamt or Race and Settlement Main Office) documents for the defendant in question.

Peiper (or "Jochen" as he preferred, perhaps reflecting SS distaste for names of biblical origin), commander of the SS battlegroup that spearheaded the drive of the Sixth Panzer Army into the Ardennes. Peiper was born in Berlin in 1915, the son of Hauptmann (Captain) Waldemar Peiper, who fought and was seriously wounded in the colonial campaigns in Africa during World War I.[2] The young Peiper received a thoroughly middle-class education, attending the Goethe Oberrealschule (high school) although not achieving the Abitur which would have permitted him to attend a university or technical college. His political views—or those of his parents—were reflected in the fact that he was an early member of the Hitler Youth at a time when a young German could still easily avoid membership. In 1933, he joined an SS cavalry company but seems never to have sought or achieved membership in the Nazi Party.[3] The SS Cavalry, it might be noted, was established by Himmler as part of an effort to attract socially "respectable" elements to the SS and had no executive function. It was, in fact, the only branch of Himmler's black corps to be excluded from the verdict of criminality by the postwar International Military Tribunal.[4]

The ascetically featured and well-bred young Peiper probably mixed well with the gentry of his riding unit but craved more than decorous gallops through the countryside surrounding Berlin. On February 17, 1934, the nineteen-year-old Peiper wrote to the headquarters of SS Superior District East (whose chief was none other than Sepp Dietrich, simultaneously commander of the infant Leibstandarte SS Adolf Hitler), applying for active SS membership as an officer candidate and proclaiming the intention of making the SS his career.[5] In January 1935, Peiper was called to an SS officer

2. "Personalangaben des SS-Sturmbannführer Peiper, Joachim," Berlin Document Center Malmedy Defendants' Files (hereafter BDC/MDF).
3. "Personal-Nachweis für Führer der Waffen-SS," "Personalangaben," BDC/MDF.
4. Hohne, *Orden,* pp. 129-30; *Nazi Conspiracy and Aggression. Opinion and Judgement,* p. 102.
5. Peiper to SS Oberabschnitt Ost, February 17, 1934, BDC/MDF. Peiper was

candidate's training course which was followed by admission to Junkerschule Braunschweig. Upon graduation and the completion of the standard platoon-leader course at the SS training installation at Dachau, Peiper was commissioned an SS-Untersturmführer in ceremonies on April 20 (Hitler's birthday), 1936. He was immediately posted to the Leibstandarte SS Adolf Hitler in which he was to serve until the end of World War II, with one significant interruption. In July 1938, Peiper was transferred to the personal staff of the Reichsführer-SS, Heinrich Himmler, for what was initially specified as a three-month period. Himmler must have been more than satisfied with his young aide, however, for Peiper remained on the Reichsführer's staff far longer than three months and rose to the rank of First Adjutant on November 1, 1939.[6] This stage in Peiper's career constitutes further evidence of the difficulty in attempting to fully dissociate the Waffen-SS and its military functions from the hideous realization of the racial aspects of the Nazi Weltanschauung for which the SS was responsible. As adjutant, Peiper frequently accompanied Himmler on official tours of inspection and on one occasion witnessed an early experiment involving the fatal gassing of living subjects.[7]

During the Polish campaign, Peiper was assigned to Hitler's military headquarters but rejoined the Leibstandarte's field force for operations in the Low Countries and France in the spring of 1940, winning the Iron Cross First and Second Class.[8] Although no longer part of his entourage,

---

part of what might be considered an "SS family." His brother became an officer in the SS-Totenkopfverbände, while two brothers of his future wife were SS officers, one in the SD. See Peiper to RuSHA, February 6, 1939, BDC/MDF.

6. "Personalnachweis"; "An die Leibstandarte SS Adolf Hitler," June 30, 1938; Himmler to Peiper, n.d., BDC/MDF.

7. Cross-examination of Joachim Peiper, Dachau, June 22, 1946, *U.S. v. Valentin Bersin, et al.* (hereafter "U.S. v. Bersin"), U.S. National Archives Record Group No. 153, Roll 3, Frames 000189–90, transcript pages 1968-1969, hereafter cited in the following form: 153/3/000189-90 (1968-1969).

8. "Personal-Nachweis für Führer der Waffen-SS," BDC/MDF; Jochen Peiper, "Kommentar zum Buch *Massacre at Malmedy* von Charles Whiting" (unpublished manuscript), p. 1.

the twenty-five-year-old officer, now SS-Hauptsturmführer (captain), obviously retained Himmler's favor, for the Reichsführer ordered that two automobiles "liberated" in France by Peiper and Max Wünsche, another of the bright and good-looking SS officers in favor with Nazi leaders, be maintained at Hitler's headquarters for the duration of the war as the personal vehicles of the two men. Himmler thoughtfully noted, however, that he intended to provide Peiper and Wünsche with *German* automobiles at the end of the war.[9]

Army psychiatrists who had examined Peiper prior to his admission to Junkerschule Braunschweig had found him to be intelligent but egocentric and mistrustful of others, the latter quality, perhaps, helping to explain his enthusiasm for a career in the SS, an organization formed to combat the real and imagined enemies of a movement with which Peiper had early identified himself. His chronic efforts to impress others with his "connections," also noted by the psychiatrists, must have made his tenure on Himmler's personal staff an intensely satisfying experience, although the possibility advanced by his examiners that he would prove to be a critical and difficult subordinate must not have materialized in the presence of the Reichsführer. Peiper was also found to be strong of will and inclined to attempt to realize that will in quick, impulsive thrusts, qualities that may be significant in understanding his battlefield conduct.[10]

Peiper, like the Waffen-SS itself, was to rise to military prominence on the battlefields of Russia. The unit to which he belonged, the Leibstandarte SS Adolf Hitler (soon to become a motorized and then armored division), had entered combat in Russia in July 1941, penetrated six hundred miles to the Don River by November, and had then suffered extremely heavy casualties in the bitter defensive fighting of the winter of 1941 to 1942. Shipped to France for reorganization and refitting, the division returned to meet an even more

9. Himmler to Wolff, June 29, 1940, BDC/MDF.
10. "Gutachten des Prüfauschusses Braunschweig," April 4, 1935, BDC/MDF.

critical situation in the winter of 1943.[11] By that time Peiper had risen to the rank of SS-Sturmbannführer (major) and the command of the Leibstandarte's Third Battalion, Second Panzergrenadier (Motorized Infantry) Regiment. In fierce fighting against odds around Kharkov, operations in which Waffen-SS units predominated, Peiper commanded his battalion with great skill and daring. On March 6, 1943, he led it far beyond the objective assigned and succeeded in establishing and holding a bridgehead across the Msha River, setting the stage for the capture of the key strongpoint of Walki and the German recapture of Kharkov. For his achievement, Peiper was awarded the Knight's Cross of the Iron Cross, Nazi Germany's most prestigious military decoration. Peiper also provided an example of personal daring which goes far to explain his success as a combat leader; he expected much of his men but demanded more of himself and displayed sangfroid which excited the admiration of his youthful troopers. One of many anecdotes that has survived describes Peiper's destruction of an onrushing T-34 tank with a rifle grenade at a few meters' range. Peiper grinned, observing, "That should suffice for the close-combat badge, boys."[12]

As Germany's military fortunes declined, Peiper's reputation as a cool and resourceful performer in the clutch was further enhanced and was reflected in his assumption of the leadership of Leibstandarte's Panzer Regiment. In command of a battlegroup in the Zhitomir sector, he played a significant role in the successful efforts of the army's Forty-eighth Panzer Corps to disrupt the offensive plans of the Russian 16th Army during December 1943. Faithful to Waffen-SS doctrine concerning the employment of armored infantry, Peiper personally led a night attack on the village of Pekart-

11. Weingartner, *Leibstandarte*, pp. 74-75.
12. "Fernschreiben an Führerhauptquartier. Vorschlag zur Verleihung des Ritterkreuzes an SS-Stubaf. Joachim Peiper, Kdr. III/2 Pz.Gz.Rgt.," March 7, 1943; 'Vorschlag Nr. (?) für die Verleihung des Deutschen Kreuzes in Gold," February 26, 1943, BDC/MDF. Ernst Günther Krätschmer, "Der Soldat: Jochen Peipers militärischer Werdegang," *Der Freiwillige*, September 1976, p. 5.

schina, roaring into the area with guns and flamethrowers blazing from his SPWs (Schützenpanzerwagen, half-tracked armored personnel carriers). The village was totally destroyed and, as an after-action report laconically put it, the enemy "annihilated." In the following two days, Peiper's battle-group penetrated thirty kilometers into the Russian rear, put to flight the field headquarters of four Russian divisions, and claimed twenty-five hundred Russian troops killed, a figure that might be contrasted with a total of *three* prisoners taken during the same period. Peiper was to receive the Oak Leaves to his Knight's Cross for these exploits.[13] This was war as the Waffen-SS on the Russian Front knew and practiced it—the product of a racist and Social Darwinist Weltanschauung applied in a military situation of increasing desperation against a tough and often ruthless and fanatical enemy. It was also a modus operandi that could be carried to other theaters. In July 1943, the First SS Panzer Division "Leibstandarte SS Adolf Hitler" was shipped from Russia to Italy on Hitler's orders to strengthen Germany's hold on her crumbling ally. Following the surrender of Italy to the Allies in September, elements of the Leibstandarte, including Peiper's Panzer-grenadier battalion, participated in the early phases of anti-partisan operations in the north of the peninsula. Following the capture of two of his men by communist guerrillas in the Piedmontese town of Boves, Peiper attacked the town, destroying numerous buildings and killing thirty-three inhabitants.[14] A legitimate military operation or a criminal act? It is in the nature of guerrilla operations to render such distinctions

13. "Eichenlaub für Kommandeur SS-Pz. Rgt. 'LSSAH,'" BDC/MDF.
14. Heeres Gruppe B, "Anlage zum Tätigkeitsbericht der Abt. Ic, Abschluss-bericht der Entwaffnungsaktion in Nord Italien," September 19, 1943, U.S. National Archives Microfilm Publication, Records of German Field Commands—Army Groups, T-311/276/000065-67; "Besonderes Feindnachrichtenblatt," September 22, 1943, T-311/276/000084-86; "Stellungnahme des Einheitsführers," n.d., T-354/624/0000363; Klietmann, *Dokumentation*, p. 80. See Michèle Cotta, "L'énigme Peiper," *L'Express*, No. 1306 (19-25 Juillet, 1976), p. 28; Peiper, of course, regarded himself as guiltless (personal communication to author, March 13, 1976).

extraordinarily difficult if not impossible to make. The Waffen-SS, moreover, was less inclined than most twentieth-century combat organizations to ponder such questions.

Closest to Peiper in age and background among those Malmédy defendants who can be classified as officer "core types" was Fritz Kamp.* A tall, well-educated, middle-class youth who had achieved the Abitur, Kamp joined the Nazi Party in 1933 and the SS Political Alert Unit Württemberg (shortly to become Battalion Four of the SS-VT Standarte "Deustchland") in August 1934. Kamp attended Junkerschule Bad Tölz from October 1937 to July 1938 earning high marks in ideology and was commissioned SS-Untersturmführer on November 9, 1938 (the anniversary of Hitler's abortive "Putsch" of 1923), at the age of 23. Although his career was not as spectacular as Peiper's, Kamp's performance more than satisfied his superiors; wounded once in France in 1940 and twice in Russia, he had risen to the command of Leibstandarte's Reconnaissance Detachment by the spring of 1943 and was recommended for the Knight's Cross for his cool and skillful leadership during desperate fighting in the Tarnopol-Proskuroff sector in the spring of 1944, earning plaudits from Sepp Dietrich as one of his "best" commanders.[15]

Johannes Metzger cut a fine figure as an SS officer, having been described by a superior as "tall, slender, and of Nordic appearance." He had completed his studies at a Gymnasium and, with Abitur in hand, had gone directly into the Leibstandarte in the fall of 1935. Although a member of the Nazi Party and a man of reasonably high educational attainments, Metzger is unusual in that his career did not involve attendance at a Junkerschule. Instead, he was promoted from SS-Oberscharführer (master sergeant) to SS-Untersturmführer in September 1940 after having been decorated with the Iron Cross First and Second Class for service as a squad leader in

15. "Dienstlaufbahn"; "Abgangszeugnis der SS. Junkerschule Tölz," July 28, 1938; "Vorschlag Nr. 91 für die Verleihung des Deutschen Kreuzes in Gold"; "Vorschlagsliste für die Verleihung des Ritterkreuzes des Eisernen Kreuzes," May 4, 1944, BDC/MDF.

the campaigns of 1939 and 1940. Metzger may have been a difficult subordinate, which could explain his failure to have been chosen to attend a Junkerschule. A fitness report of 1940 described him as arrogant and excessively self-conscious. But he functioned in the Balkan campaign of 1941 as the commander of a reconnaissance platoon with "prudence and energy" and advanced through a battalion adjutancy to the adjutancy of the Second Panzergrenadier Regiment by February 1943. On the eve of the Ardennes offensive in which he would command a battalion, he was described by his regimental commander as an excellent officer, battle-tested, and combining a high level of theoretical knowledge with experience. He was rated, moreover, "ideologically solid," and his conduct as an SS officer was judged "exemplary and irreproachable."[16]

Fifteen officers among the Malmédy defendants can be categorized as "junior" officers, having commanded no unit larger than a company up through the Ardennes offensive. Here, biographical information is less complete than that available for more senior officers, but some useful generalizations can, nevertheless, be made. Data on six of the fifteen demonstrates or strongly indicates middle-class origins, while three were the sons of manual workers.[17] Information on the remaining six is insufficient to make a judgment as to social status. Unlike those designated as "core types," not all the junior officers had clearly elected careers in the SS. One, to be sure, had joined the Totenkopfverbände (concentration camp guard units) in February 1939 and had later served as an ideological instructor in Poland, but ten of the fifteen did not

16. "Lebenslauf des SS-Hauptsturmführers [Johannes Metzger]"; "Beurteilung des SS-Untersturmführer [Metzger, Johannes]," July 22, 1941; "Beurteilung fur den SS-Oberscharführer [Metzger]," September 6, 1940; "Beförderung in der Waffen-SS," BDC/MDF.

17. One officer, who eventually commanded a company, had not even completed the Volksschule and had worked as a carpenter before joining the Leibstandarte in 1936. At least two had the Abitur. Surprisingly, only one was the product of a "Napola" (National-politische Erziehungsanstalt or National Political Educational Institution), elite Party schools intended for the training of the future Nazi leadership. BDC/MDF.

enter the SS until after the war had begun, raising the possibility that some, at least, might not have joined had it not been for the pressure of war and the inevitability of military service. One had been involuntarily transferred from the Luftwaffe in 1943. Only five of the fifteen can be clearly established as having been Party members while seven had attended Junkerschulen. None combined Party membership, attendance at a Junkerschule, and prewar SS membership.

As might be expected, the combat achievements of the younger officers prior to the Ardennes offensive were much less imposing than those of their seniors. Information on their battlefield experience is limited. One was twice-wounded; another, once. A third had won the Iron Cross First and Second Class; a fourth, the Iron Cross Second Class only. Two were of marginal utility as combat leaders. One was termed by his superiors as "intellectually rigid," "imprecise in his orders," but a man who made up for his shortcomings through "will and *Härte.*" Another, one of the many ethnic Germans recruited by the manpower-hungry wartime Waffen-SS, had difficulty adjusting to German discipline and communicated poorly in the German language. He may have attempted to compensate for these flaws and to achieve acceptance by his German comrades through the demonstration of ideological fervor, for he was judged an "enthusiastic and self-sacrificing National Socialist fighter" by a superior officer in November 1943.[18]

Three general officers were among the seventy-four Malmédy accused and represent two differing categories of senior leadership in the Waffen-SS. These men ranged in age from the early forties to the early fifties at the time of the Ardennes offensive. All three had reached adulthood long before Hitler's appointment to the German chancellorship in January 1933, and all had been otherwise employed before having joined the SS.[19]

18. An officer-defendant spoke feelingly of having been transferred from the Luftwaffe to the Waffen-SS and of having desperately attempted to return to the former. U.S. v. Bersin, 153/4/000722 (3235). See also BDC/MDF.

19. BDC/MDF.

Sepp Dietrich was born a peasant. Following eight years at the Volksschule (elementary school), he worked as a hotel menial before enlisting in the Bavarian Army in 1911. During World War I he served with distinction as a noncommissioned officer and was probably as heavily decorated as was possible for an enlisted man in the caste-ridden German military of that time. There followed service as a low-level police official, combat with the Bund Oberland Free Corps in Upper Silesia, and dead-end jobs in commerce before he took the fateful step of joining the Nazi Party and the SS in 1928. Dietrich rose rapidly in the ranks of the infant SS due to unpolished but genuine leadership and administrative talents. Most crucial to the attainment of the influential position that he was later to achieve, however, was his absorption into Hitler's personal entourage as bodyguard in the fall of 1932. A few months later, he accompanied Hitler to the Reich Chancellery and was called upon by the Führer in March 1933 to organize the "palace guard" which was to become the Leibstandarte SS Adolf Hitler. Dietrich's loyalty to Hitler was demonstrated during the "Blood Purge" of late June to early July 1934 when he, stifling whatever scruples he may have had, aided and abetted in the murder of numerous old Party comrades.[20]

Unlike the much younger "core type" officers who were required to conform to the image of the SS-Führer inculcated at the Junkerschulen and in SS ideological literature, Dietrich was sufficiently powerful, largely as the result of his personal access to Hitler, to constitute a quasi-independent force within the VT-Waffen-SS.[21] Only nominally subordinate to Heinrich Himmler, Dietrich never felt himself to be an "SS man" in the full ideological sense of that term as it was understood by the Reichsführer-SS. To be sure, his own experiences in the nihilistic atmosphere that pervaded the elite assault formations of the World War I German Army and the

20. See Weingartner, *Leibstandarte*, pp. 12-13.
21. See, for example, Himmler to Dietrich, March 5, 1938, T-175/33/2542516-17. For an uncritical portrait of the wartime Dietrich, see Lehmann, *Die Leibstandarte*, I, 15-20.

later Free Corps and his dependence on Adolf Hitler for status and advancement prevented him from overtly rejecting the ideological underpinnings of the Nazi movement. But the necessary associations between the Leibstandarte and the German Army, which increased as time went on, created in Dietrich a conflict of loyalties similar in microcosm to that experienced by the VT-Waffen-SS as a whole and tempered only by the fact that the army, itself, became increasingly politicized.

During World War II, Dietrich assumed progressively greater command responsibilities, culminating in the leadership of the Sixth Panzer Army prior to the Ardennes offensive.[22] Although he was not the military nullity some have suggested, Sepp Dietrich's rise from regimental to army command within the space of five years was due less to his leadership talents than to Hitler's conviction that he represented an elemental force which could secure a victory that had eluded the traditional militarists of the German Army. The untutored Dietrich *was* an elemental force and, as such, unpredictable. His battlefield conduct prior to the Ardennes offensive ranged from the granting of a chivalrous armistice— almost eighteenth century in its courtliness—to the Greek Epirus Army, whose surrender the Leibstandarte accepted in April 1941, to orders issued six months later in retaliation for the murder of six Leibstandarte troopers by their Russian captors, which, contemporary German sources claimed, led to the shooting of four thousand Russian prisoners.[23] These extremes of behavior reflected not only the vastly different ideological significances of Greeks and Russians in the Nazi Weltanschauung but also the conflicting forces at work within Sepp Dietrich and, indeed, the whole of the Waffen-SS.

The background of Hermann Priess, commander of the

---

22. Sometimes mistakenly referred to as "Sixth SS Panzer Army." That designation was not applied to Dietrich's army until after the Ardennes offensive.

23. Weingartner, *Leibstandarte*, pp. 54-55; Stein, *Waffen SS*, pp. 272-73.

First SS Panzer Corps during the Ardennes offensive, was similar in many respects to that of Dietrich, although Priess was ten years his junior. Born the son of a Mecklenburg butcher, Priess combined attendance at the Volksschule with assistance to his father, followed by a year's work in the post office of his home town of Marnitz. Apparently bored by drudgery of this kind and probably stimulated by tales of World War I heroism, the seventeen-year-old Priess volunteered for the German Army in January 1919. No sooner enlisted than demobilized, Priess joined the von Brandis Free Corps, fought in the Baltic area, and participated in the capture of Riga (where he was wounded) in May 1919.[24] The spirit that pervaded these Free Corps, a reflection of despair over Germany's humiliation and defeat as well as of the nihilism fostered by the frightful wartime "trench experience," is effectively conveyed by this eyewitness description of the German withdrawal from the Baltic under Allied pressure in the fall of 1919:

> The soldiers of the Iron Division and the German Legion [to which Free Corps von Brandis belonged] unloaded all their despair and fury in one wild powerblow against the Letts. . . . Villages burst into flames, prisoners were trampled under foot . . . chaotic revenge and joy in destruction.[25]

Following his return to Germany, Priess subjected himself to a stricter discipline, enlisting for a twelve-year term of service as a cavalryman in the highly selective one-hundred-thousand-man post-Versailles Germany Army. After mustering out, the thirty-year-old Mecklenburger found employment as a low-level civil servant before deciding to tie his future to that of the victorious Nazi movement by joining the Party and SS in March 1933. As a long-service army non-commissioned officer and reservist, Priess was prime material for the armed SS and was assigned in the summer of 1934 to

24. "Lebenslauf des SS-Oberführer Hermann Priess," BDC/MDF.
25. Waite, *Vanguard*, p. 131.

the newly established Political Alert Unit Hamburg as a member of its officer corps. In the later SS-Standarte "Germania," for which the Political Alert Unit Hamburg served as a cadre, Priess was trained as an artilleryman and commanded a section of the SS-VTs first artillery regiment during the Polish campaign. Transferred to the new SS-Totenkopf Division commanded by the brutal Theodor Eicke, Priess assumed command of that division's artillery regiment in August 1940. Eicke seems to have found in Priess a kindred spirit and praised him lavishly as "unusually reliable," "unspoiled" (probably meaning primitive when used by Eicke), and a man willing to commit himself "recklessly" at any time for the goals of the Party. To Priess's guns was attributed the survival of the SS-Totenkopf Division in the perilous Demyansk pocket in the winter of 1942, an exploit for which Priess was awarded the Knight's Cross.[26]

Priess ultimately took command of the Totenkopf Division following the death of Eicke in action and distinguished himself for raw bravery and tenacity rather than tactical insight. Field Marshal Erich von Manstein praised him as the "leading fighter of his brave division," while General Ferdinand Schörner found Priess an "iron soldier" and "*the* man for these times" (July 1944) but one who needed an "intelligent assistant."[27] Schörner had been impressed by Priess's resolute conduct in the field but, perhaps, driven to question his mental stability as the result of Priess's refusal in the summer of 1944 to relinquish command of his division although seriously ill with dysentery. Himmler suggested that he be assigned a specialist whom he couldn't terrorize but may well have been pleased by such evidence of inner-directed *Härte*;

26. "Beurteilung des Obersturmführers Priess der SS 2," May 18, 1936; "Beurteilung des SS-O'sturmbannführer, Kommandeur des SS-Totenkopf Art. Regt.," September 29, 1940; "Dienstlaufbahn"; Recommendation by Max Simon for Ritterkreuz for Priess, March 10, 1943. BDC/MDF. For a thorough account of the Demyansk crisis, see Sydnor, *Soldiers of Destruction*, pp. 208-54.

27. Fernschreiben, Heeresgruppe Süd, September 5, 1943; "Stellungnahme zur Beurteilung über Gruppenführer und Generalleutnant der Waffen-SS Priess, Kommandeur der 3. SS-Panzer Div. 'Totenkopf.'" BDC/MDF.

in any event, the Reichsführer appointed him commander of the First SS Panzer Corps in November 1944, the command that would carry him into the Ardennes and also into the courtroom at Dachau in 1946.[28]

In an entirely different category from either Dietrich or Priess was Fritz Kraemer. Information on Kraemer's formative years is not available, but he served as a lieutenant in the Stettin and Berlin municipal police and was sent to the Berlin War Academy in October 1934 for command training as part of the Nazi effort to circumvent the military limitations of the Treaty of Versailles. In May 1935, shortly after Germany had reintroduced military conscription, Kraemer was promoted to captain and simultaneously transferred to the army. Unlike the untutored Dietrich and stolid Priess, to whom war was largely a matter of instinct, Kraemer was a military intellectual of the type that characterized the Prussian-German General Staff Corps. When World War II began, he was a staff officer with the Thirteenth Panzer Division where he remained until December 1942, then being posted as Oberquartiermeister (senior quartermaster) to the army's First Panzer Corps, and almost simultaneously awarded the Knight's Cross. He was later rated by his superior as "an above average" divisional staff officer and a "model" Oberquartiermeister, demonstrating "great severity toward himself and heart for his troops."[29]

Kraemer's membership in the Waffen-SS was not of his own volition. Sepp Dietrich had probably come to know Kraemer in the course of operations in which the Leibstandarte and Thirteenth Panzer Division had fought together in Russia. In any event, it was obvious that Dietrich would require expert technical assistance in the command of the SS Panzer Corps which began to be organized for him in the spring and summer of 1943. The Waffen-SS was unable to

28. "Angelegenheit Gruppenführer Priess, Kommandeur 3. Pz. Div. SS T," July 11, 1944; Himmler to Priess, November 6, 1944. BDC/MDF.

29. "Dienstlaufbahn"; "Beurteilung zum 1. März, 1943"; "Antrag auf Freigabe des Oberst i.G. Fritz Kraemer," July 28, 1944. BDC/MDF.

supply the necessary talent from its own ranks and therefore "borrowed" Kraemer from the army, an occurrence that was not unique. Kraemer was seconded to the SS for service as chief of staff of the First SS Panzer Corps in June 1943 and given the right to wear the uniform of an SS-Oberführer (senior colonel) in September while retaining his army commission. Himmler was desirous of terminating this ambiguous and implicitly humiliating situation, and on August 1, 1944, Kraemer was formally absorbed into the officer corps of the Waffen-SS. Following a brief period as commander of the Twelfth SS Panzer Division "Hitler Jugend" in October and November while that division was being rebuilt after the fierce summer battles in France, Kraemer was appointed chief of staff of Sepp Dietrich's Sixth Panzer Army, then being readied for the Ardennes offensive.[30]

One officer brought to trial in the Malmédy case falls into none of the categories established in this analysis. Karl Schiff* entered the SS in November 1931, soon after having graduated from medical school (he was then in his mid-twenties), and joined the Nazi Party the following year. His activities in the prewar period are not clear, but shortly after the outbreak of war he was sent to Poland with an SS Totenkopf unit. A brief tour of duty with the Waffen-SS Division "Das Reich" was followed by an appointment as SS garrison physician for the Lublin area. His duties were described by his superior, SS-Gruppenführer and Lieutenant General of Police Sporrenberg, as providing normal medical services to SS personnel in and around Lublin but also functioning as "head of Section IV in the office of the SS and Police Leader Lublin *with the widest responsibilities*" (italics mine).[31] In characteristic Nazi fashion, bland language masked stark horror, for Schiff's duties included the supervision of the "health" of

30. "Dienstlaufbahn," and "Beurteilung," BDC/MDF; Fritz Kraemer, *Commitment of 6 Panzer Army,* U.S. National Archives Foreign Military Studies Collection, A–924, p. 4.
31. "Dienstzeitbescheinigung"; "Beförderung in der Waffen-SS," BDC/MDF.

Jews held in labor camps in the Lublin area and the selection of those no longer fit to work for gassing at the nearby Maidenek extermination camp. At the end of 1943, Schiff was transferred to the Leibstandarte SS Adolf Hitler and became regimental surgeon of the First SS Panzer Regiment, with which he was to serve during the Ardennes offensive.[32]

The overwhelming majority of the Malmédy defendants (fifty-one) were enlisted men and noncommissioned officers. Almost half (twenty-three) were Sturmmänner (acting corporals). Extreme youth was their most obvious characteristic, twenty-two having been twenty years of age or under and the youngest, a bare sixteen at the time of the Ardennes offensive. A typical Sturmmann had an elementary school education, had worked as a manual laborer, and had participated in Nazi youth organizations. Only one Sturmmann was a Party member. Combat experience varied from none prior to the Ardennes offensive (for four Sturmmänner) to two years. Most (probably fifteen) had seen action in France following the Normandy invasion. Seven had probably fought in the East as well.

Eight of the fifty-one were Rottenführer (corporals). Several of these had been transferred from the Luftwaffe and most had been drafted. Unlike the Sturmmänner, the Rottenführer, with two exceptions who were seeing their first action in the Ardennes, had experienced at least twenty months of service and had probably fought in Russia.

Noncommissioned officers of the rank of Scharführer (sergeant) and above (numbering twenty among the defendants) had long service experience, averaging fifty-two months. One remarkable case, who had served "on the home front" from May 1940 until August 1944, was seeing his first action in the Ardennes. Normandy had been the first field experience for a second. The remainder had had considerable combat experience, including large doses of the brutal war in the

---

32. Promotion proposal by Sporrenberg, n.d. BDC/MDF.

East.[33] All but one, who had been transferred from the Luft-waffe, had volunteered for the Waffen-SS. Of these, only five had joined the SS before the outbreak of war. Wilhelm Schoettel* was a noteworthy member of this group. He was born in 1919, the son of a glassblower, and learned the trade of glass grinder. In November 1938 (for economic reasons, he would claim at the trial), he volunteered for the Leibstan-darte SS Adolf Hitler. Schoettel never joined the Nazi Party and during World War II spent 680 days in actual combat, revealing himself to be a noncommissioned officer of rare courage and presence of mind as well as one blessed with more than a modicum of good luck. In heavy street-fighting in Kharkov in March 1943, Schoettel's tank was hit by anti-tank fire as it approached a Russian barricade. The only member of the crew to survive, he immediately assumed command of another tank and smashed through the Russian obstacle.[34]

Four months later, Schoettel, then in command of an ar-mored platoon, found himself at the focus of one of the larg-est tank battles of the war. Early in July 1943, German forces undertook their last large-scale offensive in Russia, an effort to pinch off the huge Kursk salient. On July 12, the Russians launched a massive armored counterstroke with 850 tanks and self-propelled guns west of Prokhorovka. Schoettel was among the first to observe the approach of Russian armor and threw his tank platoon into the enemy flank, being cred-ited with the destruction of six T-34s. Schoettel distinguished himself in several other engagements on the crumbling Rus-sian Front and acted with equal bravery and dash in Nor-mandy during the summer of 1944. In the course of a Cana-dian attack on the Leibstandarte's positions near Tilly la Champagne on August 1, 1944, Schoettel's tank was hit re-peatedly by artillery fire, which knocked off a tread and ren-

33. BDC/MDF.
34. U.S. v. Bersin, 153/4/000725 (3236); "Vorschlag Nr 469 für die Verleihung des Deutschen Kreuzes in Gold," BDC/MDF.

dered the cannon and turret machine gun inoperable. The immobilized and largely helpless vehicle was quickly surrounded by Canadian infantry, but its crew, led by Schoettel, defended it with small arms until rescued by a German counterattack.[35]

Rather different was the record of Franz Niemann.* He was born in 1915, completed the eight years of the Volksschule, then learned the trade of cloth finishing. He joined the SS in June 1933 and became a member of the Nazi Party. At a time that cannot be established with certainty but may have been as early as May 1934, he transferred to the SS-Totenkopfverbände and was assigned to duty at the Oranienburg concentration camp. In the spring of 1940, Niemann was, himself, arrested and sentenced to two years' incarceration in a concentration camp by a Higher SS and Police Court. He would later maintain in the presence of his American captors that his offense had been to make food "available" to political prisoners, perhaps a euphemistic and self-serving reference to profitable activity on the camp black market. Niemann was interned initially at Dachau but was transferred in July to Sachsenhausen concentration camp where he was left to meditate on his sins until November. Then, the manpower needs of the expanding Waffen-SS resulted in Niemann's release to the punishment company of the Totenkopf Division's engineer battalion. Seriously wounded in October 1941 in the Ukraine, Niemann returned to active duty with the Leibstandarte after his recuperation and seems to have served with that unit until the end of the war.[36]

The information on which these biographical sketches are based is, at best, fragmentary and tells us relatively little of the "mind sets" of the persons under examination. Specifically, to what degree did they conform to the official image

35. *Ibid.*
36. U.S. v. Bersin, 153/4/000734-35 (3247-48); "Dienstlaufbahn" and "RuS Fragebogen," BDC/MDF.

of the Waffen-SS as a body of ideologically dedicated soldiers? Membership in the Hitler Youth, and all but the most senior defendants had belonged to it, is of limited significance. While a vehicle by which German youth was indoctrinated with an ideology that differed from the "SS ideology" only in degree of virulence, it was an organization through which most German males of an age distribution similar to that of the Malmédy defendants would have passed, whether destined for SS membership or not.[37] As an index of comparative ideological commitment, it is therefore useless. Party membership was also of limited import, even among professional Waffen-SS officers. All SS men were encouraged to join the Party but suffered no disabilities if they did not, as Peiper's career amply demonstrates. SS men were committed to defending the Nazi movement with their lives; alongside that commitment, Party membership was an insignificant formality.

Another possible index of ideological dedication is religious affiliation. The Nazi movement was unquestionably anti-Christian, although this quality was muted for political reasons. The SS, however, as an ostensibly exclusive elite within the movement, could afford to be somewhat more stringent in this regard and attempted to substitute for traditional religious creeds a vague pantheism with overtones of a romanticized ancient Germanic paganism. In order to avoid the negative connotations of descriptive terms such as "paganism" and "heathenism," Himmler in 1936 ordered that SS converts to this spiritual mélange be designated gottgläubig (believing in God), "God" being understood as an impersonal life-force pervading the universe.[38] SS men were encouraged to withdraw from the traditional Christian de-

---

37. Membership in the Hitler Youth became compulsory in 1936 for all children between the ages of ten and eighteen. Karl Dietrich Bracher, *The German Dictatorship,* trans. Jean Steinberg (New York, 1970), p. 261.

38. Order signed by Personalreferent beim RFSS (Schmitt), November 6, 1936, T–354/366/4070648.

nominations, although this seems never to have been an overt requirement.[39] Whether or not an SS man declared himself to be *gottgläubig* probably did have considerable positive correlation with the degree of his ideological commitment. It required him publicly to proclaim a rupture with what, in many cases, was an important element of childhood experience and family tradition, a move that could not often have been made lightly. Significantly, the percentage of SS men who had declared themselves *gottgläubig* by 1938 was highest in the Totenkopfverbände, that branch of the SS whose members' duties diverged most decisively from traditional norms. Unfortunately, religious affiliation can be determined for only twenty-six of the Malmédy defendants, but of these, eighteen had declared themselves to be *gottgläubig* while five adhered to the Protestant and three to the Roman Catholic churches. Fourteen of the eighteen *Gottgläubige* were officers, representing 64 percent of the total number of officers among the defendants; and all the officers whose religious persuasion can be ascertained were *gottgläubig*.[40]

But what of the act of volunteering for SS duty? Himmler was wont to think of his SS as an organization whose members had voluntarily dedicated themselves to ideologically motivated struggle.[41] Even in the VT-Waffen-SS, this was undoubtedly true of some members. But many had joined simply as a means of discharging their military obligations and had selected the VT-Waffen-SS rather than the army because it appeared to be vaguely more glamorous or seemed to offer the likelihood of more rapid advancement. It is reasonable

39. The "encouragement" could assume coercive forms. See Höhne, *Orden*, pp. 417-18.

40. BDC/MDF.

41. In this context, it is relevant to note that the monthly magazine published by the Waffen-SS veterans organization (HIAG) is entitled *Der Freiwillige* (*The Volunteer*), this, in spite of the fact that perhaps one third of wartime Waffen-SS men were conscripts (estimate in *Nazi Conspiracy and Aggression. Opinion and Judgement*, p. 99).

to assume that the ranks of the ideologically fervid were larger among those who had volunteered for SS duty rather than among those who had been conscripted. All categories, however, were represented among the Malmédy defendants.

The Malmédy defendants were neither an undifferentiated body of fanatical "storm troopers" nor were they uniformly "soldiers like any others." In forming a composite impression of the group, one must consider "pure" soldierly types such as Fritz Kraemer and Wilhelm Schoettel along with those who had functioned as more direct instruments of Nazi ideological aims, such as Karl Schiff and Franz Niemann, as well as reflect upon the ambiguities in the careers of Dietrich, Priess, and Peiper. One must also avoid the simplistic notion that the conduct of the Malmédy defendants in the Ardennes was, in some sense, predetermined. They were responding to a situation only partly of their own making, although the specific way in which they responded to it was, of course, strongly conditioned by training and combat experience.

III. DASH FOR THE MEUSE

Even in the fall of 1944, after the summer battles in northwestern France had exacted a frightful toll in German troops and equipment, Hitler believed it possible to destroy a major fraction of Allied forces in northwestern Europe and, thus, decisively alter the course of the war. A new panzer army, the Sixth, was organized under the command of Sepp Dietrich as the battering-ram which, with the support of Manteuffel's Fifth Panzer Army, was to break through lightly held American positions in the rugged and heavily wooded Ardennes of southeastern Belgium, strike northwest to the Meuse River and race for the port of Antwerp eighty miles beyond, thus splitting the Allied forces in northern France and the Low Countries and, simultaneously, depriving them of a major port of supply.[1]

Before so daring and desperate a plan could be implemented, the SS panzer divisions which now formed a major part of German striking power had to be hastily rebuilt. German industry was still capable of providing the tanks and guns for another attempt at blitzkrieg, and men could still be found to operate them, but many of them were very young, hastily trained, and inexperienced. Frantic efforts

1. Literature on the Ardennes offensive or "Battle of the Bulge" is extensive, although much of it is quite superficial. The best work is that by Hugh M. Cole, *The Ardennes: Battle of the Bulge (U.S. Army in World War II)* (Washington, D.C., 1965). On Hitler's thinking, see pp. 19-32.

were made in the waning months of 1944 to whip them into shape in terms of technical training and emotional fervor. Although Americans did not occupy a place on the Nazi scale of demonology comparable to that assigned to Russians, most of them being conceded racial qualities comparable to those possessed by Germans, they were, nevertheless, "the enemy" and guilty of horrendous crimes. Propaganda that circulated among Waffen-SS personnel of the Sixth Panzer Army during the fall of 1944 stressed the ostensible rapine and pillage of which American troops were guilty in those areas of western Germany that they had already occupied. This was a new factor in the consciousness of the German fighting man, for never before in the course of World War II had enemy soldiers been in control of territory and citizens of Germany proper. It served to sharpen hatred of the Anglo-American enemy which was already at a high level as the result of the heavy and often indiscriminate bombing of the German cities. It was hoped that enthusiasm, generated by a desire to "get at" the enemy and by evocations of memories of the past combat "glories" of the Waffen-SS, would compensate for inexperience and substandard training.[2]

Hitler's "own," the First SS Panzer Division "Leibstandarte SS Adolf Hitler," was to lead the way for Sepp Dietrich's army. It was indicative of the reputation that he had achieved as a daring and resourceful leader of armor that the twenty-nine-year-old commander of the Leibstandarte's First SS Panzer Regiment, SS-Obersturmbannführer (Lieutenant Colonel) Jochen Peiper, should have been given the critical assignment of dashing for the Meuse and establishing a

---

2. See Fritz Kraemer, *Commitment of 6 Panzer Army*, U.S. National Archives Foreign Military Studies Collection, A-924, p. 5; "Ausbildungsplan für die Zeit vom 23.10-20.11.44," T-354/615/000811-18. For examples of pre-attack propaganda, see "Keiner dünke sich besser," *Politische Wochenschau, Informationsdienst der Abt. VI, LSSAH,* November 29, 1944, T-354/624/000588-89; "Warum sind sie uns nicht gewachsen?" *Politische Wochenschau,* December 6, 1944, T-354/625/000145-46; "So haust der Feind," *Politische Wochenschau,* November 29, 1944, T-354/624/000590.

bridgehead at Huy, it was hoped within twenty-four hours after the opening of the offensive.[3]

Hitler had first declared his intention of launching a major offensive in the West on September 16, but secrecy was strictly enforced, and knowledge of the impending operations filtered down from the top only slowly. SS-Brigadeführer (Brigadier General) Fritz Kraemer learned of it on November 16 when he assumed the post of Sixth Panzer Army's chief of staff. The fact that the army was being prepared for an offensive might have been suggested by training exercises in the waning days of October, which presumed conditions almost identical to those that the Germans would face in December.[4] Whatever Jochen Peiper's suspicions might have been, they were greatly sharpened when on December 11 Kraemer approached him at the Leibstandarte's bivouac area near Euskirchen west of Bonn and asked him how long he thought an armored regiment would require to travel fifty miles (the approximate distance as the crow flies from German lines to Huy). Peiper apparently preferred empiricism to speculation (although he must have often ridden similar distances in his combat career) and took one of his regiment's Panther tanks on a night ride of the prescribed distance behind German lines.[5] Although moderately colorful in the recounting, this excursion is of questionable value since the roads were superior to those that Peiper would encounter in the actual offensive, the distance to Huy over these roads was much greater, enemy opposition absent, and only one vehicle was involved. Nevertheless, Peiper, now convinced that a major westward push was in the offing, could attempt to give his panzer and SPW drivers advice on

3. *An Interview with Obst. Joachim Peiper,* U.S. National Archives Foreign Military Studies Collection, ETHINT 10, pp. 5-9.

4. Cole, *Ardennes,* p. 1; Kraemer, *6 Panzer Army,* p. 8; LSSAH, "Der Kommandeur, an alle Kompanien," October 18, 1944 [two documents], T–354/615/000808-10.

5. ETHINT 10, p. 2.

negotiating the difficult terrain that they were soon likely to encounter.

Peiper was not present at the conference attended by Hitler and his army and corps commanders at Bad Nauheim on December 12 but received his marching orders from the headquarters of SS-Gruppenführer (Major General) Hermann Priess, commander of the First SS Panzer Corps, on the following day. By the morning of December 14, Peiper's command had melted into the heavily wooded pre-attack assembly area in the Blankenheim Forest about ten miles east of the Belgian frontier. Before noon, Peiper was called to divisional headquarters with other officers of the division to receive detailed orders in preparation for the attack. The conference was scheduled to begin at 11:00 A.M., but due to roads jammed with traffic, Peiper arrived late and had to be filled in by the commander of the First SS Panzer Division "Leibstandarte," SS-Oberführer Wilhelm Mohnke and his chief of staff, SS-Obersturmbannführer Dietrich Ziemssen.[6]

Peiper was less than pleased with his assignment. The offensive was to commence in the predawn hours of December 16, and its outcome would largely depend on Peiper's success in reaching the Meuse with all possible speed. The route assigned to him ran for long distances over narrow dirt roads which snaked through hilly and heavily wooded terrain, forest tracks that Peiper contemptuously described as "fit for bicycles," not tanks.[7] The routes had been chosen for the relative paucity of bridges that would have to be negotiated—bridges that could readily be destroyed by the enemy (an important consideration as events would prove) and which, even if intact, might not support the weight of Peiper's tanks: twenty-six-ton Mark IVs, fifty-ton Panthers, and seventy-two-ton Royal Tigers. Even more discouraging was the revelation that two trainloads of gasoline destined for the

---

6. Peiper testimony, U.S. v. Bersin, 153/3/000124-25 (1903-04).
7. ETHINT 10, p. 7.

German attack force had not arrived. Peiper could, therefore, count on starting out with full fuel tanks but with no reserves and would have to capture large stocks of gasoline along his line of march if his advance was not to stall for want of fuel.[8] Mohnke emphasized the absolute necessity of a rapid breakthrough without concern for flank security and a willingness for self-sacrifice. He further stressed that at Bad Nauheim Hitler had expressed special confidence in "his" Leibstandarte and expected it to "fight fanatically."[9] The Führer had long come to count on the elite divisions of the Waffen-SS to achieve the "impossible."

Peiper returned to his own command post—a forester's cabin in the Blankenheim Forest—by two o'clock and began to prepare his troop dispositions.[10] In addition to four tank companies of his own First SS Panzer Regiment, his command included the unit that he had led with such notable success in Russia in 1943, the Third Battalion of the Second Panzergrenadier Regiment, now commanded by SS-Sturmbannführer (Major) Johannes Metzger, an additional Panzergrenadier company, two companies of motorized combat engineers, an anti-aircraft company, a few of the Royal Tiger tanks of the First SS Panzer Corps' 501st Heavy Tank Battalion and, somewhat incongruously, a company of landbound paratroopers of the Luftwaffe.[11] According to German custom, this composite group was identified by the name of its commander and, hence, was known as Kampfgruppe Peiper (Battlegroup Peiper). It was a powerful fighting force, although hardly overwhelming in view of its assignment. Attached to Kampfgruppe Peiper but not under its tactical control was a detachment of SS-Sturmbannführer Otto Skorzeny's 150th Panzer Brigade, English-speaking German soldiers

8. *Ibid.*, pp. 7-8.
9. Peiper testimony, U.S. v. Bersin 153/3/000124-25 (1903-04).
10. *Ibid.*, 000125-27 (1904-06).
11. Prosecution testimony, U.S. v. Bersin, 153/1/000201 (196); Peiper "Kommentar," p. 2.

dressed and equipped as Americans, whose job it was to spread confusion and panic behind enemy lines.[12]

Peiper had commanded composite battlegroups in Russia with considerable success, operating with reckless daring, skill, and ruthlessness.[13] But the task that now confronted him was quite different from leading such a force on the plains of the Ukraine with vast areas over which to deploy. In the Ardennes, Peiper calculated, his march column would be strung out over fifteen miles of narrow forest roads with little opportunity to maneuver should enemy resistance be encountered. He planned, therefore, to concentrate forces at the head of his column powerful and flexible enough to cope with any problem that might confront them—strong elements of tanks and Panzergrenadiers as well as self-propelled anti-aircraft guns and combat engineers.[14]

At a conference with his subordinate commanders held in the forester's cabin at around 4:00 P.M., Peiper explained the objectives of the forthcoming offensive and stressed that, in view of the grave disabilities under which the Kampfgruppe would be operating, the only chance for success lay in the maximum possible speed, surprise, and the ruthless commitment of men and materiel. The leading elements of the Kampfgruppe were to stop for nothing and drive with single-minded purpose for the Meuse. Crucial to later events would be the question of instructions issued concerning prisoners of war. In what may have been a self-serving postwar (but pre-investigation and -trial) statement, Peiper averred that he had transmitted an order from divisional headquarters which stated that it was not to be the job of the armored spearhead to collect prisoners; that task, rather, was to be left to the

---

12. ETHINT 10, p. 6.
13. A Kampfgruppe Peiper similar in organization to the above but lacking Royal Tigers had fought in Russia in December 1943. See "Vorschlag für die Verleihung des Eichenlaubes zum Ritterkreuz des EK," December 27, 1943, BDC/MDF.
14. ETHINT 10, p. 9.

following infantry. The order supposedly further warned of possible resistance by Belgian guerrillas, which was to be broken "ruthlessly" if encountered.[15]

On the morning of December 15, Peiper attended a final conference at the headquarters of the corps commander. Priess gave the assembled divisional and regimental leaders a "pep talk" which was followed by an overall review of the attack plan by the corps chief of staff. Immediately thereafter, Peiper called a second meeting of his battalion commanders, issued final orders, and sent his subordinates back to their units. Between that time and the small hours of December 16, the same process would be followed through battalion, company, and platoon levels: announcement of the impending attack, the issuance of orders, and an "inspirational" address of greater or lesser length and eloquence according to the oratorical talents and inclinations of the individual commander.[16]

Kampfgruppe Peiper's mission began inauspiciously. The Twelfth Volksgrenadier Division, under the command of General Gerhardt Engel, had been given the assignment of punching a hole in the front of the U.S. Ninety-ninth Infantry Division in the Losheim sector through which Kampfgruppe Peiper would then hurl itself on its critical drive to the Meuse.[17] Peiper moved to Engel's headquarters in the predawn hours of December 16 in order to be able to commit his force to battle the moment Engel had achieved a breakthrough. Artillery preparation began at 5:30 A.M., Engel's infantry moving forward one half-hour later; but instead of the prompt jump-off that he expected, Peiper found himself still at Engel's headquarters by early afternoon. The bridge northwest of Losheim, which the Germans had themselves blown during their eastward retreat months earlier, could not

15. Peiper testimony, U.S. v. Bersin, 153/3/000125-27 (1904-06).
16. *Ibid.*, 000129-30 (1908-09).
17. Cole, *Ardennes*, p. 260.

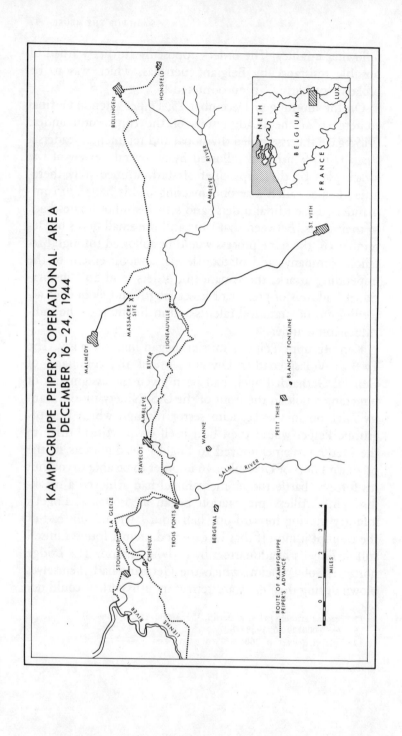

KAMPFGRUPPE PEIPER'S OPERATIONAL AREA
DECEMBER 16–24, 1944

HONSFELD

BÜLLINGEN

AMBLÈVE RIVER

ST VITH

MASSACRE SITE

LIGNEAUVILLE

MALMÉDY

AMBLÈVE RIVER

BLANCHE FONTAINE

STAVELOT

WANNE

PETIT THIER

SALM RIVER

LA GLEIZE

TROIS PONTS

BERGEVAL

STOUMONT

CHENEUX

LIENNE RIVER

NETH

BELGIUM

FRANCE

LUX

ROUTE OF KAMPFGRUPPE
PEIPER'S ADVANCE

MILES
1   0   1   2   3   4

be repaired due to the presence of the Twelfth Volksgrenadier Division's horse-drawn artillery, which clogged the approaches to the bridge and prevented combat engineers from reaching it with their equipment. Peiper's response was typically energetic. After a fruitless personal effort to direct traffic and restore order, Peiper took his lead vehicles onto the road around 4:00 P.M. with orders to run down anything in their paths. An overland detour around the bridge was found and Losheim entered by forward elements of the Kampfgruppe after dark.[18] Peiper's orders now called for his battlegroup to proceed via the bridge northwest of Losheim to Honsfeld. A radio message from divisional headquarters informed him that that bridge, too, was unusable and directed him to detour southwest to Lanzerath before swinging north into Honsfeld where he was to assume command of elements of the Ninth Regiment, Third Parachute Division. These, it was suggested, might be used for flank protection on the thrust into Lanzerath.[19]

The detour through Lanzerath cost Peiper his first significant losses. Leaving the main road at Losheim, the Kampfgruppe cut across snow-covered fields studded with recently laid American mines and, probably, older German devices. The result was that Peiper reached Lanzerath weaker by three tanks and five SPWs.[20] Disdaining sleep, as he would do throughout the offensive, Peiper conferred with the Luftwaffe colonel commanding the parachutists concerning American dispositions between Lanzerath and Honsfeld. Concluding that the parachutists knew nothing and had attempted no serious reconnaissance, Peiper set out for Honsfeld at 4:00 A.M. the next day (December 17) and entered the town at dawn, finding it occupied by American troops (Company B of the 612th Tank Destroyer Battalion), most of

18. ETHINT 10, pp. 13-14.
19. *Ibid.*, pp. 14-15; *An Interview with Obst. Joachim Peiper*, U.S. National Archives Foreign Military Studies Collection, ETHINT 11, pp. 3-4; Peiper testimony, U.S. v. Bersin, 153/3/000141-42 (1920-21).
20. Peiper testimony, U.S. v. Bersin, 153/3/000141-42 (1920-21).

whom were still asleep. Resistance was light, and Peiper recalled seeing only a few soldiers "jumping from house to house" as his command car pushed through.[21] The men of the Ninth Parachute Regiment were left behind to deal with residual resistance and await further orders. Fighting in Honsfeld was far from over, however, for two Panthers of the First Panzer Regiment's Second Company, which lagged far behind the point of the Kampfgruppe, were "knocked out" as late as 11:00 A.M. while passing through the town.[22]

Peiper's battle plan now called for a thrust to Moderscheid—about four miles in a direct line west of Honsfeld—through Hepscheid. The route through Büllingen (Bullange) was a better one, and German intelligence indicated that stocks of American gasoline might be found there. That route had been assigned to Twelfth SS Panzer Division "Hitler Jugend," Leibstandarte's sister division in the First SS Panzer Corps, operating to the north; but sounds of battle coming far behind from the northeast led Peiper to conclude that their route of march could be safely "borrowed."[23]

Büllingen was reached at around 8:00 A.M., and after destroying a dozen American liaison planes on the airstrip outside the town, the Kampfgruppe was able to refuel with fifty-two thousand gallons of captured gasoline. Peiper recalled seeing perhaps a dozen American prisoners at the airfield and some sixty in Büllingen itself being directed to the rear in captured American trucks. It was in Büllingen, too, that Peiper claimed to have witnessed Belgian civilians firing on SS troopers from the windows of houses.[24]

While fuel was being poured into the tanks of Peiper's lead vehicles with the assistance of American prisoners, Büllingen came under artillery fire. As each tank and SPW was

21. ETHINT 10, pp. 14-15; Peiper testimony, U.S. v. Bersin, 153/3/000142-43 (1921-22).
22. *Kampfgruppe Peiper (15-26 Dec. 44)*, U.S. National Archives Foreign Military Studies Collection, C-004, p. 3.
23. ETHINT 10, p. 16.
24. *Ibid.*; Peiper testimony, U.S. v. Bersin, 153/3/000145 (1924).

fueled, it departed in haste but found the going painfully slow on the muddy road from Büllingen to Moderscheid. Two American ambulances and their crews were captured two miles outside Büllingen, and as Peiper drove westward, sharing the meager comforts of the SPWs of his two lead battalion commanders, additional American vehicles were intercepted and, Peiper later recalled, routinely directed toward the rear.[25]

Between one o'clock and one-thirty in the afternoon, elements of Kampfgruppe Peiper were approaching the road intersection at Baugnez about four kilometers southeast of Malmédy.[26] According to Peiper's postwar recollections, he had paused to question an American prisoner while the point of the column continued on. His efforts at interrogation were suddenly interrupted by the roar and crackle of cannon and machine-gun fire. Riding to the point, he found five tanks and an equal number of SPWs firing at a range of about five hundred yards at a column of American trucks which had been proceeding south on the road from Malmédy to St. Vith. Peiper professed distress over the expenditure of ammunition occasioned by the chance encounter and grief over the destruction of "beautiful" American trucks which German forces desperately needed and ordered that firing be halted. In the din and confusion of battle, it required several minutes for his order to be understood by his SS troopers. Perceiving that this lightly armed American convoy presented no danger to his own heavily armed and armored force, Peiper showed little concern for the mopping-up operation and ordered his leading elements to press forward.[27] The American unit surprised at the Baugnez crossroads was Battery B, 285th Field Artillery Observation Battalion,

25. ETHINT 10, p. 17; C–004, p. 4; Peiper testimony, U.S. v. Bersin, 153/3/000146 (1925).

26. Recollections of the time vary slightly. C–004, p. 4; Peiper testimony, U.S. v. Bersin, 153/3/000148 (1927); Cole, *Ardennes*, p. 261.

27. Peiper testimony, U.S. v. Bersin, 153/3/000148-50 (1927-29), C–004, pp. 4-5.

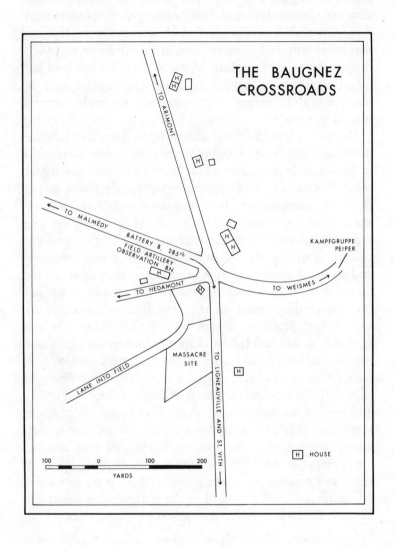

THE BAUGNEZ
CROSSROADS

TO ARIMONT

H
H

H

TO MALMÉDY

BATTERY B, 285th
FIELD ARTILLERY
OBSERVATION BN.

H

TO HEDAMONT

H

KAMPFGRUPPE
PEIPER

TO WEISMES

LANE INTO FIELD

MASSACRE
SITE

TO LIGNEAUVILLE AND ST. VITH

H

100   0   100   200

YARDS

H HOUSE

Seventh Armored Division. What came to be known as the "Malmédy Massacre" would follow. But Jochen Peiper's primary interest lay with the next objective, Ligneauville, one mile to the south.

In Ligneauville, the point of the Kampfgruppe encountered elements of the U.S. Ninth Armored Division, including several well-concealed Sherman tanks. Charging at high speed, the lead Panther tank, commanded by the battalion adjutant, was struck by a 75-mm shell from one of the Shermans and burst into flames. Peiper, in an SPW fifty yards behind the hapless Panther, saw the American tank's cannon traversing onto his own vehicle, whose driver hastily pulled back behind a house. Another SPW, less circumspect, was destroyed. The redoubtable Peiper, in a fine example of the Waffen-SS brand of personal combat leadership, seized a Panzerfaust (a short-range antitank rocket launcher) and began to stalk the offending Sherman. Before he could get within range, the American tank erupted in flames from a hit by a high-velocity shell from a German self-propelled gun. In other brief but deadly engagements, Kampfgruppe Peiper accounted for an M-10 tank destroyer and an additional Sherman.[28]

While waiting for lagging elements of the Kampfgruppe to close up, the SS troopers cared for their wounded, Peiper himself bandaging the badly burned face and hands of the battalion adjutant. According to Peiper's later recollections, several American prisoners were rounded up and left behind with those German wounded too badly injured to travel on.[29]

By now, twenty-four hours had elapsed since the start of Kampfgruppe Peiper's race to the Meuse and almost thirty-six hours since the formal beginning of the German offensive; yet, the objective at Huy still lay fifty miles to the west. Peiper planned to take Stavelot, the next village on his line

28. Peiper testimony, U.S. v. Bersin, 153/3/000155 (1934); John S. D. Eisenhower, *The Bitter Woods* (New York, 1969), p. 238.
29. Peiper testimony, U.S. v. Bersin, 153/3/000156 (1935).

of march, and its bridge across the Amblève River. The town, some six miles west of Ligneauville, could be approached only by the main road, as the terrain to the left of the road fell off precipitously and to the right rose steeply. The road, moreover, curved sharply just as it entered Stavelot, an ideal point on which defenders might train their guns.[30] Yet, had Peiper attacked immediately upon arriving in the vicinity of Stavelot as night began to fall, there is little doubt that he could have taken the bridge and the town, for the only American troops present were a squad of the 291st Combat Engineers Battalion, then in the process of barricading the approaches to the bridge.[31] For reasons that are still obscure but probably involved Peiper's overestimation of American strength, the attack was postponed until the next morning, by which time troops of the Third Panzergrenadier Battalion had arrived in force. During the night, however, the town's defenses had been reinforced by a company of the U.S. 526th Armored Infantry Battalion and a platoon of three-inch antitank guns. When Peiper's attack took place, the capture of the Amblève bridge required the sacrifice of several vehicles and caused more than a score of casualties.[32] This error in judgment was overshadowed by another, for the point of the Kampfgruppe passed within a few hundred yards of a major American gasoline dump outside Stavelot.[33] One must conclude that the quality of the Kampfgruppe's reconnaissance in this action left more than a little to be desired.

Resistance in the town, moreover, might not have been totally neutralized. As his column passed through Stavelot, Peiper later asserted, it received fire from what he took to be Belgian resistance fighters. He further claimed that German wounded, left temporarily unguarded at an aid station, were

30. ETHINT 10, pp. 18-19.
31. Cole, *Ardennes*, p. 265; Cf. ETHINT 10, pp. 18-19; C–004, p. 7.
32. Cole, *Ardennes*, p. 266; ETHINT 10, pp. 19-20.
33. This was the U.S. First Army's dump at Francorchamps, ETHINT 11, pp. 7-8; Cole, *Ardennes*, pp. 266-67.

tortured by armed Belgian civilians. Hot water was ostensibly poured on some, others were threatened with shooting, one was wounded by a knife-wielding civilian.[34] Had this been true, or had the men of Kampfgruppe Peiper, many of whom had experienced guerrilla warfare in the East and were highly conscious of such possibilities, believed it to have been true, then events that transpired later in the day at La Gleize become easier to comprehend.

In war, bridges are the bane of the attacker and often the salvation of his intended victim. Weak defenders can often halt a vastly superior offensive force, a fact made a cliché by the legend of Horatio. Kampfgruppe Peiper had been delayed for twelve hours in its hesitant efforts to cross a loop of the ambling Amblève River at Stavelot. In its drive for the Meuse at Huy, the battlegroup faced the necessity of crossing still another bend of the river and its tributary, the Salm, and therefore aimed for the bridges at Trois Ponts at the confluence of the two.

As the Kampfgruppe approached the bridge over the Amblève, it became clear that Trois Ponts would be vigorously defended. Peiper hastily took cover under a railroad overpass as enemy fire streamed across the river. As his lead vehicles bore down on the Amblève bridge, it and the Salm bridge a short distance beyond were destroyed by explosive charges. Trois Ponts had been ably denied the Kampfgruppe by Company C of the Fifty-first Engineer Battalion, U.S. Army.[35]

In retrospect, Peiper regarded his failure to capture the bridges at Trois Ponts as the most crucial setback of the offensive. West of the Amblève and Salm, the terrain became much more favorable for the movement of armored vehicles, and Peiper believed that had he been able to push through Trois Ponts, assuming sufficient fuel (a major qualification),

34. Peiper testimony, U.S. v. Bersin, 153/3/000159 (1938). See also C-004, p. 8.

35. Peiper testimony, U.S. v. Bersin, 153/3/000160 (1939); Eisenhower, *Bitter Woods,* pp. 245-47.

his Kampfgruppe would have been able to cover the remaining distance to the Meuse that day (December 18). Denied the Trois Ponts crossings, he was now forced to swing north along the valley of the Amblève, hoping to find another bridge, southwest of La Gleize, intact.[36]

According to his testimony at his postwar trial, it was shortly after passing Trois Ponts on the morning of December 18 that Peiper received the first inkling that all had not proceeded smoothly and cleanly at the crossroads southeast of Malmédy on the previous afternoon. The commander of the Kampfgruppe's Royal Tiger tanks, then toiling ponderously near the end of the column, arrived forward and informed Peiper that a "mix-up" had taken place at "Ligneauville" (by which he presumably meant Baugnez, a short distance to the north) and that a large number of prisoners of war had been shot.[37] Peiper had neither time nor inclination to pursue a matter so tangential to the tactical problems at hand. The column pushed on as rapidly as the roads and terrain would allow and reached La Gleize early in the afternoon. The passage through the town seems to have been without incident; no Americans were encountered, and the civilian population had either fled or remained hidden. With the morning's experiences at Trois Ponts (and a possible encounter with guerrillas at Stavelot) still fresh in mind, the point of the Kampfgruppe approached the Amblève bridge southwest of La Gleize. Figures were observed near the bridge. According to Peiper, gunners in the lead Panther "spontaneously" opened fire with their machine guns at a range of four hundred yards. The battlegroup's commander recalled seeing nothing of the results of this fire as his lead vehicles rumbled over the bridge.[38]

Kampfgruppe Peiper had thus far eluded the attentions of the Allied air power which had decimated the German ar-

36. ETHINT 10, pp. 20-21.
37. Peiper testimony, U.S. v. Bersin, 153/3/000160 (1939).
38. *Ibid.*, 000161.

mored formations, including the First SS Panzer Division "Leibstandarte," during the previous summer. In fact, overcast weather, which would severely limit the activities of enemy aircraft, had been one of the prerequisites of the German offensive. Air operations had not been entirely halted, however, and it was the misfortune of the leading elements of the Kampfgruppe to be detected by American planes skimming below the cloud cover just as they had crossed the bridge southwest of La Gleize. In a brief but sharp attack by fighter-bombers, the Kampfgruppe lost three tanks and five SPWs. Perhaps even more serious than the loss of heavy equipment was the fact that, due to the narrowness of the road, the wrecked vehicles could not be bypassed but had to be laboriously dragged to the side of the thoroughfare. In this way, two and one-half hours elapsed before the Kampfgruppe could resume its march.[39]

Realizing that his offensive strike was close to irretrievable failure, Peiper sent the Third Panzergrenadier Battalion racing ahead with orders to seize the bridge near Veucy over the Lienne River in an effort to maintain westward momentum. Cheneux was passed without incident and the bridge reached after dark. Before any of Peiper's vehicles could cross, that bridge too was dynamited by a demolition team of the U.S. 291st Engineer Battalion. In vain, Peiper dispatched reconnaissance patrols to seek out other possible crossing points. One patrol found a small span north of Veucy but was ambushed in crossing by American troops, probably elements of the U.S. Thirtieth Infantry Division. Its commander was one of the few survivors and reported that although a bridge had been located, it was far too weak to bear the weight of the Kampfgruppe's tanks. From the south came the same discouraging report: a bridge had been found but it could not accommodate heavy armored vehicles. With fuel running low and American resistance obviously stiffening, Peiper decided

39. ETHINT 10, p. 21; Peiper testimony, U.S. v. Bersin, 153/3/000163 (1942).

around midnight to double back to La Gleize and resume the
march up the valley of the Amblève through Stoumont to the
bridge beyond, a desperate expedient as the road was extremely narrow and flanked by steep terrain.[40]

Forward elements of the Kampfgruppe reentered La Gleize
in the early morning hours of December 19. Peiper dispatched his First Panzer Battalion on the three-mile journey
to Stoumont. The town proved to be held by a battalion of
the U.S. Thirtieth Infantry Division equipped with antitank
guns and two 90-mm antiaircraft pieces, powerful weapons
that could be used against ground targets as the Germans had
long used their famed "88s." Furthermore, the American
battalion was soon reinforced by ten Sherman tanks of the
743rd Tank Battalion.[41] The attack began at about 9:00 A.M.
A fierce two-hour engagement ensued, in the initial stages of
which the German armored spearhead was driven back. Peiper ordered Pringel,* the battalion commander, to resume
the advance and recalled later how his subordinate had approached each of his tanks with Panzerfaust in hand, threatening to destroy any tank that fell back an additional meter.
Simultaneously, Peiper coordinated the resumption of Pringel's attack with an assault by Panzergrenadiers and paratroopers which, by late morning, succeeded in driving the
Americans from the village and pushing westward to the vicinity of the railroad station two miles beyond. Prisoners were
collected and sent back under guard to La Gleize.[42]

Peiper had, himself, returned to La Gleize by early afternoon. There, he received an ominous report from the commander of his reconnaissance battalion. Stavelot had been
recaptured by American troops from the small force that Peiper had left there, a situation that meant that Kampfgruppe
Peiper's only link to the main body of German forces to the

40. ETHINT 10, p. 21; C–004, pp. 8-9; ETHINT 11, pp. 8-9; Peiper testimony,
U.S. v. Bersin, 153/3/000165 (1944); Cole, *Ardennes*, p. 268.
41. C–004, p. 9; Cole, *Ardennes*, pp. 339-40.
42. C–004, p. 9; Peiper testimony, U.S. v. Bersin, 153/3/000167 (1946).

east had been severed. The battalion commander was immediately ordered to turn back, retake Stavelot and hold it, although the likelihood that this might be accomplished was much reduced by the fact that Peiper could spare him no tanks.[43]

In fact, the offensive drive of Kampfgruppe Peiper had come to an end. With his fuel supplies almost exhausted and ammunition stocks running low, Peiper could advance no further. He could now do no more than consolidate his forces in defensive positions and hope that the First SS Panzer Corps would soon provide him with reinforcements, fuel, and ammunition, although the events of that day in Stavelot were not encouraging.

The following three days were characterized by bitter fighting in the area around Stoumont, La Gleize, and Cheneux (from which an effort was made to hold the nearby bridge). Stavelot could not be retaken, and the possibility of reinforcement and resupply was rendered even more remote by the cutting of the road between La Gleize and Trois Ponts early on the afternoon of December 20.[44] Unable to react effectively to American movements with vehicles now largely immobilized and troops short of ammunition, the Kampfgruppe could not escape increasingly destructive artillery fire and, ultimately, encirclement by the U.S. Thirtieth Infantry Division and Eighteenth Airborne Corps. It fiercely resisted the tightening American ring. Particularly heavy fighting took place between troops of the Kampfgruppe and units of the U.S. 119th Infantry Regiment for possession of St. Edouard's Sanitorium on the western edge of Stoumont. Driven out on the morning of December 20, Peiper's Panzergrenadiers recaptured the building that night in a bloody and nerve-wracking operation reminiscent, on a small scale, of the battle for Stalingrad in which the occupiers of the building

43. ETHINT 10, p. 22; C-004, pp. 9-10; Peiper testimony, U.S. v. Bersin, 153/3/000169 (1948).

44. C-004, p. 12.

were cleaned out room by room. The commander of the Ninth Panzer Pioneer Company distinguished himself in this action by personally leading his men with grenades and Panzerfaust in the attack on the sanitorium.[45] Further clashes with the 119th on the following day resulted in more prisoners being placed in the Kampfgruppe's bag, among them the commander of the regiment's Second Battalion, Maj. Hal D. McCown, who would later play a significant role in the Malmédy trial.[46]

At midday on December 21, Peiper called a conference of his battalion commanders to discuss what was obviously a desperate situation. The meeting was interrupted by a radio message from the headquarters of the First SS Panzer Division informing Peiper of an impending attack by the balance of the division to relieve the beleaguered Kampfgruppe.[47] The objective was now simply survival until help arrived, and in order to maximize the defensive powers of his dwindling command, Peiper ordered the abandonment of Stoumont and the concentration of all remaining forces in the area in the tiny village of La Gleize. Most of those Americans who had been captured in the past days' fighting around Stoumont and Cheneux and housed in the Kampfgruppe's command post in the chateau of Froide Cour a short distance east of Stoumont were now marched to La Gleize. German wounded who could not be moved and injured American prisoners were left behind in the chateau under the supervision of one German and two American medical aid men.[48]

The situation in La Gleize was grim. Overlooked by hills excellent for artillery observation, the village came under a heavy American bombardment against which the fifty-odd houses which comprised the village could offer only scant pro-

45. Peiper testimony, U.S. v. Bersin, 153/3/000177 (1956); "Vorschlag Nr. 112 für die Nennung im Ehrenblatt des Deutschen Heeres," February 25, 1945, BDC/MDF; see also Cole, *Ardennes,* pp. 349-50.
46. Peiper testimony, U.S. v. Bersin, 153/3/000179 (1958).
47. C-004, pp. 12-13.
48. *Ibid.,* pp. 13-14; Peiper testimony U.S. v. Bersin, 153/3/000178 (1957).

tection. To the north and east, forested terrain almost abutted La Gleize and offered excellent cover for attacking infantry. In short, La Gleize was not a place where Kampfgruppe Peiper could long survive, particularly since food supplies were scant and stocks of gasoline and ammunition virtually exhausted. An effort to resupply the Kampfgruppe by air on December 22 achieved little. Only three aircraft appeared over La Gleize, and a mere 10 percent of their modest load could be recovered by Peiper's men.[49]

If it was to remain in La Gleize and avoid annihilation, the battlegroup required immediate reinforcement and massive resupply, but it was not forthcoming. At around noon on December 23, Peiper received a radio message from Mohnke informing him that the relief column had got "stuck" and ordering him to attempt a breakout.[50] Peiper realized that escape through the heavily wooded and enemy-infested countryside was remotely feasible only if all possible encumbrances were left behind, for no fuel remained for the Kampfgruppe's mechanized equipment. Germans and captured Americans wounded during the fighting in and around La Gleize remained in the aid station which had been established in the village church, cared for by SS-Untersturmführer Dr. Willibald Dittmann, medical officer of the Third Battalion, Second Panzergrenadier Regiment, assisted by several American medical aid men.[51] Close to one hundred and fifty healthy American prisoners were, in effect, set free as the remnant of Kampfgruppe Peiper slipped out of La Gleize in the predawn hours of December 24.

One American prisoner was forced to accompany the German column. Peiper hoped to exchange the senior American prisoner of war, Major Hal McCown, for the wounded whom he had been forced to leave behind. This anachronistic effort, however, came to nought. During a brief fire fight with an

---

49. *Ibid.,* 000181 (1960); C–004, p. 15.
50. ETHINT 10, p. 23; Peiper testimony, U.S. v. Bersin, 153/3/000182 (1961).
51. C–004, p. 16.

American outpost south of Trois Ponts on Christmas Eve, Mc-Cown was able to dart into the surrounding brush and escape.[52]

Some eight hundred footsore German soldiers snaked painfully across country through snow cover that was sometimes fourteen inches deep and succeeded in breaking through American lines running along the Salm River north of Bergeval, making contact with friendly forces near Wanne early Christmas morning.[53] Peiper, who claimed not to have slept during the nine days that had elapsed since the beginning of the offensive and who had been slightly wounded in the breakout, collapsed and was carried to the aid station that had been established in Wanne by the surgeon of the First SS Panzer Regiment. Demonstrating remarkable resilience, Peiper was able to make a full report to the corps commander, Priess, on the following morning and that afternoon established his own command post in the small chateau of Blanche Fontaine southeast of Wanne at Petit Thier.[54]

Kampfgruppe Peiper was now dissolved into its component units, the remnants of which were placed at the disposal of the parent division which was soon to enter combat in the Bastogne sector. For the First SS Panzer Regiment, now bereft of tanks and other heavy equipment, the Ardennes offensive was over. From his new headquarters, Peiper dealt with the aftermath of his abortive thrust to the Meuse, overseeing efforts to put his regiment back into fighting shape and evaluating the performances of his subordinates. He, himself, was proposed by Mohnke for the Swords to his Knight's Cross.[55] Kampfgruppe Peiper had failed to secure its objectives but

52. McCown testimony, U.S. v. Bersin, 153/3/000055-56, 000060-61 (1834-35, 1839-40).

53. C–004, pp. 16-17; Eisenhower, *Bitter Woods,* p. 279. This was not the total number of survivors, for some elements of the Kampfgruppe remained strung out along the line of march.

54. Peiper testimony, U.S. v. Bersin, 153/3/000183-84 (1962-63).

55. "Vorschlag nr. 1 für die Verleihung der Schwerter zum Eichenlaub des Ritterkreuzes des EK," BDC/MDF.

for reasons largely beyond its commander's control. That it had fought well under exceedingly adverse conditions is beyond dispute.

But had Kampfgruppe Peiper conducted itself in conformity with the laws of war? That, of course, would be the focus of a lengthy postwar investigation and trial. Peiper's superiors had learned through Allied radio of American assertions that large numbers of American prisoners of war had been killed on December 17 near Malmédy; the United States government had, in fact, promptly lodged a protest with the German government through Switzerland.[56] Sepp Dietrich later claimed to have undertaken an internal investigation of the incident, but there is no evidence indicating that Peiper disclosed to his superiors the "mix-up" resulting in the deaths of American prisoners of war which he later testified had been revealed to him on December 18.

Significantly, however, the summary of Peiper's exploits during the Ardennes offensive included in the document proposing him for the Swords to his Knight's Cross (and which must have been based on Peiper's own after-action report) refers to the Kampfgruppe's "annihilation" of an enemy motorized column at Baugnez.[57] Although no date is given, there can be no doubt that the event alluded to here is that which came to be known as the Malmédy Massacre. But what is the significance of its inclusion in a report recommending Peiper for a high decoration? The difficulty in formulating an answer is compounded by the ambiguity of the word *Vernichtung*, which can as well be translated "extermination" as "annihilation," and which could be interpreted to mean in this context either the elimination of the enemy formation as an effective fighting force without implying the

56. See memorandum of Secretary of State Stettinius to President Roosevelt, January 1, 1945, and copy of directive to the American legation in Bern, both in the Roosevelt Library.
57. See "Vorschlag" cited in note 55.

deaths of all of its members or the actual killing of the human components of that formation.

Was Peiper, at the time he reported to Mohnke on December 26, unaware of the questionable aspects of the Baugnez incident? This is conceivable but conflicts with Peiper's later claim to have been informed of the "mix-up" on December 18. It is also conceivable that Peiper, aware of the fact that a large number of prisoners had been killed by members of his Kampfgruppe and that the Americans were making propaganda capital of it, attempted to cover for himself and his subordinates by describing the Baugnez incident in vague and ambiguous terms. But, given the combat "traditions" of the Waffen-SS, established in over three years of savage and ideologically charged warfare on the Eastern Front and justified by the ruthless ethos of Himmler's "Black Corps," the possibility that both Peiper and Mohnke understood *Vernichtung* to include the killing of prisoners of war must not be overlooked. To quote once more a pregnant excerpt from an SS propaganda article, the Waffen-SS had "learned to be fearfully harsh" when it served a purpose.[58]

58. See Chapter I, note 19.

IV. MANHUNT

As Kampfgruppe Peiper was searching for a bridge to carry it westward across the Amblève on December 18, the following terse message was received from the U.S. First Army by Twelfth Army Group and Supreme Headquarters, Allied Expeditionary Force (SHAEF):

> SS troops vicinity L8199 captured U.S. soldier, traffic M.P. with about two hundred other U.S. soldiers. American prisoners searched. When finished, Germans lined up Americans and shot them with machine pistols and machine guns. Wounded informant who escaped and more details follow later.[1]

Thirty Americans would eventually be identified as having escaped from a field southwest of the Baugnez crossroads from which the bodies of seventy-two GIs would later be recovered.

The investigation of what appeared to be a war crime of major proportions could not begin in situ, for the field at the crossroads remained behind German lines until mid-January. In the meantime, both the Inspector General of the First Army, Col. Rosser M. Hunter, and the SHAEF Standing Court of Inquiry, which had been established by General Eisenhower in August 1944 to investigate allegations of war crimes

---

1. *Report of Supreme Headquarters Allied Expeditionary Force Court of Inquiry re Shooting of Allied Prisoners of War by the German Armed Forces Near Malmedy, Liege, Belgium, 17 December, 1944* (hereafter cited as "SHAEF Report, Malmedy"), Appendix A to Exhibit 3, U.S. National Archives, Modern Military Branch, Record Group 319 (hereafter NA, RG 319).

committed against Allied personnel, began to assemble the meager evidence available.[2]

On January 14, 1945, officers of the First Army's Inspector General's section followed troops of the U.S. Thirtieth Infantry Division onto the field southwest of the Baugnez crossroads. Heavy snow had fallen in the area shortly after December 17, and the field was found to be covered with a layer of whiteness two to five feet thick. It was initially feared that the bodies assumed to be lying beneath the snow cover might have been booby-trapped by the Germans, but an examination by combat engineers of the Thirtieth Division revealed these fears to have been unfounded. A team made up of Graves Registration personnel, Signal Corps photographers, and a physician then combed the field, attaching a numbered placard to each body and photographing it as found.

Although dead for almost a month, the bodies were frozen and, hence, well preserved. After being photographed, they were trucked to Malmédy and placed in a heated building. When thawed to a point permitting the removal of clothing, each body was rephotographed, subjected to medical examination, then placed in a bed sack and turned over to a Graves Registration detail for burial.

Most of the bodies were found to have multiple bullet wounds of the face, chest, and abdomen. Some had wounds in the temple, forehead, or behind an ear; and, in most cases of this nature, only one wound was to be found. The temple wound of one corpse was surrounded by powder-burns. Other bodies showed post-mortem damage by shell fragments and, in a few cases, eyes were found to have been punctured and even removed with sharp instruments. The back of the skull of one corpse had been crushed as if by a heavy object. The investigators noted that the dead Americans had not been systematically robbed. Money was found on most, some still

2. SHAEF Report, Malmedy, p. 1.

wore watches, and a few had cigarettes. It did not escape the examiners' attention that a "considerable" number of bodies had been frozen with arms still above their heads.[3]

On January 27, 1945, the Inspector General's Office of the First Army completed its initial report, a body of information deemed sufficient to establish a prima facie case that war crimes had been committed against U.S. personnel and, specifically, that in a field southwest of the Baugnez crossroads on the afternoon of December 17, 1944, approximately "one hundred twenty" American prisoners of war had been murdered.[4] A few members of Battery B, 285th Field Artillery Observation Battalion had succeeded in escaping capture while their column was under fire and had fled into the woods along the road while a few others, including an MP who had been directing traffic at the road junction, had found refuge in a nearby barn. On several occasions after the Germans had shot down the mass of American prisoners, efforts were made by survivors, who had feigned death, to run from the field and into the woods. Early reports from survivors indicated that parties of Germans had walked among the recumbent American forms, shooting and clubbing those who appeared to be still alive.[5]

It had not been difficult for U.S. Army Intelligence to determine through the interrogation of prisoners and the examination of captured documents that Kampfgruppe Peiper had been operating in the area where the alleged atrocities had been committed and, further, to ascertain the identity of those units which had been components of the Kampfgruppe. But which of the over one thousand members of Peiper's force had participated in the killings? As of January 27, 1945, American authorities were in possession of the name of one Waffen-SS trooper who had been in the vicinity of the crossroads at anywhere near the material time. Information

---

3. U.S. v. Bersin, 153/1/000876-79 (850-53).   4. *Ibid.*, 000474 (461).
5. *Ibid.*, 000476-80 (463-67).

supplied by a Belgian civilian indicated that, some hours after the massacre, a Mark IV tank had fired its 75-mm cannon with uncertain purpose into the civilian's farmhouse adjacent to the field where the American prisoners had been shot. The intrepid Belgian had emerged from the house and protested the bombardment to the tank's commander who, with rare punctiliousness, presented the irate farmer with a slip on which were written the commander's name and field post number to be used in claiming compensation for damages from the German government. Thus did Unterscharführer (Sergeant) Hermann Braun* of First Company, First SS Panzer Regiment, become the first German positively identified in the American investigation of the Malmédy Massacre.[6]

Three days after the completion of the First Army's initial report, SHAEF's Court of Inquiry opened hearings on the Malmédy case in a facility belonging to the U.S. Hospital at Harrogate, Yorkshire, England. Acting president of the SHAEF court was Lt. Col. J. H. Boraston of the British Army, joined on the bench by the Canadian Lt. Col. B. J. S. MacDonald and the American Lt. Col. John S. Voorhees.[7] The court considered the evidence assembled by the First Army and questioned additional witnesses. In the latter category, the most compelling testimony was supplied by twenty-six-year-old S. Sgt. Henry Roy Zach of the U.S. Thirty-second Armored Regiment.

On the morning of December 17, 1944, Zach and a party of two junior officers and seven other enlisted men had driven south in a small convoy through Eupen and, by late morning, had reached the vicinity of Moderscheid. Driving at high speed around a sharp curve, the Americans narrowly avoided colliding with a column of German tanks and half-tracks halted on the road. Before they could pull back to cover, Zach and his companions found themselves gazing into the muzzles of German rifles and machine pistols. Offer-

6. *Ibid.*, 000481 (468).
7. SHAEF Report, Malmedy, pp. 2-3.

ing no resistance, the Americans immediately surrendered to the Germans whom Zach readily identified by their collar tabs as members of the Waffen-SS.

The Americans were ordered to insert their four jeeps into the German column. This unlikely procession continued down the road before cutting across country in what Zach recalled was a southerly direction. The terrain encountered off the road was more easily negotiated by the German tanks and half-tracks than by the American jeeps; the vehicle in which Zach was riding quickly burned out its clutch in deep mud and had to be abandoned. Its occupants were ordered to clamber onto the hulls of German tanks and there rode uncomfortably for an hour before the column regained a road and joined a larger motorized force at the Baugnez crossroads by early afternoon.

As the column halted, Zach and his companions were hustled off the tanks on which they had been riding and directed to join a large group of American prisoners (Zach estimated their number at "about fifty") already standing in a field along the road. The Americans were perfunctorily searched, and Zach recalled that the Germans seemed most interested in obtaining cigarettes.

Zach's testimony suggested that the situation in the field was characterized by some confusion. All the prisoners seemed to have their hands raised, but there was considerable "shifting and jostling" so that Zach, to his good fortune as events would prove, found himself in the rear of the group, i.e., that part farthest from the road. He was nevertheless able to see a tracked vehicle mounting a heavy gun maneuvering on the road and seemingly attempting to depress its weapon in order to cover the prisoners. Having failed in this, the vehicle was removed and replaced by two SPWs, each mounting 7.9 mm machine guns on flexible mounts. Shortly thereafter, heavy automatic weapons fire was opened on the prisoners, although Zach was unable to see where the firing had originated. He immediately fell to the ground as bullets thudded into earth and flesh (Zach was struck in the leg and hip). After what seemed to Zach a quarter-hour but which was almost certainly a much shorter period, the firing stopped and the German vehicles could be heard moving off a few minutes later. Zach dramatically described the subsequent movement on two occasions of small numbers of Germans through the field finishing off survivors.[8]

But Zach lived. After successfully feigning death until dark, he crawled to the smoldering remains of a nearby outbuilding which had burned that afternoon. Although hearing renewed fire coming from the direction of the road, he escaped additional injury and succeeded in concealing himself in the ruins until discovered the next morning along with two other wounded survivors by Capt. Edward W. Schenk of the 955th Field Artillery Battalion, then traveling in his command car from Butgenbach to Malmédy. Schenk later testified to having seen "numerous" bodies of American soldiers around the burned outbuilding and to having been informed by civilians that the bodies were those of Americans who had sought refuge in the building and who had been shot while escaping the blazing structure which the Germans themselves had set alight.[9]

In addition to Sergeant Zach's lengthy and detailed statement, the SHAEF Court of Inquiry also considered the testimony of twenty-nine other survivors of the massacre as well as information provided by German prisoners of war and four Belgian civilians who had been in the vicinity of the crossroads at the material time. Although noting that not all witnesses agreed on every detail of the grisly event, the court believed that it had been established "beyond question" that a large body of American prisoners had surrendered, that their surrender had been accepted and that, having done

8. This narrative is taken from the sworn statement of S.Sgt. H. R. Zach, Exhibit No. 6, dated January 23, 1945, in SHAEF Report, Malmedy.
9. *Ibid.;* sworn statement of Captain Edward W. Schenk, Exhibit No. 10, dated January 26, 1945, in SHAEF Report, Malmedy.

nothing to forfeit their rights as prisoners of war under the Geneva Convention, seventy-two had been killed in a manner "unprovoked, deliberate and brutal." Lending additional gravity to the offense was the fact that seven of the seventy-two were noncombatant medical personnel, while others had already been wounded when captured; both were categories entitled to special protection as prisoners of war. In addition to the seventy-two killed at the crossroads, the thirty survivors had been clearly subjected to assault with intent to commit murder.[10]

The SHAEF Court of Inquiry also pointed in directions along which the case would later be expanded far beyond the matter of the crossroads victims. Evidence received by the court suggested that American prisoners had been killed elsewhere in the area in which Kampfgruppe Peiper had operated. Staff Sergeant George Clevinger, for example, testified that he and five other enlisted men had surrendered to German troops at Ligneauville on December 17 and had then been lined up and shot. Clevinger was only grazed by a bullet and successfully played dead until the Germans departed. Other witnesses testified to having seen the bodies of Americans who had seemingly surrendered at Heppenbach and near St. Vith. The court expressed the belief that these stories, if confirmed, would suggest that the shooting of prisoners of war was official German policy during the offensive and that orders to that effect must, at some point, have been issued.[11]

What had the SHAEF Court of Inquiry achieved as it made its final report in March 1945? Its major conclusion, that seventy-two American prisoners of war had been killed at the Baugnez crossroads on December 17, 1944, in violation of international law, was only a modest advance in detail over the report made more than a month before by the Inspector General's Office of the First U.S. Army; and its suggestion of

10. See SHAEF Report, Malmedy, "Findings of the Court" and "Summary of Evidence."
11. SHAEF Report, Malmedy, Summary of Evidence.

additional atrocities was based on what was, as yet, flimsy evidence. Yet, it is difficult to find fault with the recommendations made by the court: that Allied personnel in contact with German prisoners of war be ordered to attempt to identify captured members of the component units of Kampfgruppe Peiper and that such prisoners be interrogated concerning their activities during the Ardennes offensive; further, that one line of investigation be devoted toward attempting to determine whether or not a general order requiring the shooting of prisoners of war had been issued to German troops.[12]

As long as hostilities continued, little could be done. Following the Ardennes offensive, the First SS Panzer Division returned to the Eastern Front with the Sixth SS Panzer Army to fight an unequal battle with the onrushing Red Army in Hungary and Austria before surrendering to American forces near Steyr in May 1945. Along with hundreds of thousands of other German soldiers, the survivors of what had been Kampfgruppe Peiper were herded into American prisoner-of-war compounds. Peiper, who had risen to the rank of SS-Standartenführer (colonel) following the Ardennes offensive and had found himself in command of the remnants of a division at the end of the war, temporarily eluded capture and sought to reach his home in the company of several SS comrades. He was apprehended within a dozen miles of his goal, prudently discarding the weapons he had retained when capture appeared imminent.[13]

Now, the building of the Malmédy case and the rounding-up of suspects could begin in earnest. In June, Lt. Col. Martin H. Otto, Chief of the Investigation Section of the War Crimes Branch, United States Forces European Theater (USFET), assigned the Malmédy file to Capt. (later Maj.) Dwight Fanton. Fanton, a graduate of Yale Law School, had worked briefly for the Aetna Life Insurance Company and the Bridgeport law firm of Pullman and Comely before joining the U.S.

12. SHAEF Report, Malmedy, Recommendations.
13. Peiper testimony, U.S. v. Bersin, 153/3/000188-89.

Army in April 1942. He spent the duration of the European war stateside in the Quartermaster Corps, and it was not until June 1945, when the need for personnel trained in law became desperate as a result of burgeoning war crimes investigations and trials, that he was posted to Europe.[14]

When Fanton received it, the Malmédy file was composed of nothing more than the report of the Inspector General, First Army, and the SHAEF Court of Inquiry report. Contained in the SHAEF report were the names of forty-two known members of Kampfgruppe Peiper, and it was here, logically, that Fanton's investigation should begin. Yet, the location of members of the Kampfgruppe progressed very slowly. Some, of course, had been killed in the interval between the Ardennes offensive and the German surrender. In addition, the hard-pressed staffs of overflowing POW cages were little inclined to cooperate. "Wanted" notices on members of Kampfgruppe Peiper went without response. Even Peiper, whose name and purported crimes had been widely publicized and whose location should have been readily ascertainable, remained lost in the labyrinthine network of prisoner-of-war facilities. Sepp Dietrich, who was found in a POW cage near Wiesbaden, confirmed that Peiper had survived the war, but nothing more was learned until the middle of August when the service newspaper *Stars and Stripes* published an article revealing that Peiper was to be found in the POW compound at Freising, about twenty miles north of Munich.[15] More than the chaos of the immediate postwar period, the difficulty in finding suspects indicated that, in spite of the enormous publicity given to the Allied intention to try German war criminals, the United States Army was fundamentally ill prepared for the tasks involved, a fact that

14. MMIH, pp. 476-77.
15. National Records Center, Military Government (hereafter NRC), Box 4-1/11, "Investigation of the 'Malmedy Massacre,'" report of War Crimes Branch, USFET (n.d.), pp. 1-2. Although sought by American investigators, Mohnke, the divisional commander, could not be found. Letter of Burton F. Ellis to author, February 14, 1978.

the Malmédy investigation and trial would reflect in other ways as well.

Fanton interviewed Peiper on August 25 and 26, 1945. He may have found the job, as others would, both pleasant and disconcerting, due to Peiper's fluency in English combined with his high intelligence and mordant wit. Fanton was given a lecture on battlefield tactics but learned little of substance about the massacre.[16] By that time, Fanton had begun to assemble a team of investigators, and with their assistance the "bag" of former members of Kampfgruppe Peiper gradually swelled. Still, Fanton and his team were unable to secure hard evidence against the SS troopers. In early fall, survivors of the massacre were taken to POW enclosures in the hope that they might identify participants in the killings. That this endeavor was fruitless should have come as no surprise, for the gaunt and bedraggled inmates of the camps bore little resemblance to the helmeted and cocky soldiers of December 1944. Moreover, interrogation of those identified as having belonged to Peiper's battlegroup produced no useful information.[17]

By the end of October it was distressingly evident that little had been achieved. Almost six months had elapsed since the end of hostilities in Europe, yet Fanton's team was far from having produced a case sustainable even in a military court whose judges were unlikely to be overly demanding concerning the quantity or quality of evidence brought against SS men accused of murdering American soldiers. This was an embarrassing situation in that, on the other side of the globe, Japanese General Tomoyuki Yamashita had been served with war crimes charges within a month of the surrender of Japan and was brought to trial shortly thereafter.[18] The Malmédy Massacre had received wide publicity in the United States, and the American people expected that the murderers of American boys would be given swift and severe justice.[19]

16. *Ibid.*, p. 2; cf. MMIH, pp. 270-71.
17. "Investigation of the 'Malmedy Massacre,'" p. 3.
18. A. Frank Reel, *The Case of General Yamashita* (Chicago, 1949), p. 279.
19. See, for example, "Murder in the Field," *Newsweek*, 25, No. 2 (January 8, 1945), p. 24; *Time*, 44, No. 26 (December 25, 1944), p. 19.

It was late in October that Fanton's team began a "crash" program to produce tangible results. The cooperation of Allied governments was solicited, prisoner-of-war camps were again scoured (the process now facilitated by direct telegraphic orders from USFET to camp commandants), while facilities where all Malmédy suspects could be concentrated and intensively interrogated were secured in an annex to Civilian Internment Enclosure No. 78 at Zuffenhaussen near Ludwigsburg. There, by mid-November, almost one thousand members of Peiper's former command, including six brought from prison camps in the United States, were housed in a single barracks-like structure. Again, results were meager. Many prisoners denied all knowledge of the murders, while it seemed to the Americans that a suspiciously large number of those known to have been at the crossroads at the material time claimed that the killings had been ordered by SS-Sturmbann-führer Walter Pringel, commander of the First Battalion, First SS Panzer Regiment, who had not survived the war.[20]

The American investigators concluded that some degree of collusion was taking place among the prisoners in the formulation of alibis. Indeed, it would have been remarkable had this not been the case, and the fact that the likelihood of such an occurrence had not been foreseen is further evidence of poor preparation by the army for war crimes investigation. All the prisoners were aware of the purpose behind their concentration at Zuffenhausen. It was clear to them that the "Amis" were probing an incident involving the killing of American prisoners of war, and their attitude toward those on whom culpability might appear to rest would not likely be charitable. Moreover, the fact that men were returned to a common barracks after interrogation and naturally discussed their experiences and responses to questions with their comrades would have produced a certain homogeneity of response quite independently of any conscious design. It is likely, too, that unit loyalties reasserted themselves with what amounted to the

20. "Report of Proceedings of Administration of Justice Review Board," NRC Box 4-1/11, July 1948, pp. 5-6; U.S. v. Bersin, 153/1/000103-04 (98-99).

reassembly of Peiper's command. Fanton and his team came to believe that Peiper was orchestrating a campaign of obfuscation, certainly a possibility although not a demonstrable fact.[21]

An important factor in the further development of the case was the image of the suspects held by the investigation team. It was difficult for the investigators, as, indeed, it would have been for most Americans in 1945 and 1946, to view the SS prisoners as men (many of them very young) who, although some of them might have been guilty of brutal atrocities, were also frightened and disoriented human beings. Wartime Allied propaganda and the Schutzstaffel's own widely publicized self-image had stressed the "hardness" and fanaticism of the SS man. And these, after all, were not garden-variety SS men but members of the Leibstandarte SS Adolf Hitler, "Hitler's Own" and ostensibly the cream of the crop. Not only was this a prejudgment which would have been difficult to avoid so soon after the war, but such an image offered an ego-saving explanation for the inability of Fanton's staff to build a case.

By mid-November the investigation group assigned to the Malmédy case included, in addition to Dwight Fanton, Capt. Raphael Shumacker and First Lt. William R. Perl plus two civilian army employees, Morris Elowitz and Harry Thon. Lieutenant Colonel Burton F. Ellis and Lt. Col. Homer B. Crawford, both of the investigation section, War Crimes Branch, USFET, took an intense interest in the case and had assisted in the location of suspects. Later, they would formally be assigned to the Malmédy team. It was Ellis, a tax attorney in civilian life, along with Perl, who suggested that those prisoners most likely to have been materially involved in the massacre, about five hundred in number, be removed to facilities that would permit their segregation one from another,

21. See Ellis affidavit of October (?), 1948, MMIH, pp. 1217-18; that the American investigators had no hard evidence for such collusion is suggested by Fanton's memorandum to Ellis, February 19, 1946, in MMIH, p. 294.

thus preventing future collusion in the formulation of statements and rendering the suspects more vulnerable to interrogation by isolating them psychologically.[22] A traditional penal facility provided with individual cells would be ideal for the purpose. Occupation authorities provided a drab, forbidding structure, parts of which were almost a century old and which was already being used to hold political internees, at Schwäbisch Hall, east of Heilbronn. Prisoners began to be transferred there early in December, and it would be at Schwäbisch Hall that the prosecution case would be built.[23]

In striking contrast to the long, sterile period that had preceded the move to Schwäbisch Hall, the Malmédy investigators now made significant progress. On December 17, 1945, one year to the day after the Malmédy Massacre, Heinz Reinhardt,* who had commanded the Second Company, First SS Panzergrenadier Regiment during the offensive, made a statement under oath to Lt. William R. Perl which, in awkward official translation, read as follows:

I am stating herewith the facts as given below: On the afternoon of the day before the attack on the Eiffel [sic] Mountains started— according to my knowledge it was the fifteenth of December, 1944—a meeting of the company commanders was held at the CP of the armored group. On this occasion Pringel stated that the impending battle would be the decisive battle. Amongst other things he said that we should behave toward the enemy in such a way that we create amongst them panic and terror and that the reputation for spreading panic and terror through our behavior should precede our troops so that the enemy should be frightened even to meet them. Amongst other things he also stated in connection with this that no prisoners should be taken. On my own, I added nothing to his talk nor did I take anything away from it, but on the same evening I repeated to my company in the Blankenheim Forest what Pringel had told us.

22. "Investigation of the 'Malmedy Massacre,'" p. 4; MMIH, p. 614.
23. See "SOP [Standard Operating Procedure] No. 1," December 5, 1945, MMIH, p. 1227.

This disposition I made on my own without influence by either threats or promises and I wrote it down in my own handwriting. It consists of two pages. I am fully aware of the importance and holiness of an oath.

Reinhardt, Heinz
SS *Obersturmführer*
17 December 1945[24]

Standing alone, Reinhardt's statement was of limited significance, although Perl would later characterize it as a major "break" in the case which laid the foundation for other confessions.[25] As had been true of statements elicited in earlier interrogations, Pringel had been singled out as the source or, at least, the transmitter of an order that seemed relevant to the killing of prisoners of war (assuming the "no prisoners" meant that Americans who were captured should be killed, an interpretation which, in company with an encouragement to spread "panic and terror" among the enemy, would not seem unreasonable). Reinhardt had admitted to having passed on this order to his subordinates. If he had done so, other officers had presumably done the same. That Reinhardt would have transmitted what he had taken as an order without adding or removing anything is certainly in harmony with the strict and unquestioning obedience to orders required of every SS man. Reinhardt's personality, moreover, well suited him for the role of passive conduit for superior orders. His instructors at SS Junkerschule Bad Tölz had described him as "very deferential in the presence of superiors" and as one who attempted to compensate for limited intellectual gifts through "extraordinary diligence."[26] It seems reasonable to assume, too, that those same qualities tended to make Reinhardt vulnerable and cooperative when confronted by American interrogators.

But many others besides Reinhardt were to make sworn statements between December 1945 and April 1946. On

24. Prosecution Exhibit P-15-A, U.S. v. Bersin, 153/1/000271 (258).
25. MMIH, pp. 614-15.
26. "Allgemeine Beurteilung der Persönlichkeit," BDC/MDF.

December 28, 1945, Hannes Pfordtner,* former ordnance sergeant of the Headquarters Company, First SS Panzer Regiment, signed a sworn statement which supported an expansion of the case beyond the crossroads incident. Pfordtner described a bizarre scene which he claimed had taken place around the beginning of 1945 at the chateau near Petit Thier, Peiper's headquarters following the breakout from La Gleize. Late one morning, while he was cleaning an outbuilding near the chateau, he saw the tattered figure of an American soldier stagger out of the nearby woods. Investigating, Pfordtner observed that the American who, it seems, had been hiding in the woods (perhaps since the beginning of the German offensive) was near collapse from exposure and hunger. With the assistance of another SS man, Pfordtner half led, half carried the American to Peiper's command post within the chateau. They found their commander in the company of the regimental surgeon, Karl Schiff, and another unidentified officer. Peiper examined the prisoner's paybook and attempted to question him in English, but the American's condition was so weak that he could reply only in unintelligible sounds. The surgeon cursorily examined the prisoner and observed that his hands were badly frostbitten. Pfordtner then claimed to have asked, "Should I bring him up?" meaning by "up," to the first aid station located on the second floor of the chateau. Peiper and his surgeon exchanged a pregnant glance, following which the surgeon motioned toward the door with his thumb and growled (according to Pfordtner), "Get the swine out and bump him off." In the company of the SS man who had earlier assisted him with the prisoner, Pfordtner, by his own admission, took the American a short distance up the road to a nearby field and shot him several times with his Luger in the back below the left shoulder, killing him instantly. Peiper, in a sworn statement of March 26, 1946, and Schiff, in a deposition dated April 9, 1946, would admit to the essential features of Pfordtner's narrative.[27]

27. Prosecution Exhibit P-123-A, U.S. v. Bersin, 153/2/000423-29.

The incident described in Pfordtner's statement had nothing to do with the crossroads killings or, indeed, with any aspect of Kampfgruppe Peiper's role in the Ardennes offensive. The role had ended approximately one week earlier, after which the Kampfgruppe had been disbanded and Peiper's permanent command, First SS Panzer Regiment, had been withdrawn into reserve. But the killing of the starved and frostbitten American was undisputably a war crime; moreover, the callous attitude on the part of Peiper and his regimental surgeon, as described by Pfordtner, and Pfordtner's own unquestioning willingness to carry out an illegal command reinforced an image of brutality and unwavering obedience to orders into which the shooting of the prisoners at the crossroads could comfortably fit.

In his sworn statement of January 5, 1946, Otto Klein,* a twenty-three-year-old Rumanian Volksdeutscher from the Siebenbürgen and former SS-Rottenführer in the Third Platoon, Seventh Company of the First SS Panzer Regiment, provided crucial information concerning the crossroads incident. Klein, assistant gunner in Panther tank number 731, commanded by SS-Hauptscharführer (Master Sergeant) Wilhelm Schoettel, recalled that his company commander, SS-Hauptsturmführer Sigmund Rinker* had urged his company prior to the attack to fight "recklessly and cruelly" and, in order to "strike terror" into the enemy, to take no prisoners. Klein went on to describe the scene at the Baugnez crossroads as his tank arrived early on the afternoon of December 17. Many Americans stood with raised hands in the field along the road, covered by the machine gun of an SPW parked on the road. The commander of the SPW signaled Klein's tank to stop and engaged its commander in conversation. Klein claimed to have heard the SPW commander inform Schoettel that orders had come from "up front" to kill the prisoners and that Schoettel's assistance was required. The tank commander protested that he was short of 7.9 mm ammunition for his machine guns but, observing that Klein already had his pistol in hand, ordered him to fire at the Americans. Klein fired one shot (according to his account) whereupon the machine gun on the SPW opened fire, mowing down rank after rank of prisoners. One prisoner who remained standing after the SPW ceased its fire was shot by Klein.[28]

Schoettel seemed to confirm the broad outlines of Klein's confession two days later. He stated that, as his Panther had entered the intersection, he had observed two or three SPWs parked on the road opposite a large group of American prisoners standing in a field. Schoettel believed these SPWs to be of the Ninth Panzer Pioneer Company. As Klein had stated, the commander of one of the SPWs had called on Schoettel for assistance in shooting the prisoners, but, due to a shortage of machine-gun ammunition, Schoettel had limited himself to having "permitted" Klein to fire into the prisoners with his pistol. One SPW had opened fire "simultaneously or immediately thereafter," joined by machine pistol fire from a soldier standing in the same SPW. According to his statement, Schoettel ordered his tank's advance resumed scarcely a minute after the firing had begun.[29]

As the winter months wore on, additional information on the apparently criminal activities of Kampfgruppe Peiper was accumulated, particularly after leadership of the investigation team was assumed in February by the energetic Lt. Col. Burton Ellis, who had actively sought formal assignment to the case.[30] Many of the statements in the investigator's growing file supplied dramatic detail. A twenty-seven-year-old former SS-Hauptscharführer asserted in his statement of February 16, 1946, that prior to the Ardennes offensive Pringel had addressed all tank commanders in his battalion and had ordered that everything that came before the muzzles of their guns was to be "bumped off" and that those who demonstrated consideration for the enemy would be shown

28. Prosecution Exhibit P-38-A, *ibid.*, 1/000559-64 (540-45).
29. Prosecution Exhibit P-39-A, *ibid.*, 000578-81 (559-62).
30. MMIH, pp. 523, 1059.

no consideration by him. The informant, who commanded a Mark IV tank in the Sixth Panzer Company, added with feeling that Pringel's method of demonstrating displeasure toward a subordinate had been to require him to go into battle exposed on the hull of a tank. Essentially the same order to kill all enemy personnel who came within range was repeated, according to this statement, by his company commander.

The former Mark IV commander was remarkably candid and even more detailed regarding his own activities. Due to engine trouble, his tank had become separated from the rest of the company and had reached the Baugnez crossroads late on the afternoon of December 17. Upon turning left onto the main road, he had seen a column of abandoned American trucks and a large number of bodies in the adjacent field. Investigating the grisly scene, the tank commander detected a slight movement on the part of one of the "corpses." Seizing the American soldier by the collar, he pulled him to his feet and discovered that he was, in fact, unwounded. Of a seemingly practical bent, the SS sergeant relieved the American of his watch and jacket, then gestured for him to remove his boots. As the prisoner was complying, the German admitted to having shot him in the back of the neck with his 9 mm Belgian automatic pistol and twice more in the chest as he fell. In the meantime, the gunner of his tank had swung the vehicle's turret around and proceeded to fire a twenty-five to thirty round burst into the field with the coaxial machine gun. The tank commander ordered the firing stopped, then watched as a Panther pulled up behind his Mark IV and discharged two crewmen who walked into the field and fired pistol shots although at what, the German claimed not to have been able to see. Still another vehicle, an SPW, halted as its commander investigated the source of what had been a considerable volume of shooting. He was brought into the picture by the Mark IV commander who matter-of-factly discussed his recent shooting of the American who had unsuccessfully feigned death.

The SS sergeant's justification for his behavior fit in well with an image of the Waffen-SS as a combat organization whose battlefield conduct was characterized by a consciously high level of brutality. He explained that he had been on bad terms with his commanding officers and had been transferred from the battalion supply company to the Sixth Panzer Company as punishment. His murder of the American at the crossroads, he suggested in his sworn statement, had simply been an effort to restore himself to the good graces of his superiors by demonstrating zeal and obedience to orders.[31]

Numerous other statements provided additional and sometimes contradictory detail concerning the crossroads killings. They further indicated that those killings were only a minority of the total number of American prisoners shot by Kampfgruppe Peiper during the Ardennes offensive. It seemed that parcels of American POWs had been shot at many points along the Kampfgruppe's line of march with, perhaps, as many as two hundred having been killed at La Gleize.

One of the lengthiest and most detailed accounts of carnage at the Baugnez crossroads and elsewhere was offered by an enlisted member of the Third Panzer Pioneer Company. As his unit entered Honsfeld on December 17, the soldier saw a group of approximately fifteen dead and unarmed Americans who, he assumed, had been killed following surrender. Later, six to eight American prisoners were encountered on the road to Büllingen marching eastward without guard. When the prisoners were ten to fifteen meters away from the German vehicles, an SS sergeant shouted, "Ready! Bump 'em off!" at which point several SS troopers, including the signer of the statement, fired at the Americans, apparently killing them all. Farther on, two additional small groups of American prisoners were fired upon. In Büllingen, two SS men known to the deponent entered a house and captured seven Americans. These were added to a group of fifteen to twenty Americans captured by several other SS troopers. The author of the statement later "heard" that all had

---

31. Prosecution Exhibit P-60-A, U.S. v. Bersin, 153/1/000822-28 (796-802).

been killed. Beyond Büllingen, according to this account, two more small groups of disarmed Americans marching to the rear without guard were shot. The informant's group then reached the Baugnez crossroads sometime between 1:00 and 2:00 P.M. Near the north end of a field or pasture in which stood "sixty to eighty" American prisoners lay a Panther tank on the right side of the road with its turret guns swung to the one o'clock position (which would have brought them to bear on the prisoners). On the left side of the road just south of the Panther was parked an SPW around which stood its crew. Two other SPWs were parked on the right side of the road south of the tank. The informant's SPW parked in front of the latter.

> . . . My recollection is that the first firing I heard was pistol fire from Holzapfel's* SPW [the one immediately south of the Panther]. While we were firing with our machine gun, I saw *Rottenführer* Hans Moeller* firing into the prisoners with his machine pistol. I saw *Unterscharführer* Holzapfel and *Unterscharführer* Blettner* also firing with their machine pistols into the prisoners. Pioneer [Engineer] Rapp* was firing with his rifle; *Rottenführer* Udo Bohlen* was firing with either a rifle or a pistol. . . . I also saw *Rottenführer* Hans Eck* shooting with a rifle. The machine gun in the Panther at the north end of the pasture was being fired. We fired approximately 75 rounds from the front machine gun. Then I went to the rear machine gun, loaded it and started shooting into the American prisoners.
>
> As soon as the first firing began, all of the American prisoners who were in the field fell to the ground. While I was still in my SPW manning the machine gun, I saw the following additional people shooting into the American prisoners: *Sturmmann* Ernst Haase* with his machine pistol; *Sturmmann* Manfred Schmidt* with his fast-firing rifle; *Unterscharführer* Fatzinger* with his machine pistol; Pioneer Altgeld* and Pioneer Unger* both with rifles; and Pioneer Foertsch* and Denkhoff* both with rifles.
>
> It was during the time that I was firing the rear machine gun on our SPW that Hannauer's* SPW pulled up on the right hand side behind my SPW. When Hannauer's SPW came to a halt, I

saw *Sturmmann* Dausner* firing the machine gun from Hannauer's SPW. After the machine gun fire had ceased, our SPW was driven down the road toward Engelsdorf and also halted in front of an American truck. . . . Hannauer's SPW stopped behind the American trucks. . . . Then I saw Moellenbruck's* SPW for the first time stop behind Hannauer's. . . .

After our SPW was parked in front of the American truck, I threw the brass out, then dismounted and started walking back in the direction of the pasture. I was walking along the ditch by the side of Hannauer's SPW when I saw Moellenbruck firing into the pasture from his SPW with his machine pistol. The men who were walking with me from our SPW at this time were Driemeyer* and Follen.* When we reached the pasture, we entered it and stood for a few minutes to observe the Americans who were still moving or otherwise showing signs of life. As we observed those who were still moving, the three of us chose different targets and went toward them in order to shoot them. . . . I shot four or five wounded American soldiers with my pistol. I shot only one round into the heart of each wounded man. At the time I fired, my pistol was one to one and a half meters from the American soldiers at whom I fired. All of these men were moving or otherwise showing some sign of life before I fired, and after I shot them, they didn't move any more and I am sure I killed each man at whom I fired.

While I was standing at the place previously described I saw the following among the prisoners, more or less at the south end of the group. . . : *Unterscharführer* Fatzinger, Pioneer Driemeyer, Pioneer Follen, Pioneer Karlsen,* Pioneer Foertsch, Pioneer Denkhoff, Pioneer Altgeld, Pioneer Unger and Pioneer Manfred Schmidt. Of this group I actually saw Fatzinger fire five or six bursts with his machine pistol. I saw Driemeyer firing with his pistol; I saw Follen firing with his pistol; I saw Denkhoff shooting with a rifle; I saw Fatzinger fire with his rifle; and I saw Schmidt shooting with his fast-firing rifle. . . .

In comparable detail, this deponent described the shooting of American prisoners in Stoumont and repeated hearsay descriptions of many other killings, noting that ''I saw and heard about so many cases of POWs being shot, that I cannot remember details of each case.''[32]

Nevertheless, the deponent would appear to have done remarkably well. It was no mean feat to have remembered in minute detail events which had taken place under what must have been considerable emotional stress, events which, moreover, had taken place over a year earlier. Other deponents were able to match that performance. Another enlisted member of Third Panzer Pioneer Company declared in a statement of March 6, 1946,

> . . . We entered La Gleize on the Stoumont Road. . . . We made a turn after the church and later dispersed our vehicles among the trees. . . . A guard was left with our SPWs and then we crossed the street and went to a house. . . . *Rottenführer* Bollmann* of the First Platoon had his SPW parked by the side of the house. I stayed in the cellar of this house until late afternoon when someone came and told me that *Unterscharführer* Fatzinger, who was wounded, wanted to see me in the church. I then left the house and walked up the street toward the church. As I walked up the street, I met *Rottenführer* Hans Moeller and Ernst Batz.* When the three of us reached a point on the street in front of the church. . . , we saw eighty to one hundred American prisoners standing on the school ground behind the school building across the street. They were being guarded by some German soldiers. . . . Then Moeller, Batz and I entered the church and after I had been in there a short while I heard machine pistol and rifle fire coming from the direction of the school. I do not know how to estimate the number of rounds or bursts that I heard, but there was a good deal of shooting. I was in the church about 15 or 20 minutes and left with Batz. . . . We stopped and looked behind the school and saw the bodies of these American soldiers lying on the ground. As far as I could observe, they were not moving and showed no signs of life. . . .[33]

Affidavits of a similarly highly detailed nature would later be instrumental in convicting seventy-three SS men of war

32. Prosecution Exhibit P-49-A, *ibid.*, 000696-711 (677-92).

33. This is a fraction of a very long and detailed statement. See Prosecution Exhibit P-46-A, *ibid.*, 000664-76 (645-57).

crimes but would also occasion no little skepticism as to their validity.

Not only had American prisoners of war fallen victim to the guns of Kampfgruppe Peiper but also, according to the sworn statements of SS prisoners, a substantial number of Belgian civilians. Thus, a member of the Eleventh Company, Second SS Panzergrenadier Regiment, stated in a deposition of March 12, 1946, that on December 18 between Stavelot and La Gleize, he had witnessed a member of his company fire his machine pistol from an SPW at two Belgian civilians working along the road, hitting both.[34] The commander of Tank 101 of the First Company, First SS Panzer Regiment, affirmed in a sworn statement of March 13, 1945, that the radio-man/machine-gunner of his vehicle had fired three to four machine-gun bursts into a group of women while passing through Stavelot on the morning of December 18.[35] A member of a penal group attached to the Ninth Panzer Pioneer Company admitted, in a statement of March 26, 1946, to having blown out the brains of a forty-year-old woman as she stood in her kitchen in Büllingen.[36] Other depositions indicated that civilians had been killed at many other locations.[37]

Had this apparently widespread and indiscriminate slaughter been the result of undisciplined bloodlust, or had it been directed from above? The bulk of the statements secured during the winter and early spring of 1945 to 1946 indicated the latter. One SS-Unterscharführer asserted that his company commander in his pre-attack "pep talk" had ordered company members to "fight in the old SS spirit" and followed that directive with the oblique but seemingly unmistakable elaboration: "I am not giving you any orders to shoot prisoners of war, but you are well-trained SS soldiers. You know

---

34. Prosecution Exhibit P-95-A, *ibid.*, 2/000120-24 (1237-41).
35. Prosecution Exhibit P-78-A, *ibid.*, 1/001035-41 (1004-10).
36. Prosecution Exhibit P-57-A, *ibid.*, 000777-85 (752-60).
37. See, for example, the following prosecution exhibits: P-86-A, *ibid.*, 2/00034-35 (1151-52); P-90-A, *ibid.*, 000074-80 (1191-97); P-114-A, *ibid.*, 000357-61 (1467-71).

what you should do with prisoners without me telling you that."[38] A private swore that his company commander had said, "There is an order not to take prisoners of war; also, civilians who show themselves on the streets or at the windows will be shot without mercy."[39] Many sworn statements secured by the American investigators recalled pre-attack orders from commanding officers in words virtually identical to these.

The sworn statements made by SS prisoners also indicated that a conscious effort had been made to stimulate hatred and, thus, to morally justify the murder of Americans soon to be encountered in the Ardennes. An SS-Unterscharführer claimed that the commander of the company to which he belonged had incited his men with the following harangue: "Think of it, that American gangsters have made our cities into a heap of rubble, millions of women and children were killed. If you think of all that, you know what you as SS men have to do in case you capture American soldiers."[40] A platoon leader supposedly characterized the impending offensive as an operation "against the murderers of our mothers, fathers and children."[41] With slight variations, this was a frequent theme in the statements sworn by SS prisoners under interrogation.

But what of the commander of the ill-starred SS battlegroup, the dashing and resourceful Jochen Peiper? In his statement of December 28, 1945, Hannes Pfordtner had implicated Peiper in the "mercy" killing of the starved and frostbitten American prisoner at Petit Thier. But statements subsequent to Pfordtner's suggested that Peiper had been far more deeply implicated in criminal acts. No deponent placed Peiper at the crossroads at the time of the killings, and it seems certain that he had passed that point prior to the incident, but several statements involved him in other killings.

38. Prosecution Exhibit P-24-A, *ibid.*, 1/000391-95 (376-80).
39. Prosecution Exhibit P-92-A, *ibid.*, 2/000105-07 (1222-24).
40. Prosecution Exhibit P-67-A, *ibid.*, 1/000911-13 (884-86).
41. Prosecution Exhibit P-46-A, *ibid.*, 000664 (645).

An SS-Hauptsturmführer on the staff of the First SS Panzer Regiment asserted that Peiper had personally questioned an American POW in Stoumont on the afternoon of December 19 and had then ordered him shot.[42] An SS-Obersturmführer (first lieutenant) of the Ninth Panzer Pioneer Company swore in his statement that he had heard Peiper state on December 22 in La Gleize that he had ordered some prisoners of war to be shot because they had refused to work.[43]

The subject of pre-attack orders was prominent in sworn statements relating to Peiper's culpability. Most of the relevant statements indicated that Peiper's regimental order did not actually require the shooting of prisoners of war but suggested that situations could arise in which such shootings might prove necessary. In that context, Peiper's own sworn statement of March 11, 1946, deserves to be quoted at some length:

. . . On the 14th December 1944 I was ordered to the Division Command Post, which was located in Blankenheim [Forest], where I had but a short conversation with the Division Commander, *Oberführer* Mohnke. The field order and the other material, such as maps, disposition of the enemy, and so forth, I received from the "Ia" [operations officer] of the division, *SS-Obersturmführer* Ziemssen. I did not read the material given to me at the Division Command Post, because I was in a hurry, and was also in a bad mood, because I disagreed with the entire preparation for the undertaking which looked highly defective to me.

I then returned on the same day to my Command Post, which was located in a forester's house in the Blankenheim woods. First, I ordered my adjutant, *Hauptsturmführer* Axel Steiner,* to call a commander's meeting for the same day at about 1600 hours. This left me about two hours, which I used to study the material handed to me at the Division. The very first impression of the terrain which I got, with the aid of maps, reassured my opinion that it was a desperate undertaking. I can remember that in this material, among other things, was an order of the

42. Prosecution Exhibit P-127-A, *ibid.*, 2/000457-59 (1567-69).
43. Prosecution Exhibit P-55-A, *ibid.*, 1/000766 (741).

Sixth SS Panzer Army, with the contents that, considering the desperate situation of the German people, a wave of terror and fright should precede our troops. Also, this order pointed out that the German soldier should, in this offensive, recall the innumerable German victims of the bombing terror. Furthermore, it was stated in this order that the enemy resistance had to be broken by terror. Also, I am nearly certain that, in this order, it was expressly stated that prisoners of war must be shot where the local conditions should so require it. This order was incorporated into the Regimental Order, which was drawn up on my command by *Hauptsturmführer* Johannes Metzger, *Sturmbannführer* Fritz Kamp (although he arrived a little late), *Obersturmführer* Hannsen,* *Sturmbannführer* Dr. Schiff, *Hauptsturmführer* Pfeil,* and I believe also the major who commanded the anti-aircraft battalion attached to me. In addition, *Hauptsturmführer* Steiner was at least temporarily present. At this meeting, I did not mention anything that prisoners of war should be shot when local conditions of combat should so require it, *because those present were all experienced officers to whom this was obvious* [italics mine].

In the meantime, the regimental orders were written and were picked up by the battalions, either during the night or on the following day.

It is possible, although I don't know for sure, that the paragraph of the regimental orders, which dealt with the prisoners of war, and was taken from the Army order without receiving any additions, was not sent to the battalions in writing, but for reasons of security was only looked at in the Regiment, and remained there to avoid this order falling into enemy hands.

The above Army order, about which I have just talked, was signed by *SS Oberstgruppenführer* and *Generaloberst* [General] Sepp Dietrich. I know, however, that the order to use brutality was not given by Sepp Dietrich out of his own initiative, but that he only acted along the lines which the Führer had expressly laid down.

. . . On the morning of 15 December, 1944, I was at the Command Post of the 1st SS Panzer Corps, where the commanding general, *SS-Gruppenführer* [Major General] Priess used the words as they were in the Army Order, in which he talked about the manner in which to treat the enemy and fight him. Anyhow,

out of all his words emerged that we had to fight with brutality
and that this was expressly desired by the Führer. . . . [44]

Peiper thus seemed to admit the existence of superior
directives permitting the shooting of prisoners of war when
local conditions of combat "required" it. But there appeared
to be a logical inconsistency in Peiper's sworn statement, for
if it was "obvious" to all "experienced officers" that prisoners of war had to be shot under pressing circumstances, why
should orders cut at any level contain such "obvious" and
therefore presumably redundant information? Further confusion and additional ambiguity were introduced on March 22,
1946, in the sworn statement of the former commander of the
Ninth Panzer Pioneer Company. According to this officer,
Peiper had alluded to the necessity of abandoning standards
of battlefield conduct hitherto obtaining in the Western
Theater as early as November 1944, long before orders for the
Ardennes offensive had been received, and had observed cyn-
ically that "a bad reputation [acquired in Russia, presuma-
bly] carries with it obligations." The deponent then claimed
to have read a "secret" regimental order at Peiper's headquarters (but, confusingly, on December 12 or 13, before
Peiper had received his marching orders) in which it had been
explained that Kampfgruppe Peiper, in the impending
offensive, would have as its mission deep penetration of the
enemy's positions and that, while the Kampfgruppe was
strong in firepower, it was weak in infantry and under no circumstances would be permitted to disperse its forces. All
tasks other than deep and rapid penetration would have to be
left to the masses of infantry that would follow the Kampfgruppe. "Therefore, the situation can arise when prisoners of
war have to be shot. . . ." All officers who read this order, according to the deponent, were required to sign a statement
pledging them to secrecy. The author of the March 22 statement also recalled the contents of the "open" regimental
order that was distributed to subordinate units. It contained,

44. Prosecution Exhibit P-11-A, *ibid.*, 000167-71 (162-66).

he averred, references to the "terror bombing" of German cities and the opportunity for revenge that would present itself in the impending offensive. The informant could not remember whether or not the order had specifically mentioned prisoners of war but was certain that it had not *forbidden* the taking of prisoners.[45]

By indicating that Peiper had expressed the opinion that standards of battlefield conduct would have to be "changed" for the next offensive long before orders for that offensive had been received, the statement of March 22 seemed to place upon Peiper a heavy burden of initiative and, therefore, personal guilt, no matter what the nature of the orders he might later have received from above. Statements made in March and April 1946 by the former commander of the Sixth Panzer Army, Sepp Dietrich, his chief of staff, Fritz Kraemer, and the former commander of the First SS Panzer Corps, Hermann Priess, were ambiguous on the subject of orders that had been received and issued on the army and corps levels. Dietrich recalled that, at the Bad Nauheim conference of December 12, 1944, Hitler had ordered his commanders to fight "hard and recklessly" and to "act with brutality" and without "humane inhibitions." He stated that the order which he subsequently issued to the Sixth Panzer Army had contained the phrases used by the Führer, but he vehemently denied that the order had demanded, or even suggested, that prisoners be shot. Kraemer, who as chief of staff actually drafted the orders issued to the army, admitted having stressed the importance of speed and ruthlessness and that civilian resistance would have to be broken by terror but had mentioned prisoners only in the context that they were not to be the concern of lead units in the offensive but were to be left to slower following elements. Hermann Priess claimed to have regarded Hitler's address at Bad Nauheim as "propaganda" and had not interpreted it to mean that fighting

45. Prosecution Exhibit P-55-A, *ibid.*, 000757-60 (732-35).

methods on the Western Front were to be changed. He remembered nothing in the orders received from the Sixth Panzer Army indicating that prisoners of war should be shot.[46] Thus, by April 1946 the American investigating team, now headed by Lt. Col. Burton Ellis, had accumulated a substantial body of evidence. Beginning with the uncontestable fact that a large number of American prisoners of war had been killed on December 17, 1944, at the Baugnez crossroads south of Malmédy, the investigators had assembled much additional evidence which, in spite of contradictions and ambiguities, suggested that large numbers of prisoners and a substantial number of Belgian civilians had been murdered elsewhere by Kampfgruppe Peiper and that these murders had likely been carried out in obedience to orders which had passed from Hitler through Sepp Dietrich, Fritz Kraemer, and Hermann Priess to Peiper's battlegroup. Implicit in most of the evidence was an image of the Waffen-SS as a ruthless and brutal combat organization which had constituted the executive instrument par excellence for orders of this kind.

While some testimony would be secured from American soldiers, Belgian civilians, and German prisoners of war not involved in war crimes, the overwhelming weight of evidence assembled by the American investigators consisted of the sworn statements of SS prisoners who were implicated in criminal acts. In most cases, the implicated prisoners had both confessed to crimes which they, themselves, had committed and had accused other prisoners of deeds frequently more heinous. Without these statements, the case against the SS prisoners would have been thin indeed.

A skeptic might have expressed incredulity concerning the minute detail contained in some of the sworn statements and would, perhaps, have questioned the veracity of certain of the accusations and counter-accusations contained therein. But,

46. Prosecution Exhibit P-6-A, *ibid.*, 000131 (126); Prosecution Exhibit P-10-A, *ibid.*, 000163-64 (158-59); Prosecution Exhibit P-8-A, *ibid.*, 000143-44 (138-139).

in the spring of 1946 with the end of the bitter European war less than a year past and memories of Nazi atrocities still fresh and frequently reinforced by new revelations, Americans willing to exercise skepticism on behalf of SS men were few. The case against Kampfgruppe Peiper and the three general officers responsible for its orders appeared overwhelming.

V. JUSTICE AT DACHAU— PRELIMINARIES AND PROSECUTION

Concentration Camp Dachau—a complex of barbed wire and low wooden buildings northwest of Munich—is now a tourist attraction. It has a special significance, for it was the earliest component of what would become the vast camp system run by the SS and dedicated to human suffering and death. The camp was liberated on April 29, 1945, by troops of the U.S. Forty-fifth Infantry Division, the dead buried, the survivors set free. But Dachau had yet another function to perform before becoming a lurid curiosity to be gawked at and photographed by camera-toting visitors. It was to serve as an internment center for suspects and witnesses in war crimes cases and as the site of war crimes trials which were to continue until the end of 1947, involving over fourteen hundred defendants.[1]

In the middle of April 1946, the transfer of several hundred prospective defendants and witnesses from Schwäbisch Hall to Dachau was undertaken and completed.[2] The irony of incarceration in Dachau cannot have been lost on the Waffen-SS veterans, many of whom had been participants in officer training courses conducted at the nearby SS training facility. A few of those soon to be tried had, themselves, been

1. Earl F. Ziemke, *The U.S. Army in the Occupation of Germany 1944-46* (Washington, 1975), p. 253; Office of the U.S. High Commissioner for Germany, *6th Quarterly Report on Germany,* Table II, P. 41.
2. "Investigation of the 'Malmedy Massacre' by War Crimes Branch, USFET," in MMIH, p. 1226.

among the tormentors at camps similar to Dachau. The SS men were subjected to a gentler authority, one which, nevertheless, might ultimately deprive them of their lives.

The lawyers among the Malmédy investigation team were transmuted into the prosecution staff with Lieutenant Colonel Ellis as chief prosecutor. Ellis, along with Lt. Col. Homer B. Crawford, Capt. Raphael Shumacker, First Lt. Robert E. Byrne and Mr. Morris Elowitz, might not have been adequately prepared for war crimes work but had become familiar with the Malmédy case and its cast of characters over a period of many months.[3] Equally unprepared for such judicial proceedings but without the advantage of long association with the Malmédy case was defense counsel, appointed early in April by the Deputy Theater Judge Advocate, Col. Claude B. Micklewaite. Micklewaite selected as chief defense counsel Col. Willis M. Everett, Jr., recently arrived in the European theater from the United States. Unlike Ellis, who entered the Malmédy case with enthusiasm, Everett was horrified by his assignment. An Atlanta attorney who, like Ellis, had virtually no courtroom experience in civilian life, Everett had been activated from the reserves in 1940 as Director of Security and Intelligence for the Fourth Corps area with headquarters in Atlanta. He arrived in Europe in the spring of 1946 with expectations of being assigned to a nonjudicial role in U.S. military government. He accepted his job as chief defense counsel with reluctance based in part on an awareness of his own professional inadequacies but rooted, too, in initial repugnance for the ostensible crimes of his prospective clients. Everett's only consolation lay in assurances from Micklewaite that he would be given well-qualified assistants and that his function as chief defense counsel would be primarily that of coordinator.[4]

Everett had reason to be satisfied with the staff he was

3. Lt. William R. Perl was designated "special assistant" to the prosecution. U.S. v. Bersin, 153/1/000009 (4).

4. Willis M. Everett to family, April 10, 1946, in Everett Papers (hereafter EP); Everett deposition of October 10, 1949, MMIH, p. 1556.

given. Of six army attorneys, designated "assistant defense counsel," one, Lt. Col. Granger G. Sutton, had had extensive courtroom experience in private life. A civilian member of the defense staff, Herbert J. Strong, had been born and raised in Germany and was, therefore, fluent in the German language, a rare but invaluable facility among both the prosecution and defense staffs. In addition to appointed counsel, the defendants were permitted to engage native German counsel to supplement the efforts of their U.S. army attorneys. A number of defendants from among the commissioned ranks did so, producing a satellite body of six defense attorneys whose value was severely limited by linguistic problems and unfamiliarity with American legal procedure. The greatest disability weighing upon the defense staff was the fact that scarcely a month elapsed between its appointment and the commencement of the trial. Approximately half of that time was consumed in organizational details, leaving little more than two weeks for the effort to prepare a defense case.[5] It was, therefore, a confused and pessimistic defense staff that assembled in the courtroom at Dachau for the opening session of the trial on May 16.

In common parlance, it would be referred to as "the Malmédy Massacre trial"; officially it was designated "U.S. vs. Valentin Bersin, et al.," the name of that twenty-five-year-old ex-tank-commander in the Second Platoon, First Company, First Battalion, First SS Panzer Regiment, being alphabetically first on the list of seventy-four officers and men of the Waffen-SS whom the government of the United States charged with "violations of the laws and usages of war."[6] Of that number, all but three had been members of Kampfgruppe Peiper. The three exceptions were Sepp Dietrich and Fritz Kraemer, former commander and chief of staff, respectively, of the Sixth Panzer Army, and Hermann Priess, sometime commander of the First SS Panzer Corps. Of the

5. *Ibid.*, pp. 1556-57; Dwinnell testimony, MMIH, p. 405.
6. Charge Sheet, MMIH, pp. 1191-92.

seventy-one defendants who had fought in December 1944 with Kampfgruppe Peiper, twenty had been commissioned officers and fifty-one of enlisted or noncommissioned rank. As they filed into the courtroom on the morning of May 16 and took places in banked rows of seats to the right of the judges' bench, they were, in the eyes of the United States government, no longer prisoners of war, having lost that status by unilateral declaration of the U.S. Army as of April 26. The defendants were now "civilian internees" of a specific category: accused war criminals. As such, they were no longer protected by the provisions of the Geneva Convention of 1929 relating to prisoners of war and, in fact, had been discharged as prisoners of war "in order to preclude the possibility of legal complications."[7] This had no necessarily sinister implications but was clearly intended to simplify and hasten the trial process by avoiding possible claims that defendants were entitled to be tried only according to procedures that would be used in trying nationals of the captor government.

The Malmédy defendants were to be tried before a General Military Government Court, the highest of three grades of military government courts, reserved for important cases. Much bitterness would later be occasioned by confusion concerning the purpose and procedures established for these courts. The primary purpose of military government courts was not to realize an abstract concept of "justice," although that fact did not preclude the possibility of justice being done. Rather, as stated clearly in the *Technical Manual for Legal and Prison Officers*, the central function of the courts was preservation of the security of Allied Forces, to which procedural "technicalities" were to be subordinated. Nowhere was this as clear or, ultimately, as controversial as in those regulations establishing rules of evidence. While "in

7. Internal route slip, Headquarters, U.S. Forces, European Theater. Subject: Discharge of German Prisoners of War, April 26, 1946. U.S. vs. Bersin, 153/6/000705.

general'' military government courts were to base their verdicts on the "best" evidence available, no evidence, however tenuous, was to be excluded if, in the opinion of the bench, it had a bearing on the case at hand. Conversely, the bench was free to exclude any evidence it considered irrelevant.[8] Overwhelming and potentially arbitrary authority was therefore vested in the army judges who determined what evidence was to be accepted and what excluded and on that basis arrived at a verdict, on the agreement of two-thirds of the bench, and passed sentence.

An eight-man bench was assembled to judge the Malmédy case. Presiding officer was Brig. Gen. Josiah T. Dalbey of Headquarters, Third Infantry Division, while the crucial position of law member, that officer trained in the law whose function was to interpret applicable law and determine procedure, was occupied by Col. Abraham H. Rosenfeld. The remaining six members of the bench were line officers holding the rank of colonel.[9]

General Dalbey called the court to order under the glare of photographers' floodlights (much of the trial would be filmed) at 10:00 A.M., May 16, 1946. Members of the bench and of the prosecution and defense staffs as well as stonographers and interpreters were introduced, and the charges against the seventy-four defendants were read by Lieutenant Colonel Ellis: ". . . That the accused, charged as being parties concerned, did willfully, deliberately and wrongfully permit, encourage, aid, abet and participate in the killing, shooting, ill treatment, abuse and torture of members of the Armed Forces of the United States of America, and of unarmed allied civilians." Individual charges were listed in a separate bill of particulars.[10]

---

8. *Technical Manual for Legal and Prison Officers*, 2nd ed. (Washington, D.C., 1945), pp. 8, 37, 43.

9. "Special Orders No. 117," Headquarters, Third United States Army, 10 May, 1946, MMIH pp. 1195-96. One officer was excused from judicial service before the trial began. Another would drop from the bench during the trial.

10. U.S. v. Bersin, 153/1/000010 (5).

Following several pro forma challenges to the jurisdiction of the military government court in the Malmédy case, summarily rejected by Rosenfeld, each of the seventy-four defendants was called upon, alphabetically, by Dalbey to state his name, nationality, legal residence, and length and branch of military service, whereupon he was assigned a number according to his alphabetical position on the list of defendants which he was required to wear, emblazoned on a placard and suspended from his neck, for the duration of the trial. Thus, Valentin Bersin became defendant number 1, Dietrich received the number 11, Peiper, 42.[11] The uniformity that was introduced into the appearance of the defendants was more than counterbalanced by their motley attire, in most cases composed of odds and ends of German and American uniforms—often combinations of both, and all devoid of insignia. Peiper was clad in the field-gray tunic and breeches of a Waffen-SS officer but shod with American combat boots several sizes too large for him. All were well groomed, however, and obviously well fed and reflected their soldierly backgrounds, if not sartorially, then in the crisp manner in which they moved through the courtroom and snapped to attention with clicking heels when required to rise from their seats.

The defendants' dock, with its seventy-four occupants, represented a significant characteristic of the Malmédy trial and a major problem for the defense, second in magnitude only to the great mass of documentary evidence possessed by the prosecution. That problem lay in the obvious fact that the Malmédy proceedings were a mass trial, a condition advantageous to the prosecution, in that damaging evidence against specific individuals would tend to rub off upon all, and clearly in consonance with the U.S. Military Government's desire for "efficiency" but imposing great and, perhaps insurmountable burdens upon the defense. The defense's appreciation of the deficiencies that it faced was reflected in a motion

11. *Ibid.*, 000012-77 (7-72).

for severance addressed by Capt. Benjamin Narvid of Everett's staff to the bench on the afternoon of May 16. Narvid's motion requested that, in place of a single trial of the seventy-four defendants, two separate trials for two distinct sets of defendants be conducted, one for those whose alleged offenses were those of issuing illegal orders and another for those defendants accused of having executed the orders. If such a severance were not granted, the defense arguments of many individual defendants would clearly be mutually antagonistic as they sought to shift the burden of responsibility onto one another, particularly in efforts by subordinate figures to claim superior orders as a mitigating circumstance.[12]

In the prosecution's counterargument, Capt. Raphael Shumacker introduced the conceptual framework within which Ellis's team was to present its case and did so with the highly emotional and inflammatory rhetoric that would characterize its presentation. It was appropriate for all defendants to be tried jointly, Shumacker argued, in that all had been members of a criminal conspiracy:

> . . . If it be true, as alleged in the charge, that the named accused acted together in this shooting and killing of prisoners of war, each accused became a cog-wheel in a monstrous slaughter machine. Now each such cog-wheel or group of cog-wheels comes into court and demands a severance as a matter of right because their teeth mesh less smoothly when they drip with blood than when oiled with prospects of victory. . . . They demand, we submit, retail justice for wholesale slaughter.[13]

Again, Rosenfeld sided with the prosecution, citing as precedents the recently completed Dachau and Mauthausen Concentration Camp cases (Rosenfeld had participated in the latter) in which forty and sixty-one men, respectively, had been tried. Yet another defense motion offered by Lt. Wilbert Wahler requesting greater specificity in the charges brought against the defendants met a similar fate. The denial of that

12. *Ibid.*, 000078-80 (73-75).
13. *Ibid.*, 000081 (76).

motion brought the first day of the trial to an end on a note less than encouraging to the defense.[14]

On the morning of May 17, the trial began in earnest. Through defense counsel, all defendants entered pleas of "not guilty" to the charges brought against them.[15] The prosecution, thereupon, began its presentation with a slashing opening statement in which it stressed the ostensibly conspiratorial aspects of the offenses and, of course, the loss of American and Belgian lives. Hitler, himself, stood at the apex of the conspiracy that the prosecution now proceeded to outline. At the Bad Nauheim conference in December 1944, Hitler had commanded that enemy resistance in the impending offensive be broken by terror. Sepp Dietrich, lending greater specificity to the Führer's wishes as he interpreted them for the Sixth Panzer Army, urged his subordinates to remember the victims of Allied bombings of German cities and to shoot prisoners of war, at least when combat conditions "required" it. That order, the prosecution maintained, was passed down through corps and divisional levels and ultimately to the companies and platoons that comprised Kampfgruppe Peiper, commanders conveying the murderous intent of the order with varying degrees of callousness, which the prosecution was able to exemplify with excerpts from the defendants' sworn statements.

Mass carnage was the result of these orders. The prosecution declared itself prepared to prove the murder of from "538 to 749" prisoners of war and "over 90" Belgian civilians while suggesting that, in fact, the slaughter had been even greater. In addition to the 72 Americans killed at the crossroads, the prosecution alleged that the SS troops had killed from 28 to 40 prisoners in six incidents at Honsfeld, 62 to 90 prisoners and at least 9 Belgians in thirteen separate incidents at Büllingen, 48 to 58 prisoners at Ligneauville, 8 prisoners and at least 73 Belgians at Stavelot and vicinity, at least 6

14. *Ibid.*, 000082-84 (77-79).
15. *Ibid.*, 000096-97 (91-92).

civilians in three incidents at Wanne, at least one civilian at Lutre Bois, 41 to 51 prisoners of war in two incidents at Cheneux, at least 4 civilians in two incidents at Trois Ponts, 104 to 109 prisoners and at least one Belgian civilian in twenty-four separate incidents at Stoumont, 175 to 311 prisoners and at least 3 Belgian civilians at La Gleize, and, finally, the single starved and frostbitten American prisoner allegedly killed on agreement between Peiper and Schiff at Petit Thier.

Noteworthy in the prosecution's opening statement was the vagueness of what Ellis and his staff claimed to be able to prove. They were able to speak only in very imprecise numerical terms of the victims alleged to have been done to death by the German defendants and were not always able to make their totals jibe. The problem was more than arithmetic. For the alleged murders other than those at the crossroads on December 17, 1944, there was little evidential material besides the sworn statements of SS prisoners and a few Belgian civilians, and much of this was confused and contradictory. During the trial it would be supplemented by the testimony of prosecution witnesses, but this would suffer from similar flaws. In a significant admission the prosecution conceded, in its opening statement, that it was "practically an impossibility to present to the Court the evidence on this mass of murders in a chronological sequence and in an understandable manner. . . ." Nevertheless, the case which the prosecution began to unfold on May 17 was a powerful one.[16]

Three weeks (with half-day sessions on Saturdays) were consumed by the prosecution in the presentation of its case. Suspended from the courtroom wall was a 1:100,000 scale map depicting the road and topography along and over which Kampfgruppe Peiper had fought during that frenzied December seventeen months earlier. On this map, witnesses identified the locations of incidents on which they offered testimony. And there was much testimony. Some former members of Peiper's battlegroup, not charged with war

16. *Ibid.*, 000097-103 (92-98).

crimes but reserved as prosecution witnesses, were called upon to corroborate the content of the sworn statements that were offered as evidence.

A particularly effective witness was the blond and baby-faced Kurt Kroll,* former SS-Untersturmführer and adjutant on the staff of Pringel's battalion. Kroll's appearance for the prosecution elicited a collective "raspberry" from the prisoners' dock which required an admonition from the bench to silence. Kroll testified that, prior to the December offensive, he had heard Pringel declare in an address to subordinates that "this humanity foolishness has stopped," an opinion that was supported by Peiper, who stated that "we will fight in the same manner as we did in Russia in the action which will follow. The certain rules which have applied in the West until now will be omitted." Kroll further claimed to have seen the regimental order in Peiper's command post but recalled nothing that related specifically to prisoners. He was able to allude only to a passage which ordered the attack to be carried out "without regard to losses of our own and without mildness toward the enemy." A maladroit effort by the defense to cross-examine the witness on the details of his cooperation with the prosecution came to nought when the prosecution's objection was sustained by Rosenfeld.[17]

Emotionally, the high point of the prosecution was reached with the presentation of testimony by American survivors of alleged SS atrocities. Virgil P. Lary, then a student at the University of Kentucky, appeared before the court on the morning of May 21 to describe his experiences at the Baugnez crossroads. Early on the afternoon of December 17, 1944, Lary, then first lieutenant, Battery B, 285th Artillery Observation Battalion, was traveling in the lead jeep of the convoy of some thirty vehicles. Approximately "one thousand meters" south of the crossroads, the convoy came under heavy fire from the high ground due east. The picture that he painted was one of confusion and American conduct which

17. *Ibid.*, 000191-221 (186-216).

fell rather short of the heroic standard portrayed by the wartime and postwar mass media.

Q. After you were fired upon, what did you do?

A. I discussed with Captain Keele,* who was in the leading jeep and who was in charge of the convoy, what would be best: to continue en route, to attempt to turn around or to abandon the vehicles and get into the ditch.

Q. What did you do?

A. The firing became so intense that we decided to get into the ditch, stopping the convoy.

Q. After you got into the ditch, what did you do?

A. We continued to lie in the ditch while the artillery and small arms fire came into the convoy.

Q. Was anyone in the ditch with you?

A. Yes. Captain Keele and Corporal Lester, driver of the vehicle.

Q. Can you describe what happened after you were in the ditch?

A. I spoke to Captain Keele and said, "Do you think that a patrol has broken through or is it too heavy for a patrol?" and he said, "The fire is too intense."

Q. Then what happened?

A. At this time, I spoke to Captain Keele and said, "Let's crawl up this ditch and attempt to make a stand for it besides [sic] that small house which we just passed."

Q. What did Captain Keele say?

A. He said, "All right."

Q. Then what did you do?

A. We crawled up the ditch for approximately 100 meters in the direction of the house, north.

Q. Did you take refuge in the house?

A. We did not.

Q. What did you do?

A. At this time I was almost opposite the house. I started to cross the road in the direction of the house. At this time, I noticed almost upon me a German tank.

Q. How did you know that it was a German tank?

A. I saw the black crosses on the side.

Q. What did you do after you saw the German tank?

A. As the personnel had their heads out of the tank, I dropped down to the ground and pretended to be dead.

Q. Then what happened?

A. The tank passed me without incident.

After yet another narrow escape, Lary succeeded in reaching the house in front of which he found fifteen to twenty American soldiers standing docilely with raised hands. Lary then claimed to have attempted to organize these men for further resistance but was reluctantly dissuaded by Corporal Carl Daub:

A. . . . Corporal Daub stated, "look up the road, Lary," and this I did and saw an entire column of armored vehicles approaching in our direction. At this time I stated, "It will be necessary for us to surrender to these people."

Q. Did you surrender?

A. At this time, no.

Q. What did you do?

A. I crossed back over the road and spoke to Captain Keele.

Q. Where was Captain Keele at that time?

A. He was still lying in the ditch.

Q. What did you say to Captain Keele?

A. I said, "Captain Keele, are you hit?" and there was no answer. I repeated the question . . . and he said, "No. Go away or they will come back and kill me."

Q. Did you have further conversation with him at that time?

A. I did.

Q. What was it?

A. I said, "Captain, come out of the ditch. Those people have gone." This he did and joined our group across the road.

After making an effort to conceal his rank, Lary and his cohorts awaited the oncoming Germans with raised hands. An SS trooper in the lead tank motioned them to begin marching to the rear, i.e., back toward the crossroads.

A. At the time we started to march back in the direction we had come or in the direction north to the crossroads. Approximately six or seven vehicles back in this column, a German stated the following as his vehicle passed us traveling south, "It's a long way to Tipperary, boys." No one in our group responded or made comment and we continued to march to the rear.

Q. Did any other German say anything further to you?

A. Yes. A German on foot came to our group and stated, "Stop, stop, I want drivers for these vehicles." We passed on and paid no attention to this man and continued to walk north in the direction of the crossroads.

Lary then described taking his place in the field with the other prisoners.

Q. Did you observe what the Germans were doing on the road?

A. At this time the half-track vehicle, mounting a cannon, was brought up and faced—or the attempt was made to face it—in the direction of our group. For some reason unknown to me, this cannon was ordered off, and it proceeded off down the road.

Q. Then what happened?

A. At this time two vehicles drove up and parked on our flanks, approximately 30 yards apart. At this time I saw a German in one of these vehicles place a machine gun over the side of the vehicle.

Q. What else did you notice on the road?

A. At this time another vehicle drove up and stopped in the center of these two.

Q. Do you know what type of vehicle this was?

A I do not recall, but I saw only one-half of a man standing in this vehicle.

Q. What else did you observe?

A. I saw the man take a pistol and aim it in the direction of our group.

Q. Did he aim the pistol more than once?

A. He did, in the following manner: his hand on his hip. Three times.

Q. Then what happened?

A. He then fired two shots into our group. At the first shot a man to my right front, approximately here (indicating), with his hands up in this manner, went down like this.

Prosecution: Let the record show the witness indicated that the man shot had his arms extended over his head and fell sideways to the left.

At the prosecution's invitation, Lary proceeded to identify one of the defendants as the man who had fired the pistol.

Q. Now, what happened after these two shots were fired?

A. At this time, I heard two machine guns open up on the group. The firing seemed to become more intense. Those of us that were not killed originally fell to the ground. I fell with my face in the mud, my feet pointed toward the road.

Q. How long did the machine guns fire at your group?

A. For approximately three minutes.

Q. Did you hear any noises after the firing ceased?

A. I did. I heard the agonized screams from the American wounded.

Q. Did you hear anything else?

A. I heard single shots which sounded or seemed like they came from pistols.

Q. Did you see any Germans come into the field?

A. I did not. My face was in the mud.

Q. Did you hear any firing in the field?

A. I did. I heard those shots that sounded like pistol shots.

Q. After the pistol shots, did the moaning and groaning cease?

A. Yes. Completely.

Q. Did you hear the Germans say anything during the shootings?

A. Only laughter.

Q. Did any vehicles pass along the road while you were lying in the field?

A. Yes.

Q. Did you hear any noises from these vehicles?

A. Yes, I heard laughter and more machine gun fire.

Lary concluded his testimony by describing his escape from the field and his success, although slightly wounded, in reaching American forces in Malmédy.[18]

Lary's testimony, despite its self-serving aspects, was compelling. In general terms, and in many specifics, it agreed with a major fraction of the sworn statements of German defendants, and the description of laughing Waffen-SS troopers firing into the forms of American prisoners could not fail to heighten animosity toward those sitting in the dock. Accounts of the brief engagement south of the crossroads and the subsequent shooting of American prisoners essentially identical to that offered by Lary were given the court by other survivors. Samuel Dobyns, however, a former private first class in the 575th Ambulance Company, Ninety-ninth Infantry Division, who had been swept into Kampfgruppe Peiper's bag of prisoners earlier on December 17, 1944, presented some interesting nuances. Under direct examination, Dobyns testified that the German whom all witnesses mentioned as having fired the initial shots at the prisoners with his pistol had been brandishing the pistol for some time, in response to which an American prisoner had cried out to his comrades, "Stand fast!" It was at that point that the pistol-wielding German had fired, hitting one of the prisoners standing in the front rank. Dobyns then admitted to having broken ranks and run to the rear, recalling that it had been only after having run some distance that he had heard the German machine guns open fire. Under cross-examination by Lieutenant Wahler, Dobyns recalled that other prisoners had broken ranks in response to the pistol fire but before the machine-gun fire had commenced.[19] Dobyns' testimony suggested the possibility that the crossroads shootings had been nothing more than a tragic error. A trigger-happy and inexperienced young Waffen-SS trooper had fired at an American prisoner in nervous response to a shout, which he could not

---

18. *Ibid.*, 000419-36 (406-23).
19. *Ibid.*, 000517-32 (504-19).

understand, from the American ranks; the prisoners had begun to scatter, precipitating the devastating reaction from the German machine guns. Testimony from some German witnesses for the prosecution was not inconsistent with such an interpretation. An enlisted man of the First Platoon, Seventh Panzer Company, recalled that his tank had reached the Baugnez crossroads on the afternoon of December 17 and had stopped behind "two or three" other German vehicles. Pringel, the battalion commander, was present at the crossroads and was heard to order the German crews not to park their vehicles too closely to one another in view of the ever-present possibility of air attack. The witness was watching the American prisoners in the field and observed the sudden burst of fire by machine guns from the vehicles ahead of him. Thereupon, the SS-Hauptscharführer in command of his tank commenced fire on the field with the machine gun atop the turret, discharging approximately fifty rounds.[20] No evidence of premeditation was contained in the witnesses' testimony, although it must be assumed that most prosecution witnesses drawn from the ranks of the Waffen-SS were hostile, reluctant to offer testimony damaging to their comrades.

While the crossroads shootings were the prime focus of the prosecution case, many other alleged atrocities remained to be proven. Ambiguity, inherent in the confused and brutal interactions of combat, was clearly evident in many of these "satellite" incidents. On the afternoon of May 28, the prosecution introduced into evidence a series of depositions which had been taken from American soldiers of the 612th Tank Destroyer Battalion during the previous year relevant to incidents that had occurred in Honsfeld on the morning of December 17. T/5 Charles L. Morris described the brutal murder of members of two tank destroyer platoons who attempted to surrender to the crew of a German tank. The tank's commander, speaking in English, ordered them to approach his

20. *Ibid.*, 000569-74 (550-55).

vehicle, whereupon he shot them down with his machine pistol.[21] Sergeant John M. Dluski succeeded in surrendering to Waffen-SS troops in Honsfeld and fell in with a column of approximately two hundred fifty American prisoners marching to the rear. He witnessed cold-blooded murder of another member of his battalion when a crewman of a German tank being passed by the column shot T/5 "Johnie" Stegle between the eyes with an American .45 automatic. Two other depositions described the killing of some Americans who attempted to surrender in Honsfeld but described also the successful surrender of others.[22] In confronting evidence such as this, the defense was at a disadvantage, since cross-examination of the sources of the information was impossible. But even when given the opportunity for cross-examination, the defense did not always operate effectively. Thus, Lieutenant Colonel Crawford of the prosecution elicited the following testimony from the gunner in a Panther tank of First Company, First SS Panzer Regiment:

Q. Did your company come to Bullingen?
A. Yes.
Q. Was your company commander present when your company arrived at Bullingen?
A. Yes.
Q. Where was he?
A. He was driving ahead of us.
Q. What did you observe as you entered Bullingen?
A. I saw Americans come out of a house about 100 meters ahead of us.
Q. How many were there?
A. Eight to ten.
Q. How were they holding their hands?
A. They were holding their hands above their heads.
Q. What firearms did they carry?

21. *Ibid.*, 000934-35 (907-08).
22. *Ibid.*, 000923-25 (896-97).

A. They were not bearing any arms.

Q. Were any of the group carrying any objects?

A. One of them was waving a white piece of cloth.

Q. How large was this cloth?

A. About 60 by 70 centimeters.

Q. At the time these American soldiers came out of the house, did you see company commander *Obersturmführer* Lottmann?*

A. Yes.

Q. Where was he?

A. He was standing in the turret of his vehicle.

Q. What did he do?

A. He motioned to the American soldiers.

Q. Show the court how he motioned.

A. (Indicating)

Lieutenant Colonel Crawford: Let the record show the witness extends his right arm and brings it back to his right shoulder.

Q. What did the American soldiers do?

A. They then ran toward his car.

Q. What happened then?

A. When they were about ten meters away from his vehicle, Lottmann's vehicle opened fire with machine guns upon them.

Q. How many bursts were fired?

A. I couldn't observe any fire. I would say there were about 50 rounds.

Q. What did the Americans do?

A. They fell forwards towards the front and remained lying there.

Q. After they fell did the firing cease?

A. No, they continued firing.

Q. Did you see these Americans after the firing ceased?

A. We continued to drive on right after that. I couldn't see them.

The witness had testified only to having seen Americans obviously attempting to surrender run toward his company commander's tank, that the tank had fired a burst of machine-gun fire, whereupon the Americans had fallen forward. Had the Americans been hit? Had the German tank actually been firing at them rather than at some other target? In view of the fact that the witness testified that the tank's machine guns had continued firing after the Americans had fallen, the latter would seem to have been a possibility worth exploring by the defense in cross-examination. Instead, the defense limited itself to examining the witness on his field of view from the tank:

Q. Did you have opportunity from the place where you were sitting to observe what you told us just before?
A. Yes.

Q. Isn't it a fact that you have only a very small slit through which you can see, that you have practically no observation possibility whatsoever?
A. This slit, that is not a slit. It's some optical arrangement.[23]

It had also been alleged by the prosecution that a substantial number of Belgian civilians had been murdered by the men of Kampfgruppe Peiper, most in and around Stavelot. Witnesses, both former SS men and Belgians, offered testimony of varying degrees of credibility. Two SS troopers, both enlisted men of the Headquarters Company of the Leibstandarte's Reconnaissance Battalion, testified to having witnessed their platoon leader shoot two adult male civilians under a railroad overpass on December 19.[24] Achille Andre and Henri Delcourt related a horrific story of having been rounded up along with nineteen other men in Stavelot and packed into a tiny 8 foot by 12 foot shed. A machine gun was set up in front of the shed and two belts of ammunition fired into the tightly packed human mass, following which several troopers entered, firing pistols to finish off those who showed signs of life. Straw was then piled on the bodies and set alight. Amazingly, eight persons, including the witness, survived and managed to escape. The defense moved to strike

23. *Ibid.*, 000976-81 (949-50).
24. *Ibid.*, 001067-87 (1036-56).

this testimony as irrelevant inasmuch as none of the defendants had been identified as participants, but the motion was denied by Rosenfeld.[25] Testimony such as this, although failing to name specific defendants, was nonetheless damaging in that it served to enhance the murderous aura that surrounded Kampfgruppe Peiper and, hence, all the defendants. Madame Regina Gregoire of Stavelot related to the court her recollection of Waffen-SS brutality. On December 19, she, her two children, and twenty-six other townspeople had sought refuge from combat in the basement of a house on the outskirts of town along the road to Trois Ponts. Shortly before nine o'clock in the evening, two grenades were tossed into the basement which, remarkably, killed no one. German soldiers then ordered the townspeople out of the basement. Madame Gregoire, who spoke German, attempted to reason with a soldier who insisted that he and his comrades had been fired on from the basement, an accusation that Mme Gregoire vigorously denied. Her efforts unavailing, two SS troopers then opened fire on the group of civilians. Madame Gregoire and her children were spared, perhaps because of her fluency in German. In the course of the succeeding four days, Mme Gregoire, her children, and other civilians were decently treated by the Germans and, in fact, were directed to places of safety by them. Under cross-examination by one of the German defense attorneys, Dr. Otto Leiling, Mme Gregoire admitted that she did not know whether or not other people were in the upper reaches of the house in whose basement she and other townspeople had sought refuge, opening the possibility that the shooting of the civilians had been in savage reprisal for shots fired from the house at Waffen-SS troopers. She also had to concede that heavy street fighting was in progress at that time in Stavelot, recalling that "there was some shooting everywhere."[26]

Antoine Colinet, innkeeper and factory worker of Stavelot,

25. *Ibid.*, 001046-52 (1015-21), 001058-64 (1027-33).
26. *Ibid.*, 001107-17 (1076-86).

told an equally harrowing tale of brutal SS conduct toward civilians. He, his wife, and infant child and another couple and their two children, while crossing a street within a few yards of four parked German tanks, were fired upon by a machine-pistol-wielding German crewman, who killed two of the adults and wounded two others.[27]

In reacting to those and other apparent instances of the killing of civilians, the defense could do little but suggest, as Dr. Leiling had done in his cross-examination of Mme Gregoire, that the killings were, in some sense, responses to guerrilla activity; but this was difficult to demonstrate in specific cases. The defense won a minor victory, however, in its cross-examination of Jean Elias, electrician of Trois Ponts, who testified to having discovered the bodies of fifteen civilians whom he knew near the village. He added proudly that he had later accompanied American troops in recapture of Aisemont. Dr. Leiling then examined the witness:

Q. You said that, together with the Americans, you captured Aisemont, is that correct?
A. Yes.

Q. Were you wearing the American uniform at that time?
A. Yes.

Q. Where did you get the American uniform?

Lt. Colonel Crawford (prosecution): May it please the Court, I do not think there is any materiality to this question at all.

President: Objection overruled.

The witness: I got it from the Maquis.

Q. What is the Maquis?
A. It is the Army of the Resistance.

Q. It is composed of Belgian civilians, is it not?
A. Yes.[28]

Although the testimony elicited by Leiling did not speak to

27. *Ibid.*, 001022-27 (991-96).
28. *Ibid.*, 001128-29 (1097-98).

any of the specific incidents of civilian killings described by the prosecution witness, it did suggest that guerrillas of the Belgian resistance had been operating in the area.

Yet, it was not the testimony of a relative handful of German and Belgian witnesses which constituted the core of the prosecution case but, rather, the mass of sworn statements that the investigation team had gathered between December 1945 and April 1946. Testimony given by prosecution witnesses tended either to be vague as to the nature of ostensible criminal acts (this was characteristic of the testimony of German witnesses) or, if reasonably specific concerning the circumstances under which prisoners and civilians were killed, then indefinite as to the individual defendants responsible for the atrocity (as was true of the testimony of Belgian witnesses). Many of the nearly one hundred sworn statements, on the other hand, associated individual SS men with war crimes which were described in exhaustive detail. If those statements were accepted by the bench as literal truth or even approximations of the truth, the case against the defendants was sealed.

It was therefore incumbent upon the defense to attempt to exclude these statements from evidence, or, failing that, to discredit them. An early effort at the former, on the grounds that according to the army's regulations for the conduct of military government courts, defendants were not to be permitted to offer sworn testimony, was overruled by the bench. Each statement, therefore, was introduced individually by the prosecution, read aloud in translation, and accepted by the bench as evidence, accompanied by testimony from interrogators averring its voluntary nature and accompanied, too, by the perfunctory objection of the defense. Indeed, the prosecution had been amply forewarned of the defense efforts to cast doubt on the validity of the defendants' sworn statements. In April, shortly after having been assigned to the Malmédy case and before the trial had begun, the defense staff received reports from SS prisoners claiming that sworn statements had been extracted from them under duress, both physical and psychological. While not convinced, Everett had been sufficiently disturbed by these allegations, and no doubt sufficiently conscious of their potential value in undermining the prosecution's case, to report them to the Judge Advocate of the Third Army, who referred the problem to Colonel Claude Micklewaite, Theater Judge Advocate. The upshot was a meeting between Ellis and Everett in Micklewaite's office and a brief investigation by Lt. Col. Edwin J. Carpenter of the Theater Judge Advocate's Office. Little evidence of physical brutality was uncovered beyond the likelihood of isolated punches having been thrown at a few defendants by unsympathetic prison guards, but it was established and admitted by Ellis that certain psychological "stratagems" had been employed by the investigators at Schwäbisch Hall in their efforts to extract sworn statements from suspects. What came to be known in the parlance of the Malmédy controversy as "mock trials" were the major instances of such stratagems, involving a court-room-like arrangement and the participation of American personnel in roles similar to those of prosecution and defense; it was apparently hoped thereby to lead the suspect to suppose that his last opportunity to tell "the truth" had presented itself and, perhaps, to suggest that matters would go easier for him if he did.[29]

For good or ill, Micklewaite decided to take no action in response to these revelations but, rather, to allow the court to determine the validity of the sworn statements on which the prosecution case primarily rested. Unavoidably, Ellis and his staff were forewarned of the direction that defense counsel would take in trying to discredit the sworn statements and attempted to undermine its impact early in the trial. In his opening statement, Ellis recalled the extreme difficulty experienced by the investigative staff in extracting information from the Waffen-SS suspects and that, therefore, "all the

29. Everett deposition, October 10, 1949, MMIH, pp. 1560-63; Micklewaite testimony, MMIH, pp. 920-21; Carpenter testimony, MMIH, pp. 883-96.

legitimate tricks, ruses and stratagems known to investigators were employed. Among other artifices used were stool-pigeons, witnesses who were not bonafide and ceremonies."[30] Punctiliously, as each sworn statement was introduced into evidence, the investigator who had elicited the statement was asked by prosecution whether duress in any form including "threats," "promises," "harsh, cruel or inhuman treatment," had been employed, questions that were invariably answered in the negative. Promptly offered as a prosecution exhibit in order to preclude a later sensational revelation by the defense was a black cloth hood similar to those which the prisoners at Schwäbisch Hall had been required to wear on certain occasions.[31] Captain Raphael Shumacker was later to explain to the court that the prisoners had been forced to wear hoods when they were being conducted between their cells and the interrogation rooms in order to prevent them from learning the identities of fellow prisoners and to render them more tractable.[32]

In its cross-examination during the presentation of the prosecution's case, the defense sought, with varying degrees of skill and persuasiveness, to plausibly suggest that many of the sworn statements were less the confessions of guilt-laden war criminals than the fabrications of an increasingly desperate investigative staff. Under cross-examination, former investigators steadfastly denied having employed physical coercion of any kind but did admit to having employed intensive methods of interrogation upon certain prisoners. Particular attention was focused on the interrogation methods used upon Arvid Freimuth, a suspect who was not present at Dachau, for he had hung himself in March 1946 in his cell at Schwäbisch Hall (but the unsigned fragment of whose statement was nevertheless introduced as evidence). Under cross-examination by Lt. Col. Granger Sutton, Lt. William Perl, who had interrogated Freimuth shortly before his suicide, ad-

30. U.S. v. Bersin, 153/1/000104 (99).   31. Ibid., 000116 (111).
32. Ibid., 000718 (699).

mitted the "possibility" of his having threatened to turn Freimuth over to the Belgians, who presumably would be less restrained in their treatment of SS prisoners than Americans, if he, Freimuth, were not forthcoming.[33] This could hardly be characterized as a flagrant case of duress, although it did call into question the truthfulness of the blanket denial that "threats," "promises," "harsh, cruel or inhuman treatment" had been used.

Dwinnell cross-examined another of the investigators, Joseph Kirschbaum, on a "mock trial" (or "schnell procedure" as the investigators preferred to term it) in which he had participated:

Q. At that schnell procedure, who else was present besides yourself?

A. There was Lt. Perl, myself and several other persons whose names I don't remember at present.

Q. Did each person have a part to play in the supposed trial?

A. Yes, Lt. Perl played a part and I played a part.

Q. What part did Lt. Perl play?

A. For myself, I played the part of the good guy and Lt. Perl played the part of the bad guy.

Q. Will you explain the part played by the good man and also the part played by the bad man?

A. Well, the bad fellow is the one who does a bit of shouting and the other one tries to calm him down.

Q. As a matter of fact, then, the good man is the one who plays the part of the prosecutor, isn't that a fact?

A. It is the first time I have ever heard of a good man as a prosecutor. . . .

Q. During that procedure you have referred to, did Lt. Perl have many conversations with [the defendant] in your presence?

A. All I know is that I was keeping the bad fellow away.

Q. How long did this procedure take?

A. Anywhere from, I would say, 10 to 25 minutes or less.

33. *Ibid.,* 2/000364-69 (1474-79).

Q. Do you know whether Lt. Perl had a conversation with [the defendant] after the procedure had concluded?

A. You are referring to the schnell procedure? Well, after the schnell procedure, I was the fellow who spoke to [the defendant] and no one else. . . .

Q. I believe you stated on direct examination that no promises were made to [the defendant]. Now isn't it a fact that you promised [the defendant] that if he would make a statement he would only get six months or possibly one year as a result of that statement?

A. I personally never made such a promise to him.

Q. Do you know whether anyone else made such a statement or promise to [the defendant]?

A. I never heard of it.[34]

Yet, it must not be supposed that extraordinary efforts were required to extract all of the defendants' sworn statements. In some cases, statements were produced and signed in the course of one or two brief and straightforward interrogation sessions. But, in many cases, the testimony of investigators revealed, sworn statements were not in the words of the defendants who had ostensibly made them. The investigators had often drafted statements on the basis of notes they had taken during investigations and had then offered these to the suspects for signature, although the investigators assured the court that each SS man had been invited to first make whatever textual changes deemed necessary. Everett and his staff had been able to make only tentative thrusts against the prosecution case.[35] They had pried open some cracks in it, to be sure, but the weight of evidence against their clients was still massive. In order to make breaches of those cracks, they would have to produce a substantial body of evidence contradicting that of the prosecution.

34. *Ibid.*, 000388-94 (1498-1504).
35. See, for example, *ibid.*, 1/000151-55 (146-50).

VI. JUSTICE AT DACHAU —
DEFENSE AND JUDGMENT

Ellis and his prosecution team concluded their presentation on June 7. The ten-day recess ordered by General Dalbey was invaluable for the defense, which had had little time before the trial to prepare its case and only limited opportunity to do so during the trial, whose sessions generally lasted from eight-thirty until five o'clock. Yet, was it likely that anything that the defense could assemble in support of their clients would be capable of neutralizing the mass of sworn statements that formed the bulk of the prosecution evidence? Everett and his staff feared that it was not. Hence, following a perfunctory motion to dismiss the case on the grounds that the prosecution had failed to prove a prima facie case, a motion denied, the defense moved on behalf of the defendants that all sworn statements be withdrawn from evidence and expunged from the trial record on the grounds that under international law and domestic military law they were inadmissible. The defense argued that as prisoners of war prior to their release from that status in April the defendants had been under the protection of the Geneva Convention of 1929 which forbade the coercive treatment that, the defense contended, had been used to extract the sworn statements. Only if the statements had been reexecuted after the status of the prisoners had changed, the defense maintained, could they be considered valid legal instruments. While the SS defendants were prisoners of war, it was argued, the laws of courts martial were controlling, and these laws would not have admitted confessions as evidence against defendants other than the deponent; moreover, under the same laws, confessions made by an inferior to a superior officer were generally held to be inadmissible, due to the difficulty of excluding the elements of duress. The argument was imaginative and seemed logically unassailable.[1] If the Malmédy defendants had been prisoners of war, then the sworn statements which were the basis of the case against them were, indeed, totally without evidentiary value.

Not to be outdone in resourceful argument, the prosecution responded with a startling rationalization. The Malmédy defendants had never been under the protection of the Geneva Convention because they had never been prisoners of war! They had become war criminals at the moment of having committed their atrocious acts and had thereby forfeited the honorable status of prisoner of war and the safeguards which, under international law, accompanied that status. The prosecution reiterated its denial that duress had been applied in securing the sworn statements but maintained that, even if it had, the statements would retain their legal validity.[2]

It was an unusual argument and probably unnecessary. The U.S. Supreme Court had held in the Yamashita case that the provisions of the Geneva Convention relating to the trial of prisoners applied only to offenses committed *after* capture, although the Convention still offered general protection against abuse.[3] Furthermore, by admission of headquarters, USFET, the Malmédy defendants had been prisoners of war until April 1946 when they had been formally discharged and documented as civilian internees of a particular category, suspected (but not convicted) war criminals. And if the defendants were already, for legal purposes, criminals, then were not the proceedings at Dachau a charade without purpose?

1. U.S. v. Bersin, 153/2/000509-15 (1616-22).
2. *Ibid.*, 000516-18 (1523-25).
3. John Alan Appleman, *Military Tribunals and International Crimes* (Westport, 1971), p. 351.

To permit the bench time to ponder the merits of defense and prosecution arguments, Dalbey adjourned the court. Little time was required to reach a decision. After twenty-five minutes, court was reconvened. The law member, Colonel Rosenfeld, expressed the will of the bench. Without explanation, the defense motion to withdraw the sworn statements was denied.[4]

No course now remained open to the defense but to introduce as much testimony as possible contradicting the sworn statements and the testimony of prosecution witnesses. General Gerhardt Engel, whose Twelfth Volksgrenadier Division had had the job of creating an entry port for Kampfgruppe Peiper a year and a half earlier at Losheim, testified that nothing that Hitler had said in his Bad Nauheim speech of December 12, 1944, could be interpreted as ordering that prisoners of war and civilians be killed. However, the limited impact of such an assertion was reduced by the witness's recollection that the Führer had referred to his dependence upon the ideologically committed personnel of the Waffen-SS for the offensive and that it was necessary that the troops be rendered "fanatical" in preparation for battle.[5] Fritz Kraemer, Sepp Dietrich's former chief of staff, denied that orders distributed by the Sixth Panzer Army had demanded the "liquidation" of prisoners or Belgian civilians but admitted that tactical directives issued by his army had referred to the possibility of resistance to the German attack by Belgian guerrillas and that such resistance, when encountered, had to be broken "at all costs." Orders from the Sixth Panzer Army, according to Kraemer, went into considerable detail concerning the collection of prisoners of war and noted only that such collection was not to be the function of fast-moving forward elements. Far from having killed its prisoners, Kraemer pointed out, the Sixth Panzer Army had taken between five and seven thousand Americans captive during the Ardennes offensive. He had first learned of the American assertion that prisoners

4. U.S. v. Bersin, 153/2/000519 (1526).
5. *Ibid.*, 000524-42 (1631-49).

of war had been shot at the Baugnez crossroads when his G-2 (intelligence staff officer) reported to him on December 20 or 21 that such a claim was being made by Allied radio. Kraemer testified that he had, thereupon, contacted subordinate units for information concerning the alleged atrocity but had received only professions of ignorance. If the testimony of its former chief of staff was to be believed, the Sixth Panzer Army had been exemplary in its efforts to abide by the laws of war.[6]

Dietrich Ziemssen had been operations officer on the staff of the First SS Panzer Division at the time of the Ardennes offensive and had been seriously wounded on December 21, 1944, in Engelsdorf (Baugnez) by American artillery fire. Ziemssen's story, too, was one of punctilious observation of international law. Prior to the offensive, the division had received routine orders from the Sixth Panzer Army concerning the collection and humane treatment of prisoners of war. As operations officer, Ziemssen himself had established two divisional prisoner-of-war collection points and had personally observed roughly eight hundred American POWs, some on foot, some in trucks, on their way to those points. No orders received or issued by the division had demanded or encouraged illegal acts, nor had such matters been mentioned orally in discussions of which he had knowledge. Divisional orders had noted the likelihood of resistance by civilians, however, and the necessity of crushing it quickly.

Ziemssen's testimony was of some weight, for not only could he claim direct knowledge of several factors crucial to the Malmédy case, but he had made written application to testify for the defense, a move not without risk, for Ziemssen himself was a potential defendant. Captain Raphael Shumacker, cross-examining for the prosecution, suggested that Ziemssen's memory had been conditioned by the realization of his own culpability in the transmission of criminal orders, to which Ziemssen responded, to the delight of the defense,

6. *Ibid.*, 000543-83 (1650-90).

that the prosecution had in fact threatened him with criminal charges if he should testify on behalf of the Malmédy defendants.[7] Other SS witnesses were to testify, with varying degrees of persuasiveness, to questionable tactics used by the investigation/prosecution team and to the absence of any conspiracy to murder civilians and prisoners of war. Yet, the impact of their testimony was very limited, for it could too easily be interpreted as nothing more than desperate efforts to rescue comrades suffering at the hands of "the enemy" and attempts to dislodge the perhaps fatal burden of confessions earlier and truthfully given. In terms of efficacy as well as drama, the high point of the defense presentation was reached on June 20 when Everett called to the witness chair Lt. Col. Hal D. McCown of the U.S. Army, then instructor in the Infantry School at Fort Benning, Georgia, and flown from the United States to Germany at Everett's request. McCown, wavy haired and with a clean cut and boyish face, embodied the World War II visual stereotype of the American soldier. His military record was impeccable. An officer in the regular army since July 1940, he had entered combat in Normandy in June 1944 as regimental operations officer of the 119th Infantry Regiment, serving in that capacity until November, when he had received command of the regiment's Second Battalion. But his presence in the Dachau courtroom was due to the fact that he had fought against Kampfgruppe Peiper in December 1944 and had been its prisoner for four days.

In articulate sentences uttered in a soft southern accent, McCown described the entry of his regiment into combat east of Werbomont on December 18 under orders to intercept Peiper's armored spearhead. While fighting over rough terrain between Stoumont and La Gleize on the afternoon of December 21, McCown was captured along with his operations sergeant and a radio man. The three were disarmed and searched by four SS troopers and marched immediately to

7. *Ibid.*, 2/000668-3/000033 (1775-1813).

Peiper's command post. Peiper attempted to interrogate the American but learned nothing other than McCown's name, rank, and serial number. Later that day, McCown was taken to a building in La Gleize whose large cellar held one hundred thirty-five American prisoners of war, the bulk of whom were members of his own regiment's Third Battalion captured two days earlier in Stoumont. He was able to ascertain that the Americans were being well treated, complaining only of poor quality food (which the Germans, themselves, were eating) and the fact that watches and rings had been taken from them.[8] McCown's testimony discomfitted the prosecution, for it served to undermine the Manichean aura which had been cast about the case by Ellis and his staff. Thus, Dwinnell asked McCown:

Q. Did you learn of any infractions of the Geneva rules?

A. I believe the two that I have mentioned [thefts and poor food] are infractions of the Geneva rules, but inasmuch as we are guilty of the same, I found no—

Prosecution: If the court please, I object to that part of the answer.

A. I found no serious infractions.

Prosecution: I move to strike that part of the answer and the court be instructed to disregard it, referring to treatment by Americans.

President: The objection is sustained and that portion of the witness's statement as regards the action of Americans will be stricken from the record and disregarded by the court.[9]

In its opening statement, the prosecution had asserted that "one hundred seventy-five to three hundred eleven" American prisoners and "at least" three Belgian civilians had been murdered by the men of Kampfgruppe Peiper in La Gleize. Numerous sworn statements had described the killings of prisoners of war in La Gleize between December 18 and December 23, including a sizable group shot on the eighteenth along the cemetery wall of the only church in the village. La Gleize was a tiny place of fifty or sixty houses, and although McCown could not claim to have explored every street and corner, he had moved about the village under guard during his four-day "visit" and had passed the church but had seen no dead civilians or American soldiers other than an American lieutenant and prisoner of war killed by shrapnel from American artillery fire.[10] On the other hand, in one of five conversations, Peiper informed McCown that nine American prisoners assigned to labor details had been shot and killed while attempting to escape to nearby American positions.[11] Thus, at least nine American prisoners had been killed, albeit, perhaps legally, without McCown's having observed evidence of it.

McCown made no secret of having been favorably impressed by Peiper and by other members of the Kampfgruppe whom he had observed. In a report written after his escape from German captivity, McCown wrote of Peiper "I have met few men who impressed me in as short a space of time as did this German officer" and described in tones of admiration the discipline and essential humanity of the enemy soldiers with whom he came into contact.[12] His testimony before the Dachau court was somewhat more restrained but, nevertheless, strongly favorable to Peiper and his men. On the evening of December 22, McCown was called to Peiper's command post in La Gleize. Remarkable in the brief relationship between captive and captor was their subsequent conversation, which lasted into the predawn hours and which seems to have been largely devoted to Peiper's expounding of the Nazi Weltanschauung and his assessment of German prospects in the war.[13] In the poisoned atmosphere of the Dachau courtroom, the revelation of the lengthy tête-à-tête between the

10. *Ibid.*, 000047-48 (1826-28).
11. *Ibid.*, 000050-51 (1829-30).
12. "Behind the German Lines," Annexe I to Part C of Intelligence Notes No. 43 dated 6 January, 1945, p. 3, *ibid.*, 6/000709.
13. *Ibid.*, 3/000047 (1826).

American major and the SS-Obersturmbannführer carried
with it the faint scent of unwholesomeness which, to some extent, may have limited favorable impact of McCown's testimony upon the bench.

McCown went on to describe yet another meeting with Peiper on the night of December 23 and 24 in the presence of
the recently captured Captain Chrisenger of the 803rd Tank
Destroyer Battalion, an event further contributing to the air
of detachment from the savagery of World War II which characterized McCown's testimony. Peiper had received orders
from divisional headquarters at around noon that day to attempt a breakout toward the east in order to restore contact
with the main body of the First SS Panzer Division. It was at
this meeting that Peiper proposed the plan whereby all American prisoners in La Gleize, then numbering about 150 be set
free save McCown, who would accompany the Waffen-SS
troopers and could, Peiper hoped, later be exchanged under a
flag of truce for the wounded and medical attendants which
the Kampfgruppe would be forced to leave behind. Chrisenger's function was to apprise McCown's superior of the proposed arrangement when the 119th entered La Gleize. Although stressing the unlikelihood that the American forces
would honor such an agreement (which in fact they did not),
McCown joined Peiper in signing a written instrument out-
lining the proposed exchange.[14]

Shortly after midnight, McCown marched out of La Gleize
with the German column. A day later, he would succeed in
escaping from his captors and would make contact with an
outpost of the U.S. Eighty-second Airborne Division. But in
his testimony describing the escape from encirclement by the
remnant of Kampfgruppe Peiper, McCown was able, once
again, to attest both to the high level of military competence
of Peiper's men and to the humane treatment accorded their
bag of prisoners, now reduced to a single major of the U.S.
Army.[15]

14. *Ibid.*, 000054-55 (1833-34).
15. *Ibid.*, 000057-61 (1836-40).

Under cross-examination, McCown could not be shaken from his straightforward testimony, although the prosecution was able to elicit from him the admission that he had not seen all of La Gleize during his captivity and, therefore, by implication, some evidence of foul play might have eluded him. McCown also conceded that he had witnessed "minor" infractions of the Geneva Convention other than those he had earlier described, such as the use of prisoners of war to carry artillery ammunition in a zone of combat, but, again, he candidly noted to the annoyance of the prosecution that these were violations of which the U.S. Army was equally guilty.[16]

By probing more deeply into the content of McCown's long evening conversation with Peiper, Ellis might have essayed to discredit the defense "star witness," and he later certainly regretted not having done so. Yet, the fact that Kampfgruppe Peiper had held approximately 150 American prisoners of war in La Gleize, had treated them as well as could reasonably be expected under extremely difficult circumstances, and had freed them unharmed was incontrovertible.

A few minor witnesses followed McCown to the stand. The defense then called Jochen Peiper, clearly the central defendant in the Malmédy trial and the man whose personality stood out decisively from the mass of defendants. In spite of his uniform, now stripped of insignia and decorations, and his ill-fitting GI combat boots, Peiper scarcely appeared the defeated enemy and prisoner with his carefully groomed hair and his attitude of controlled yet unmistakable disdain for the proceedings which he had observed unfolding in the Dachau courtroom for several weeks. In the witness chair, Peiper spoke in a faintly nasal baritone, offering his testimony in German in spite of his facility in the English language.

Testifying in his own behalf, Peiper's obvious intention was to deny the veracity of major portions of his earlier sworn

16. *Ibid.*, 00067-73 (1846-52).

statements. He had given his testimony careful thought and needed little guidance or prompting from the questioning defense attorneys, Strong and Dwinnell, as he spoke in colorful terms of his experiences at the hands of the American investigation team. Peiper had, in fact, taken careful notes on the investigation procedure and was given permission by General Dalbey to use these aides while on the witness stand.

He told a story of five weeks of solitary imprisonment in a dark cell at Zuffenhausen without opportunity for physical exercise before having been questioned by Lieutenant Perl. Peiper implied that the depressed psychological condition which resulted from this treatment made him vulnerable to Perl's interrogation tactics, which included flattery combined with efforts to impress Peiper with the hopelessness of his situation and suggestions that the fate of his comrades depended upon his conduct. In that vein, Peiper testified, Perl informed him that among the American prisoners killed at the crossroads were the sons of a senator and a business tycoon, whose influence had created a public demand for Peiper's head so powerful that not even the president of the United States could save him. Peiper's military record had been a brilliant one, Perl supposedly conceded, but the days of glory were forever gone. The American government could not permit high-ranking SS officers such as he to ever regain their freedom, quite apart from their degree of individual guilt. His life, therefore, could have only one conceivable purpose: to minimize the sufferings of his comrades by assuming personal guilt for the murders attributed to Kampfgruppe Peiper. Peiper testified that he thereupon declared his willingness to sign anything set before him if that would result in freedom for his former subordinates.[17]

This encounter between Perl and Peiper at Zuffenhausen could only have taken place prior to December 1945 when the Malmédy suspects were transferred to Schwäbisch Hall. Strangely, Perl did not take advantage of Peiper's declared

17. *Ibid.*, 000107-08 (1886-87).

willingness to "cooperate" until March 1946, several months later, when Peiper made his sworn statements, one of a routine informational nature and two of material consequence to the Malmédy case. On March 21, Peiper testified, Perl confronted him with four young officers, one his former adjutant, who declared that Kampfgruppe Peiper had received an order encouraging terrorism and the shooting of prisoners. Initially, Peiper stoutly denied the existence of such an order. But in the face of repeated assertions to the contrary and assurances by Perl that Dietrich, Priess, and Kraemer had already admitted "everything," Peiper testified, he permitted Perl to dictate to him a statement containing the fateful admissions. Even then, the defendant claimed, he had been unwilling to sign the statement before a careful reading of it but had been denied the opportunity by Perl who had demanded Peiper's immediate signature and, having secured it, had dashed off with the precious document. Subsequent vain efforts were made by Peiper to secure a copy of his statement. An English translation was ultimately shown him which he rejected as untruthful but was not permitted to revise.[18]

Peiper testified that his second material statement, sworn and signed on March 26, 1946, had been made under circumstances similar to those that had surrounded the earlier one. It was in this statement that Peiper had confessed, or appeared to have confessed, to having given his subordinates permission to shoot recalcitrant American prisoners of war in La Gleize, to having ordered a prisoner shot in Stoumont on December 19, and to having acquiesced in the shooting of the frostbitten American at Petit Thier. Again, Peiper claimed he was confronted by Perl and several former members of Kampfgruppe Peiper, one of whom, an ex-SS-Untersturmführer, appeared to the defendant to be on the brink of nervous collapse. At Perl's direction, the prisoners proclaimed that Peiper had given orders to shoot prisoners of war in Stoumont and La Gleize. Totally demoralized by this irrefutable

18. *Ibid.*, 000109-11 (1888-90).

evidence, not of his own guilt but of the breakdown of the strong spirit of comradeship which had permeated the once proud Kampfgruppe, Peiper, despairing, declared his willingness to sign whatever statement Perl might dictate.[19] The result had been an exceedingly damaging piece of prosecution evidence.

If Peiper's sworn statements were untrue and the products not of actual duress but of a form of psychic debilitation which had robbed the defendant of the will to tell the truth, then what actually had Peiper's role been during the Ardennes offensive? Lieutenant Colonel Dwinnell sought to convey his client's "revised" version of these events by reading critical portions of his sworn statements and inviting him to respond with "the truth." Peiper testified that his divisional commander, Mohnke, had ordered him to fight "fanatically" in the forthcoming offensive but that the word had held no sinister significance. It referred, rather, to the willingness for self-sacrifice which would, it was hoped, characterize the fighting spirit of the German attack force. In his later tactical presentation to his subordinates, Peiper had ordered the ruthless commitment of men and materiel and had forbidden the point of the Kampfgruppe to halt under any circumstances. But what, then, was to have been done with American soldiers who might surrender? Peiper testified that the tactical order received from the division had stated that prisoners were to be left standing where disarmed or directed to the rear, in either case to be picked up by units following the fast-moving Kampfgruppe and that he, in fact, had discussed this procedure with the commander of the Panzergrenadier unit that was to follow his own. If anyone had received orders to shoot prisoners of war, Peiper sought to suggest, it had been the so-called "150 Panzer Brigade" commanded by Otto Skorzeny, English-speaking German troops disguised as American soldiers whose function was to spread confusion among the enemy in advance of the German spear-

19. *Ibid.*, 000111-12 (1890-91).

head. Peiper testified that he had been told by one of Skorzeny's subordinates that the 150 Panzer Brigade planned to operate as did British commandos: "If we're caught, we're finished; we don't give any mercy either."[20]

As to the shooting of prisoners at Stoumont and La Gleize, Peiper professed to know nothing. But he now offered a more complex and more flattering explanation for his earlier willingness to confess to complicity in the latter block of crimes. Prior to making his sworn statement of March 26, Peiper had been informed by Perl that one of his battalion commanders had already confessed to having ordered prisoners of war killed in La Gleize. Motivated by the earlier expressed desire to assume responsibility for crimes imputed to the Kampfgruppe and by means of that assumption to ameliorate the lot of his subordinates, Peiper now claimed, he had falsely attested to having been responsible for the fatal orders.[21]

Yet, Peiper's testimony under direct examination by the defense was not totally exculpatory. While denying having issued preattack orders requiring or permitting the killing of prisoners of war, he admitted to having observed to Perl that such orders were unnecessary, as it was "obvious" to experienced officers that prisoners had to be shot "when local conditions of combat should require it." However, he claimed under direct examination that the statement had not been made in the context suggested by Perl in the statement that he had "dictated"; how it might have arisen was not explained.[22]

Much of Peiper's direct testimony consisted of a lengthy tactical analysis of Kampfgruppe Peiper's operations from December 16 to 24, 1944, which the law member, Colonel Rosenfeld, later pronounced "one of the finest dissertations of a regimental commander that I ever heard." Peiper perfunctorily denied all knowledge of the killing of prisoners of

20. *Ibid.*, 000112, 000120-22, 000129-33 (1891, 1899-1901, 1908-11).
21. *Ibid.*, 000120 (1899).
22. *Ibid.*, 000115-16 (1894-95).

war, with two notable exceptions, and said nothing concerning the shooting of civilians while noting that civilian resistance had been encountered at Stavelot by the Kampfgruppe and that a wounded German had been murdered in Stoumont by an ax-wielding Belgian. It had been on December 18 outside Trois Ponts, however, that Peiper had been informed by the commander of the Royal Tiger detachment without elaboration that a "mix-up" had occurred on the previous day which had resulted in the deaths of many prisoners.[23]

In testifying on the final days in La Gleize, Peiper admitted having been told by Pringel that some American prisoners (eight, Peiper recalled) had been shot while attempting to escape, that having been presumably a legitimate use of force. Understandably, the defendant dwelt at some length upon his correct, even friendly, relationship with Major Hal McCown to again dramatize the fact that a large number of prisoners held in La Gleize had been well treated by the Kampfgruppe. The signers of several sworn statements had alluded to a firing squad's shooting of prisoners. A shooting party had, indeed, been formed, Peiper explained. Its purpose had not been to kill American prisoners but rather to execute a member of the Ninth Panzer Pioneer Company who had been discovered in the act of removing the SS runes from his uniform collar, an act presumed preparatory to desertion.[24] Even taken at face value, this piece of testimony was of dubious usefulness to the defendants. An admission that a Waffen-SS trooper might be shot on suspicion of planning to desert indicated an attitude toward human life that might be deemed in harmony with the killing of prisoners of war and civilians. Moreover, the bench might well have questioned why a soldier preparing to desert would take pains to remove insignia identifying him as an SS man or why his superiors would consider the removal of SS insignia proof positive of an intention to desert. The inference would have

23. *Ibid.*, 000138-60 (1917-39); MMIH, 1431.
24. U.S. v. Bersin, 153/3/000177-86 (1956-65).

to be drawn that all concerned recognized that the presence of SS runes significantly reduced the likelihood of good treatment—even survival—at the hands of the prospective captor, and presumably for a reason. In addition, Peiper did himself little good in handling the subject of the frostbitten prisoner at Petit Thier. While denying that he had ordered the prisoner shot, Peiper made it clear that he had done nothing to save him, unconvincingly citing his regimental surgeon's ostensible observation that the frostbitten American, after having spent two weeks in the winter woods, could not survive being moved to medical facilities.[25]

Peiper's direct testimony in his own defense occupied the whole of the court's June 21 session. On the following morning, it was the opportunity of the prosecution to cross-examine, and Ellis, pacing combatively beside the witness chair, subjected the central defendant to a fierce interrogation. The leader of the prosecution team focused on Peiper's claims of having been subjected to inhumane conditions of imprisonment prior to having made his sworn statements. Ellis skirted the question of what Peiper had described as dungeon-like confinement at Zuffenhausen. He elicited the admission from Peiper, however, that the cell in Schwäbisch Hall, where he had spent three months before making the three depositions now being used as prosecution evidence, had been comfortably furnished.[26] But the defendant responded defiantly when Ellis suggested that his sworn statements had been vehicles of truth which Peiper was now attempting to disavow, fearing that they would carry him to the gallows:

Q. Well, you wouldn't have signed them if they weren't true, would you?

A. I already explained yesterday why I signed them which was the situation when I signed them.

Q. Well, you told me I thought here earlier this morning that you believed in the sanctity of an oath.

25. *Ibid.*, 000185-86 (1964-65).
26. *Ibid.*, 000190-91 (1969-70).

A. Yes.

Q. Do you mean to tell me now that you don't believe in the sanctity of an oath?

A. I believe in the sanctity of an oath if it's taken under fair conditions, but not if an oath is taken under false conditions and under pretext of false facts and under pressure.[27]

Ellis was acidly persistent and Peiper disdainful, even arrogant:

Q. In other words, anything that would be damaging would be untrue and anything that was not damaging would be true, is that the situation?

A. I already said before that I personally do not care at all what could do me any harm or what was not damaging to me.[28]

But if that were true and, moreover, Peiper had earlier made false confessions prompted by evidence of the breakdown of comradeship and loyalty among veterans of his Kampfgruppe, Ellis might reasonably ask, as in fact he did, from whence had come Peiper's renewed interest in "the truth"? Under Ellis's sardonic gaze Peiper soberly explained:

> The reason for this is that today I was able to find out that the comradeship, which at that time I believed to have disappeared, is not an empty illusion, and that my opinion which I had at that time could only be created [if] all of us were played against each other, and that my comrades had been forced to testify against me. This knowledge which I had here in Dachau made it my duty to testify clearly and distinctly, and to tell how conditions were in reality so that the German people would learn who we were in reality and that we fought for our Fatherland for six years desperately and fanatically.[29]

That statement seemed to drip with self-serving cant. Yet, there is no doubt that Peiper was often open and forthright on matters clearly damaging to his own position. Thus, under

---

27. *Ibid.*, 000193-96 (1972-75).   28. *Ibid.*, 000200 (1979).
29. *Ibid.*, 000205 (1984).

cross-examination dealing with his duties as adjutant to the Reichsführer-SS, he admitted having accompanied Himmler to a demonstration involving the gassing of human subjects.[30] And while denying that he had ordered prisoners of war shot in La Gleize, Peiper declared that he would have shot those prisoners if his troops had been forced to fight to the end in that village "since I thought it was impossible that all of us would die here and the next day a hundred and fifty Americans would get new weapons and fight against the German Army. I could not take the responsibility for that toward my commanders."[31] Doubtless, it did not escape the bench that the same rationale could be used in an effort to justify the killing of prisoners of war when an onrushing battlegroup could spare neither time nor men to guard.

Peiper's candor and experience as a battlefield commander again surfaced as Ellis, reacting to one of many denials of the prosecution's allegation that the men of the Kampfgruppe had been ordered to shoot prisoners, queried sarcastically:

Q. Now were all your men so undisciplined that they killed prisoners of war without orders?

A. During combat sometimes there are situations about which one cannot talk on the green table.

Q. Now, Peiper, I asked you if your men were so undisciplined that they killed prisoners of war without orders. Can you answer that question without talking about green tables?

A. That doesn't have anything to do with discipline.

Q. Well, I'll ask the question again. Were your men so undisciplined that they would kill prisoners of war without orders? Can you answer that "yes" or "no"?

A. No, this question doesn't have anything to do with discipline, and for this reason, I cannot answer it with "yes" or "no."

Q. Well, were your men so ill-trained in the rules of the Geneva Convention that they killed prisoners of war without orders?

30. *Ibid.*, 000189 (1968).
31. *Ibid.*, 000208 (1987).

A. In the answer on that question, it is the same as on the question before. During combat there are desperate situations, the answer to which is given out very fast to main reactions and which do not have anything to do with education and teaching.[32]

Peiper's cross-examination was not without moments of grim humor. Ellis questioned the defendant concerning his claim that civilians had fired on elements of the Kampf-gruppe in Büllingen.

Q. How were they dressed?

A. These were people which one could see only for an instant. They usually wore civilian headgear and a civilian jacket, but I can't give any details.

Q. Did you see any 80 year old woman firing at you from the windows there in Büllingen?

A. In those short moments I had no occasion to determine the age of the persons firing.

Q. Did you see any one-year-old baby firing at you from the window in Büllingen?

A. No, not even in Russia did I see any one-year-old babies firing.[33]

Peiper might have won the duel of wits with Ellis, but the chief prosecutor ended his cross-examination on a strong note, demonstrating several discrepancies between the defendant's testimony under direct examination by the defense and statements he had made to U.S. Army war crimes investigators in the summer of 1945. There was no claim of duress concerning these statements. Moreover, his memory of the events of December 1944 had presumably been much fresher than it was a year later, as, in fact, Peiper was forced to concede. Most damaging, perhaps, was Ellis's introduction of the fact that in August 1945 Peiper had told U.S. investigators that his men had held "about 200 or 250" prisoners of war in La Gleize, which, if true, would have left unaccounted for a sizable number beyond the 150 released by the Germans.

32. *Ibid.*, 000209-10 (1988-90).
33. *Ibid.*, 000213-14 (1992-93).

Peiper could only respond lamely that as commander of the Kampfgruppe, his mind had been on matters other than prisoners of war and that he had never known with any precision how many prisoners his troops had taken, a statement that harmonized poorly with the numerical precision with which the defendant had spoken of prisoners of war in his direct defense testimony.[34]

Following a brief redirect and recess, Peiper requested permission to make a final statement to the court before vacating the witness chair. With a laconic "Go ahead," General Dalbey assented. Peiper began:

> Early in May, here, I had a personal conversation with Lt. Colonel Ellis. This conversation occurred on a personal, human plane . . . fundamental . . . and in that connection I asked Colonel Ellis whether he, personally, really believed all of the things I am accused of here.

Ellis was on his feet:

> If the court please, I object to that, that it is irrelevant whether I believe what is going on here or whether I don't believe what is going on here. I don't believe that has any bearing on the case here.

The objection, while, perhaps, technically correct, was intriguing. Dalbey permitted Peiper to continue:

> I had told him that—Colonel Ellis surely would know that all my testimony resulted only from my attitude, that I wanted to save my men and wanted to cover that. Upon that, Lt. Colonel Ellis said, "I admire you, and I hardly know another soldier who I estimate as highly as I do you, but you are sacrificing yourself on an ideal which no longer exists. The men whom you today think you have to cover up for are bums and criminals. I'll prove that to you in the course of the trial. We are now parting as friends, and when we see each other again before [the] Court [we will be] as enemies, and I'll have to paint you in the worst bloody colors, but you'll understand that I will only be doing my duty.[35]

34. *Ibid.*, 000214-38 (1993-2017).
35. *Ibid.*, 000266-67 (2041-42).

Ellis was obviously embarrassed and, while admitting that he had made those comments to Peiper, moved that they be stricken from the trial record, a motion that was denied by Colonel Rosenfeld, with the by now thoroughly familiar qualification that the court would attach to the matter "the value it deems necessary."[36] While a point of high drama in the trial, Peiper's revelation could be of little substantive impact. The chief prosecutor had, apparently, expressed a degree of personal admiration for the major defendant which made for strange listening by those who recalled the prosecution's opening statement, but Ellis's confidence had not suggested a belief in Peiper's innocence of war crimes. At most it indicated a willingness to believe that Peiper might have attempted to assume, in some cases, responsibility for the crimes of others.

What remained of the defense presentation would be more prosaic than the testimony of McCown and Peiper. Everett and his team placed on the witness chair well over a dozen ex-Waffen-SS soldiers, most of them not defendants, who offered testimony contradicting the major accusations brought against the Malmédy defendants; that they had received and transmitted orders to murder prisoners of war and civilians and had consistently done so. Some of this testimony was credible. A former SS-Rottenführer (corporal) of the Seventh Company, First SS Panzer Regiment, spoke simply of prisoners he had taken in Büllingen on December 17 and near La Gleize on the night of December 20 to 21, 1944. In the first case, the witness's company commander had ordered him to direct the prisoners to the rear toward Honsfeld and, in the second instance, to escort a prisoner to the regimental command post.[37] Other examples of defense testimony were more difficult to accept at face value. A noncommissioned officer of the Ninth Panzer Pioneer Company solemnly assured the court that his company commander, one of the defendants, had stated that his troops should treat prisoners of war in the

36. *Ibid.*, 000267 (2042).
37. *Ibid.*, 000521-24 (2291-92).

fashion that they, themselves, would want to be treated if captured.[38] The witness's image of a Waffen-SS officer, prior to an attack, intoning a sermon based on the golden rule was hardly persuasive. Defense witnesses occasionally contradicted one another. One young ex-SS trooper testified that his company commander in a pre-attack talk to his men had said that no prisoners were to be taken. Everyone in the company had understood him to mean that surrendered Americans would be swept up by units following Kampfgruppe Peiper. Another former member of the same company testified that in his address the company commander had said nothing whatsoever concerning prisoners of war.[39]

Additional accusations of duress, including physical brutality, were made against the investigation/prosecution staff. Thus, a defense witness claimed to have been struck in the face and thrown to the floor of the interrogation cell at Schwäbisch Hall while he, himself, had been a suspect. Furthermore, he testified, American interrogators had threatened him with hanging and suggested that his parents, who lived in Poland, would be harmed unless he swore a statement accusing his company commander of having ordered the shooting of prisoners of war and confessing that he himself had shot American prisoners in La Gleize. Rather confusingly, the witness had not made the statement demanded of him at Schwäbisch Hall but claimed to have made a false statement to the prosecution later at Dachau "under the impression of Schwäbisch Hall because I was afraid."[40] In a similar vein, the former commander of the Third Panzer Pioneer Company testified that he had been compelled to swear statements attesting to the existence of orders to shoot prisoners of war, by threats of hanging and beatings, the latter ostensibly administered by Lt. William Perl. Whatever value the testimony might have had suffered when Captain Shumacker of the prosecution called attention to the respective physiques of the two men. The ex-SS officer, a powerfully built man over

38. *Ibid.*, 4/000269-73 (2788-91).   39. *Ibid.*, 3/000563-70 (2333-40).
40. *Ibid.*, 000496-504 (2271-79).

six feet tall, towered above the much shorter American lieutenant.[41]

A far more serious problem, one that the defense had foreseen from the outset, also began to manifest itself. Defendants, motivated by a natural desire for self-preservation, offered testimony which, while serving to mitigate their own guilt, at the same time tended to increase the apparent burden of guilt borne by others. Under cross-examination by Captain Shumacker, for example, a former company commander denied having ordered prisoners of war shot in Stoumont but asserted that he had "heard" on December 19, 1944, that one of his subordinates, also a defendant, had shot American prisoners on that day.[42] In like manner, an ex-platoon leader during cross-examination denied all wrongdoing but testified that he had received unequivocal pre-attack orders from his company commander, one of the seventy-four defendants, to the effect that prisoners of war were to be shot. The witness self-righteously claimed, however, not to have conveyed these orders to the members of his platoon.[43] In brief, defendants under direct examination by the defense staff naturally offered exculpatory testimony but, when pressed by the prosecution during cross-examination on incidents other than those on which they had been questioned by the defense, occasionally made statements damaging to codefendants. Given the fact that seventy-four defendants were being simultaneously tried, this was a situation virtually impossible to avoid. It had been for this reason that the defense had moved in vain for a severance at the start of the trial. Having tried in every conceivable way to undermine the impact of the sworn statements made by the Malmédy defendants, Everett and his staff now looked on in dismay as some defendants under cross-examination lent additional credibility to the crucial documents. In a forlorn effort to permit

41. *Ibid.*, 000578-85, 000609 (2348-55, 2379).
42. *Ibid.*, 000610-12 (2380-82).
43. *Ibid.*, 000432 (2207).

defendants to testify without incriminating one another, Lt. Wilbur Wahler requested the court to rule that when defendants were testifying as witnesses for other accused, limitations on the cross-examination of witnesses be observed, preventing the prosecution from questioning the defendants on matters not raised by the defense on direct examination. Such a ruling would have eased, although it would not have eliminated, the difficulties inherent in defending more than six dozen defendants. Ellis argued that such a ruling would give the defense an unfair advantage and that, in any event, defendants remained defendants and could be questioned on any matter relating to their ostensible offenses when they took the chair. In strict terms of law, the chief prosecutor was correct. The law member ruled against Lieutenant Wahler's request.[44]

Everett immediately revealed that the ruling had been a critical one for the defense. He asked that the court briefly recess in order that he might poll the dock as to the advisability of resting the case rather than allowing the defendants to continue to imperil one another by their own testimony. On Dalbey's orders, the courtroom was emptied, save for the defendants and the defense team. Everett's point of view was clear and unequivocal: the prosecution had failed to prove its case, but the German defendants might prove it for them through their testimony. Better, therefore, to stop and hope that the bench would agree that the prosecution had not done what it had claimed itself able to do. But the defendants, supported by their German attorneys had, perhaps, more accurately assessed the temper of the army judges. To them, it seemed of overriding importance to refute the sworn statements, and that could only be done from the witness chair. Everett deferred to their determination. The defense presentation would continue.[45]

Again, witnesses testified for the defense, among them,

44. *Ibid.,* 000621-26 (2391-96).
45. *Ibid.,* 000626-28 (2396-98); Everett to family, June 29, 1946, EP.

men who were themselves defendants. Again, instances arose in which defendants offered testimony prejudicial to other accused. But the defense was able to introduce additional evidence calling into question the truthfulness of some of the sworn statements. For example, the prosecution had claimed itself able to prove that at least nine civilians had been murdered by men of Kampfgruppe Peiper in Büllingen. But the defense had dispatched Miles Rulien, a lawyer recently assigned to the staff, to the village for a brief investigation. Büllingen was a community of around three hundred souls and thirty to forty houses. It was therefore not difficult for an individual to keep account of the citizenry as, in fact, the village mayor and registrar customarily did. Rulien returned with an affidavit from the official which was introduced into evidence. The document stated that only two residents of the village had died since the start of the Ardennes offensive, and one of these had expired of natural causes on May 28, 1946.[46] One citizen at Büllingen had indeed been killed as the fighting of December 1944 swept through the village. In still another affidavit submitted as defense evidence, Anton Jonsten declared that his wife had been killed on December 16 or 17, 1944, by shrapnel from American artillery fire, the fatal wound having been suffered as she ran down a street seeking shelter.[47] Of course, the affidavits were not conclusive proof that no other civilians had been killed in Büllingen. It was quite conceivable that, in the confusion of war, transient civilians might have fallen victim to Waffen-SS troopers and their deaths never recorded. But the affidavits should have introduced a strong element of doubt concerning the alleged murder of civilians in Büllingen.

La Gleize was an equally tiny community where the prosecution had alleged on the basis of numerous sworn statements that "one hundred seventy-five to three hundred eleven" American prisoners had been killed. Lieutenant Colonel Hal

46. U.S. v. Bersin 153/4/000034-37 (2558-61).
47. *Ibid.*, 000038-39 (2561-62).

McCown had testified that during his several days of captivity in La Gleize he had seen no bodies of American prisoners of war. The prosecution had sought to neutralize that testimony by eliciting from McCown the admission that he had not seen all parts of the village. The defense, however, was able to offer several affidavits by residents of La Gleize stating that they, too, had seen no evidence of prisoners' having been murdered. Father Louis Blockian, the village priest, had remained in La Gleize from December 18, 1944, when German troops had entered, until December 24, when American troops retook it. During that time, the only dead American Father Blockian had seen was the charred body of a crewman hanging from the hatch of a burned-out Sherman tank.[48] Alfred Kreutz, who lived in the village with his family, had also been present during the same period. He and his family had taken refuge from the fighting in the cellar of a house on the outskirts of La Gleize. Sometime later, the Kreutz family was forced to find shelter elsewhere, when the Germans commandeered the house, and were ultimately permitted to remain in the village church, which Peiper's men were using as a hospital. There they found German medical personnel treating their own and American wounded alike. During the entire time, moreover, Kreutz saw no dead American soldiers.[49] Maria Gregoire, another resident of La Gleize, had seen a single dead American. She, too, had found shelter in the village church and had also observed German personnel tending the wounded of both nationalities. One American, badly injured in both legs, died. No other dead prisoner had she seen. Nor had she heard of American prisoners having been murdered.[50] Armand Baltus neither saw murdered American prisoners nor had he heard from neighbors that prisoners had been killed. Specifically, he knew of no American prisoners having been shot at the church cemetery wall, and had it happened, it could scarcely have escaped his attention, for he had

48. *Ibid.*, 000300 (2819).   49. *Ibid.*, 000306-07 (2825-26).
50. *Ibid.*, 000307 (2826).

been, as he put it, "right there."[51] Numerous German witnesses testified in the same vein, but none could be as effective as the Belgians who had no stake in the outcome of the case and, if anything, would tend to be hostile toward the German defendants. Two to three hundred corpses would have been difficult to conceal or overlook in a community the size of La Gleize. If four citizens of the village and a major of the U.S. Army had failed to detect evidence of so much as one murder, much less several hundred, could much credence be reposed in the prosecution's contention or in the sworn statements that formed its foundation? With that question left in high relief, the defense chose to rest its case.[52] Everett and his co-workers had no more significant evidence to present; to place additional defendants on the stand would have achieved little and likely would have been counterproductive. And while they could scarcely be said to have demolished the prosecution case, they could legitimately hope to have raised serious doubts about its validity in the minds of the military judges.

Ellis and the prosecution team sought to patch whatever holes had been torn in the fabric of their arguments. Defense witnesses and defendants had testified with wearisome repetitiveness to various misleading and coercive methods employed by the investigation team, primarily at Schwäbisch Hall, to extract the crucial sworn statements on which the prosecution case was largely built. Now, Perl, Thon, Elowitz, Kirschbaum, and Shumacker, under examination by their fellow investigators, denied most of the accusations that had been made against them by the Malmédy defendants. But they did not deny everything. The accusations that had been made against them had been so numerous that it would have been practically impossible to respond to each one. But the investigators' failure to deny some charges may have been significant. Ellis questioned Perl concerning the statement that

51. *Ibid.*, 000308 (2827).
52. *Ibid.*, 000403 (2923).

PLATE 1. Jochen Peiper as SS-Obersturmbannführer (lieutenant colonel) decorated with the Knight's Cross and Oak Leaves. (Private Source)

PLATE 2. A Waffen-SS SPW (armored personnel carrier). Note flexible machine gun mounted forward and Panzerschreck (bazooka) hung on side. In the background is a Panther tank. (Ernst Baumann)

PLATE 4. American survivors at the massacre site. (U. S. Army photograph)

PLATE 3. Bodies are uncovered at the massacre site. (United Press International)

PLATE 5. American survivors preparing to testify. (U. S. Army photograph)

PLATE 6. The Malmédy judges. Brig. Gen. Josiah T. Dalbey and Col. Abraham H. Rosenfeld, fourth and fifth from left. (U. S. Army photograph)

PLATE 7. Prosecution staff: (left to right) First Lt. Robert E. Byrne, Joseph Kirschbaum, Lt. Col. Homer B. Crawford, Morris Elowitz, Lt. William R. Perl, Capt. Raphael Shumacker, Harry Thon, Lt. Col. Burton Ellis. (U. S. Army photograph)

PLATE 8. Prisoners' dock and defense staff. (U. S. Army photograph)

PLATE 17. Sepp Dietrich in the Dachau courtroom. To the right are Fritz Kraemer and Hermann Priess. (U. S. Army photograph)

PLATE 18. Senator Joseph McCarthy
charges the Baldwin subcommittee
with a "whitewash" in its investigation of the Malmédy trial.
(United Press International)

Peiper had alleged the investigator to have made at Zuffenhausen. Perl flatly denied having told Peiper that the sons of
a U.S. senator and a business tycoon had been among those
killed at the Baugnez crossroads, but did not deny having
told Peiper that he could never be given his freedom, that his
life was now "ruined" and without meaning, and that he
could spare his men suffering by "admitting everything."[53]
Thon was examined concerning his interrogation of a witness
who, at Dachau, had testified for the defense that he had
been beaten, threatened with hanging, and told that his parents, living in Poland, would suffer unless he produced an acceptable statement. Thon was questioned specifically about
the alleged beatings, which he denied, but not examined on
the other elements of the accusation.[54]

If the prosecution did not fully neutralize the charges of
duress, it was able to use this penultimate opportunity to express itself to offer evidence that the defendants had themselves sought to influence testimony during the trial. On at
least two occasions efforts had been made to pass notes from
defendants to witnesses containing "suggestions" as to how
the latter might testify.[55] In neither case had the notes reached
their destinations; but even though they had been without
effect, it was useful for the prosecution to call the court's attention to them. If two attempts to influence testimony had
been uncovered, perhaps many more had gone undetected.
Two possible abortive attempts to suborn perjury could therefore contribute to the discrediting of a great mass of defense
testimony.

It was on the awkward subject of La Gleize and the mass
murders of American prisoners that had allegedly taken place
there that the prosecution chose to conclude its rebuttal of
the defense case. It was an unfortunate effort, for the "evidence" now introduced was of an obviously flawed nature,

53. *Ibid.*, 000412-13 (2932-33).
54. *Ibid.*, 000422-27 (2938-43).
55. *Ibid.*, 000448-52, 000453-56 (2964-68, 2969-72).

much of it so transparently worthless that its introduction suggested either contempt for the intelligence of the bench or confidence that any prosecution evidence, no matter how lacking in substance, would weigh in the scales against the defendants. An affidavit by a private of the Second Panzer-grenadier Regiment, then a prisoner at Fort Meade, Maryland, stated that while he was lying wounded in the church at La Gleize, he had heard a rumor from other injured troopers that prisoners in and around the village had been killed and that after his capture he had heard the same from "quite a few" other men. Two other German prisoners named by the affiant as being also aware of these events, however, denied all knowledge of them.[56] Even thinner was the deposition of another ex-Waffen-SS trooper, also a prisoner at Fort Meade, who stated nebulously and irrelevantly that "nobody knew for sure" whether the American prisoners had survived. That was too much (or too little) even for the bench, which under the rules of evidence for military government courts had been most liberal in its judgment of admissible evidence, and was ordered stricken from the record.[57] Highly suspect, finally, were affidavits offered by two American soldiers who claimed to have seen and, in fact, transported large numbers of bodies of murdered American prisoners of war from La Gleize. Both documents had been helpfully entitled: "In the matter of the finding of the bodies of approximately 200 American prisoners of war at La Gleize, Belgium, who were presumably killed after their surrender to the Germans on or about 22 December 1944." Here, apparently, was eyewitness evidence of the elusive corpses, which the prosecution had insisted must exist but which no one had seen (beyond the authors of the suspect sworn statements). But what had been confidently stated in the heading was not borne out in the text. The affiants did not speak of prisoners killed "on or about 22

56. Exhibit P-132, *ibid.*, 000466-70 (2982-86).
57. *Ibid.*, 000471-76 (2987-92).

December 1944" but of having seen the corpses on or about that date in La Gleize while on assignment to transport American dead. That, of course, was an impossibility inasmuch as La Gleize had been in Peiper's hands until early on the morning of December 24. A cursory reading of the two affidavits should have made it evident that the description of the location of the bodies and the disposition conformed to the gathering, identification, and examination of the victims of the Baugnez crossroads massacre and must have taken place more than three weeks later.[58] The affidavits, therefore, were the products either of confusion on the part of the two American deponents or the result of intentional or unconscious misleading by the Security and Intelligence Corps special agent who questioned the deponents in their Georgia homes. The latter is strongly suggested by the fact that the Americans, possessed of two and eight years of formal education, seemed to have answered the questions put to them with impeccable grammar and syntax. The purported evidence was, in fact, no evidence. Again, the defense moved to strike. Its motion was denied, although the law member of the bench, Colonel Rosenfeld, noted that certain "conclusions and assumptions" contained in the affidavits would be disregarded.[59] Nevertheless, it appeared, as the defense sarcastically noted, that the prosecution was now, in effect, contending that La Gleize was not in German hands on December 22, 1944, which contradicted not only historical fact but much of the prosecution's own evidence.

On this mildly ludicrous note, the submission of evidence in the case of the United States versus Valentin Bersin, et al. concluded on the morning of Tuesday, July 9, 1946. Following a one and one-half hour recess, the court reassembled to hear the concluding arguments of prosecution and defense. Both sides planned lengthy summaries, and in order to save

58. *Ibid.*, 000476-82 (2992-98).
59. *Ibid.*, 000482 (2998).

time, there would be no simultaneous translation of the prosecution argument into German. Instead, German counsel were provided with an already prepared written translation and permitted to retire from the courtroom to read it.[60]

Captain Raphael Shumacker began the prosecution summary with a brief but pointed allusion to the weight of emotion that lay heavily upon the Malmédy case. With the naive self-righteousness that characterized the American self-image in the postwar period, the prosecution attorney spoke of the American people's having been "shocked as only a peace-loving people can be, shocked" by news of the Malmédy Massacre. Their government had vowed that the criminals responsible for the heinous deeds would be identified and brought to book. That grim but satisfying time was now approaching. The promise made to the American people was about to be fulfilled. At the conclusion of the case not only the people of the United States but of the entire world would know what "instigators and perpetrators of unrestrained Genghis Khan warfare" might expect at the bar of justice.[61] On a more subdued level, Shumacker discussed the breaches of law of which the defendants were allegedly guilty. Specifically, these included violations of Article 2 of the Geneva Convention of 1929, requiring the humane treatment of prisoners of war and of Article 46 of Section III of the Hague Convention, enjoining the ill treatment of civilians by troops of an occupying power, with the result that the accused "did willfully, deliberately and wrongfully permit, encourage and abet, and participate in the killing, shooting, ill-treatment, abuse and torture of unarmed prisoners of war and unarmed allied civilians." Unexceptionally, Shumacker pointed out

60. *Ibid.*, 000484 (3000).
61. *Ibid.*, 000486-87 (3002-03). In the development of its case the prosecution had made much of the fact that SS officers had been required to read a book approved by Himmler on the life of Genghis Khan, interpreting it to mean that the savagery of the Mongol leader had been held up as a model for the SS to emulate. That Himmler encouraged brutality is clear, but that had not been the purpose of the reading assignment. Rather, Genghis Khan was a symbol of Asiatic barbarism against which the SS was to protect "Germanic civilization."

that those who had encouraged murderous acts "by speeches and orders" bore as heavy a burden of guilt as those who had actually pulled triggers.[62]

Yet, the prosecution was no longer claiming quite what it had asserted when the trial had begun. In its opening remarks, perhaps under the influence of the Nuremberg trial, it had emphasized the supposedly conspiratorial aspects of the case, placing hundreds of murders, which it alleged, within the framework of ostensible orders demanding mass slaughter, which had originated with Hitler and had been willingly transmitted from echelon to echelon down to the companies and platoons that composed Kampfgruppe Peiper. Now, as the Malmédy trial approached its climax, the prosecution seemed to recognize that such a characterization had been a distortion or, at least, a simplification of reality. Shumacker noted the defense contention that orders to take no prisoners, when they were given, meant only that prisoners were to be left to following units. Rejecting that as a general defense of those who had given orders, Shumacker was willing to concede "for the sake of argument" that in some cases orders did not specifically require the shooting of prisoners of war but that orders and "pep talks," when couched in expressions such as "wave of fright and terror," "everything before our guns will be mowed down," "we will avenge the bombing terror," and the like would probably be interpreted by troops "trained in ruthless methods of warfare" to mean that prisoners of war were to be shot. These were well-disciplined troops, the prosecutor observed, and it would not be credible to suppose that as many troops as had killed prisoners of war had acted contrary to orders. That was a valid point, although reversed, it constituted another nail in the coffin of the "all-echelon conspiracy theory." Would well-disciplined Waffen-SS troopers have taken many prisoners of war, as Kampfgruppe Peiper had done, if they had been ordered to kill their prisoners? According to Shumacker,

62. *Ibid.*, 000487-88 (3003-04).

the prosecution had evidence to prove that, in addition to the defendants, one hundred fifty other SS troopers, dead or otherwise unavailable, had killed prisoners of war or civilians during the offensive of December 1944. Left unsaid, however, was the obvious fact that many more had had the opportunity to kill prisoners but had not done so.[63]

But what of the prosecution's evidence, so much maligned by the defense? Again the focus rested, as it had to do, on the validity of the numerous sworn statements made by the defendants. Shumacker had no alternative but to stress the perfect propriety of the methods used to secure these statements and their essentially voluntary character, the latter in no way compromised by the use of certain "ruses and subterfuges" which the prosecution had openly admitted at the start of the trial. Shumacker attempted, however, to demonstrate the truthfulness of the sworn statements with something less than compelling logic. Where had the great detail that had marked many of the statements come from, he asked, if not from the defendants themselves? The defendants, moreover, were battle-hardened combat veterans, well trained and well disciplined, the prosecution attorney pointed out. Was it conceivable that such men could be made to write and sign often lengthy accounts of their own crimes and those of others if they were not true? And why, if the statements had been secured under duress, had some SS suspects refused to confess to wrongdoing; and why had some defendants admitted to certain crimes while denying others? In brief, Shumacker stressed, the sworn statements were of indubitable validity and had to be assigned great weight by the bench in reaching its verdicts.[64]

More persuasive was Shumacker's argument in anticipation of a possible defense effort to claim the protection of "superior orders" for its clients. On this point, the law was clear and unequivocal. Law No. 10 of the Allied Control Council

63. *Ibid.*, 000489-90 (3005-06).
64. *Ibid.*, 000492-95 (3008-11).

dated December 20, 1945, concerning war crimes trials, stated that superior orders did not free a subordinate from responsibility for his acts, although they "may be considered in mitigation." Nor could that law be viewed, simply, as a self-serving legalism of the victor, for the same principle had been eloquently expressed by the German Supreme Court sitting at Leipzig in the *Llandovery Castle* case of 1921. That case, one of a series involving German war crimes allegedly committed in World War I and brought to trial at the instance of the victorious Allies, had produced an opinion that subordinate officers are liable to punishment if they obey superior orders which they can reasonably be expected to recognize as illegal. In the *Llandovery Castle* case, the manifestly illegal orders had resulted in the murder of helpless survivors of a sunken hospital ship by the crew of the submarine that had destroyed it. It was the prosecution's contention that the illegality of orders to shoot prisoners of war and civilians as described in most of the sworn statements had been just as obvious, and the orders should not have been obeyed, although there might have existed a logical conflict between this contention and the prosecution's emphasis at other points that SS men had been steeped in barbaric "Genghis Khan" methods of warfare.[65]

Shumacker sought also to neutralize any attempt by the defense to justify the alleged murders of prisoners of war and Belgian civilians on the grounds of "military necessity." Surprisingly, the prosecutor conceded that such an argument might have validity in certain extreme combat situations but denied that it could be used in exculpation of the offenses of Kampfgruppe Peiper. Here, Shumacker was near to treading on dangerous ground, for in describing a presumably hypothetical case in which "military necessity" could conceivably be used in justification of violations of the laws of war, he

---

65. *Ibid.*, 000495-97 (3011-13). On the *Llandovery Castle* case, see Sheldon Glueck, *War Criminals. Their Prosecution and Punishment* (New York, 1944), pp. 151-54.

enumerated criteria possibly applicable to the crossroads killings (a "parcel" of prisoners "shot on an isolated spot because they could not be left or taken along"). And while the prosecution had presented evidence for many other killings which did not meet Shumacker's criteria, its evidence for the crossroads killings was by far the strongest.[66]

Shumacker continued his closing argument with a rapid summary of the evidence against the Malmédy defendants, stressing, naturally, those instances in which the prosecution case seemed strongest. This consisted, primarily, of a survey of the sworn statements that had constituted the backbone of the prosecution case. Shumacker could remind the court that by no means all of these statements had been repudiated and that some of the damaging allegations contained therein had been confirmed during the trial by the testimony of prosecution witnesses.[67] As to the defense witnesses who had been called to refute that evidence, Shumacker quite rightly pointed out that almost all had been SS men, most former members of Sepp Dietrich's Sixth Panzer Army and many, friends and comrades of the defendants. Their testimony, therefore, might have been expected to be biased and prejudiced. More to the point, they had lied to save their SS "brothers."[68]

Finally, the prosecution exhorted the bench to judge the defendants in a manner commensurate with their heinous crimes. In spite of the youth of most of the accused, they were "hardened and dangerous criminals" who often murdered "spontaneously" and "with enthusiasm" and deserved rigorous judgment. In tones of high emotion, the court was informed:

> Today in America the survivors of these massacres, the mothers, fathers, sweethearts, wives and children of these comrades of

66. U.S. v. Bersin, 153/4/000498 (3014). On the subject of military necessity, see Gerhard von Glahn, *Law Among Nations. An Introduction to Public International Law* (New York, 1965), pp. 546-47: N.C.H. Dunbar, "Military Necessity in War Crimes Trials," *The British Yearbook of International Law*, 39 (1952), 442-52.

67. U.S. v. Bersin, 153/4/000498-548 (3014-64).

68. *Ibid.*, 000549 (3065).

ours who so needlessly fell, not on the field of battle, but from the tender mercies of the SS, are awaiting your findings. These comrades all would have been alive today if it had not been for the 1st SS Panzer Regiment and they must not have died in vain. From their deaths let there come a clear understanding to our former enemies that they cannot wage warfare in a merciless and ruthless manner. They must learn that the end does not justify the means! That truth, honor and mercy cannot be sacrificed for success and that the honorable soldiers of the world still have mercy on the field of battle for their captured opponents. It must be brought home to the German people that the principle of extermination which guided them in their last battle will not create for them a new and better world but will only bring disaster to their homeland and to themselves. Let their punishment be adequate for their crimes.[69]

Whether "they" represented the defendants or the German people may not always have been clear in the final sentences of the prosecution's closing remarks; but the bench was given to understand that the issues involved in the Malmédy case rose far above the perennial problem of battlefield "excesses."

On the morning of Wednesday, July 10, the defense was given a chance to summarize its evidence and exercise its dramatic skills upon the bench. Everett's team elected to divide the task among ten of the American and German attorneys with Lt. Col. John Dwinnell speaking for the officer defendants, Mr. Frank Walters for the noncommissioned officers, and Lt. Col. Granger Sutton for the enlisted men. The six German lawyers would argue for the defendants who had retained them, following which Everett planned to offer final remarks.[70]

Dwinnell spoke to the issue of the sworn statements implicating the officers, characterizing them as vague and contradictory and, in many cases, as having been secured under duress. But the thrust of Dwinnell's argument did not move

69. *Ibid.*, 000549-52 (3065-68).
70. *Ibid.*, 000485 (3001).

in the direction of denying that the officers of Kampfgruppe Peiper had been responsible for the killing of surrendered American soldiers. Rather, he sought to remind the military judges of the confusion and uncertainty which permeate combat situations and which often obscure the neat distinctions so easily enunciated in court and that the law as it applied to the taking of prisoners was not without its ambiguities. Some killings, he suggested, had been the result of "injudicious conduct in the heat of battle" rather than the products of criminal conspiracy. It was not entirely clear, he implied, that Americans killed under questionable circumstances had in every case clearly submitted themselves to their captors, thereby becoming formally prisoners of war. Dwinnell attempted to lend weight to this hypothesis by depicting the situation existing at the Baugnez crossroads as one in which some Americans, to be sure, had surrendered, but others attempted to escape while still others continued to offer armed resistance. This was doing considerable violence to the evidence, for while there had been a faint suggestion that the prisoners might have begun to flee after the firing of the initial pistol shots (quite different in significance from moving *prior* to being fired upon), there was nothing to indicate that Americans in the vicinity had been still engaged in combat. Nor, Dwinnell insisted, were combatants necessarily always obliged to accept the surrender of a defeated adversary. Defense counsel cited Wheaton's *International Law* in support of the concept that a soldier's right to be spared injury at the hands of his captors after abandoning resistance is not absolute. His opponent is obliged, in almost all situations, to grant him "quarter" upon surrender, but there is a notable exception to that rule, which occurs "when the achievement of victory would be hindered and even endangered by stopping to give quarter instead of cutting down the enemy and rushing on, not to mention that during fighting it is often impracticable so to secure prisoners as to prevent their return to combat."[71]

71. *Ibid.*, 000555-59 (3071-75).

Here was, as the prosecution had foreseen, the argument of "military necessity." Its weaknesses, however, were manifold. Quite apart from the inherent subjectivity in determining when the granting of quarter might be "impracticable," a point on which enemies or former enemies were likely to differ, it was an argument on which authorities on international law disagreed and which, moreover, conflicted with Article 23 (c) of the Hague Convention.[72] Its most obvious shortcoming, however, was that the defendants themselves had never adopted it. To have done so would have required the admission that prisoners of war had been shot, which the defendants could scarcely do while at the same time repudiating their sworn statements. There had remained, of course, the undeniable crossroads killings; but insofar as the defendants had attempted to explain these at all, they had passed them off as a "mix-up" and not the product of calculated action. Dwinnell's introduction of the argument of "military necessity," therefore, seemed to indicate that the defense did not believe the testimony of its own clients or, at least, assumed that the members of the bench would not.

In arguing for the noncommissioned officers, Walters, like Dwinnell, attacked the sworn statements for their collective inconsistency and absence of corroborating evidence, noting that under American court martial regulations, such evidence was considered insufficient to convict, an essentially irrelevant point since the laws of courts martial were not controlling in military government courts.[73] But the core of Walters's argument was that, insofar as prisoners of war and civilians were murdered at all, they had been done to death in obedience to superior orders, an assertion that, like Dwinnell's, the prosecution had anticipated. But again, like Dwinnell's argument, that of Walters seemed to contradict defense testimony to the effect that superior orders for the killing of prisoners and

---

72. Lassa James Oppenheim, *International Law* (II *War and Neutrality*) (London, 1921), pp. 169-70.

73. U.S. v. Bersin, 153/4/000566 (3072).

civilians had never existed. And not only did the argument tend to discredit much of the defense case, but it served to redirect the finger of guilt at the officer defendants, the sources of the ostensible murderous orders. Thus, in pleading the case of a noncommissioned officer who in his sworn statement had admitted having shot an American prisoner at the crossroads and who had not repudiated his statement, Walters incriminated one of the officer defendants who, supposedly, had issued the order.[74] Again, the fearful difficulty of simultaneously defending more than six dozen officers, noncommissioned officers, and enlisted men against literally hundreds of charges of murder was manifesting itself.

In speaking for the enlisted men among the defendants, Lt. Col. Granger Sutton trod an ambiguous path similar to Walters's. Many of the sworn statements were clearly the products of duress and were unsubstantiated by corroborating evidence. If crimes were committed by enlisted men, they were the result of superior orders. Here, too, in order to make the defense of superior orders credible, the defense attorney was forced to specify by name the sources of the orders that had resulted in particular murders, working at cross-purposes with his colleagues, Walters and Dwinnell.[75] The brief arguments of the German attorneys in defense of individual defendants or small groups were often more cogent than those of American counsel but probably failed to have significant impact on the minds of the army judges. Most addressed the court in German, their statements then being translated laboriously and sometimes unfelicitously into English. Moreover, they were Germans and did not always succeed in concealing their distate for the proceedings for which their former enemies were responsible.[76]

It remained only for Everett early in the afternoon of July 11 to briefly appeal less to the intellects (and thus, perhaps, obscure the many ambiguous and contradictory currents in

74. *Ibid.*, 000567-68 (3073-74).   75. *Ibid.*, 000590-95 (3106-11).
76. *Ibid.*, 000611-92 (3127-3205).

the defense case) than the emotions of the bench. In his soft Georgia drawl and in slow, deliberate cadence he described the extreme difficulty that the defense staff initially encountered in gaining the cooperation of the defendants, a problem rooted in the distrust that the defendants had felt for all Americans as a result of their ostensibly harrowing experiences at the hands of brutal and unprincipled army interrogators. Gradually overcoming the defendants' suspicion, Everett explained, he and his staff had come to understand that many of the accused had been so disoriented and frightened by the modus operandi of the investigators as to have been willing to sign anything put before them.[77] In effect admitting that atrocities had been committed by the defendants, Everett attempted to place whatever guilt his clients might bear in the broader context of human frailty under the fearful stresses of war. Each of the judges was asked to consider:

> . . . that primitive impulses of vengeance and retaliation among victimized peoples are often called forth in the heat of battle or as the culmination of a war-weary last struggle against an overwhelming enemy. Thus the spiral of inhumanities mounts which have always been the inevitable by-product of man's resort to force and arms, whether he be enemy or ally.[78]

That was an effort at evenhandedness and objectivity which had a strange ring in the summer of 1946, little more than a year after the surrender of Nazi Germany, perhaps a bit overdrawn as well; for even thirty years later, the notion of Waffen-SS troopers as instruments of "vengeance" of a "victimized" people falls short in its persuasive appeal. Everett suggested to the bench that a fair and dispassionate judgment in the Malmédy case would assist in nurturing a new "democratic nationalism" among the German people and concluded his address with words of Tom Paine which had

77. *Ibid.*, 000693-94 (3206-07).
78. *Ibid.*, 000694-95 (3207-08).

been used a short time earlier by Justice Rutledge in his dissent from the majority opinion that the U.S. Supreme Court lacked review jurisdiction in the trial of the Japanese General Yamashita, a case that bore some similarities to the Malmédy case. "He that would make his own liberty secure must guard even his enemy from oppression, for if he violates this duty, he establishes a precedent which will reach himself,"[79] not a great piece of oratory, but intensely moving to those whose lives were in the balance. Fritz Kraemer wept openly.[80] With that, the lawyers on both sides of the Dachau courtroom sheathed their verbal swords.

A ripple of excitement and, one must believe, of envy, passed through the prisoners' dock as Ellis rose to announce that USFET had ordered the withdrawal of charges against one of the enlisted defendants, an Alsatian, over whom the French government now claimed jurisdiction (and whom the French government would shortly release).[81] But the fates of the remaining seventy-three defendants still lay in the hands of the judges, who now, at approximately two o'clock in the afternoon, cleared the courtroom and retired to produce a verdict. Everett's closing statement was read in translation to the defendants, producing a renewed flow of tears from Kraemer and a handshake and thanks for the defense chief from Dietrich.[82]

Several thousand pages of evidence and testimony concerning the many defendants and long series of complex events had been accumulated since the opening day of the trial nearly two months earlier. Yet, after two hours and twenty minutes the bell announcing the reconvening of the court was sounded. Defendants, defense and prosecution staffs, and the bench filed back into the forward areas of the courtroom, while spectators, including wives of many of the accused,

---

79. *Ibid.*, 000695 (3208).
80. Everett to family, July 11, 1946, EP.
81. U.S. v. Bersin, 153/4/000695 (3208).
82. Everett to family, July 11, 1946, EP.

took their places in the rows of wooden seats reserved for them. Banks of floodlights were once again illuminated; army cameramen squinted through their viewfinders as General Dalbey called upon the defendants and the two legal teams to rise. "The Court in closed session," Dalbey intoned, addressing the defendants, "at least two-thirds of the members present at the time the vote was taken concurring in each finding of guilty, finds you of the particulars and the charge guilty."[83] The verdict was translated into German, and all resumed their seats.

Thus, without exception, the seventy-three remaining defendants were found guilty of the "killing, shooting, ill treatment, abuse and torture of members of the Armed Forces of the United States of America, and of unarmed Allied civilians," verdicts that had been reached after a period of deliberation that averaged less than two minutes per defendant. Sentencing, literally a life-and-death matter for all seventy-three, was yet to come, but each man was first to have the opportunity of making a final plea for mitigation of sentence, "last words," in effect, as far as the Malmédy trial was concerned and for some, perhaps, within hailing distance of finality in absolute terms. Little more than half of the convicted SS men, primarily the younger enlisted men, addressed the court. A majority of these men (approximately 62 percent) made statements that were essentially noncommital as to personal guilt, stressing, rather, hardships endured during youth, family obligations, family members killed in Allied air raids, and other factors which, the convicts apparently hoped, might stimulate sympathy toward them in the minds of the judges. Almost all, however, emphasized that as SS men they had been rigorously trained in the necessity of unquestioning obedience to even "impossible" orders. It is difficult to assess the significance of this oft-repeated observation; but, in some cases, it did, no doubt, represent a tacit admission of wrongdoing, particularly when coupled with emphatic assertions

83. U.S. v. Bersin, 153/4/000696 (3209).

that to have refused to carry out orders in a combat situation would have resulted in the speaker's death. Thirty percent of those who chose to make a final appeal to the bench specifically denied having committed criminal acts. One twenty-seven-year-old enlisted man, accused of having shot prisoners of war at La Gleize, asserted that he had not fired a single shot during the entire offensive. The remainder, by far the smallest group, admitted the crimes of which they had been accused; all, however, claimed extenuating circumstances. A nineteen-year-old enlisted man declared that the court had found him guilty of a crime which he had been forced to commit, namely, the shooting of two male civilians in Wanne on the orders of his superior. Disobedience was out of the question, for he had seen five comrades shot for refusing to obey orders. Yet another young enlisted man expressed regret for having shot a single American prisoner of war but also claimed the defense of superior orders. A sergeant of the Ninth Panzergrenadier Company openly conceded that he had killed an American prisoner near Cheneux, an act for which he pleaded the multiple extenuation of exhaustion, nervous instability (he had never fully recovered, he claimed, from having been buried in debris during combat on the Invasion Front during the summer of 1944), the heat of combat, superior orders, and incitement by his comrades. Seemingly more candid and, therefore, more persuasive was the effort by a young soldier to excuse his admitted shooting of Belgian civilians in Wanne. He, too, had been indoctrinated with the principle of absolute obedience to orders. The Ardennes offensive, moreover, had been his first battle experience, and he had been so terrified that he had obeyed the directives of his superiors without question. At the time of the shootings, however, he had not been conscious of committing a crime, for the civilians were asserted to have been guerrillas who had killed German soldiers.[84]

84. *Ibid.*, 000696-737 (3209-50).

The balance of the afternoon of Thursday, July 11, and the morning of the following day were occupied with the reading of the pleas of individual convicted prisoners. It was a scene to excite varied emotions. Forty statements, some simple and seemingly sincere, others transparent attempts at pathos and melodrama, a few with pretensions to literary elegance, most, the crude efforts of ill-educated minds, had been read by men whose smooth and regular physiognomies (the average of those who read statements was less than twenty-two) belied the fact that many of them had experienced the horror and exhilaration of war over a longer period of time than had any American soldier in the Dachau courtroom (or, probably, anywhere else). One young noncommissioned officer (who denied his guilt) had spent 680 days in actual combat, had had his armored mount shot from under him eleven times, and had been wounded three times. That these, in spite of a liberal sprinkling of boyish blue eyes surmounted by blond hair, were not callow youths but experienced soldiers—German soldiers—had been reflected in the snaps to attention with clicking heels and military strides which had characterized their movements between the prisoners' dock and the point before the bench from which they had made their final statements. An American officer could respect that soldierly bearing yet desire vengeance against those who had murdered and, perhaps more difficult to forgive, humiliated other American soldiers. It was to determine appropriate punishment for these men and their less voluble superiors that the Dachau court adjourned at noon. The atmosphere prevailing among the prisoners and defense counsel was not sanguine. Moments before adjournment, Everett conveyed to the bench a request from the Malmédy convicts that death penalties, where assigned, be executed by shooting rather than hanging, noting that, in a recently concluded case involving the killing of prisoners of war, the Canadian Army had sentenced Kurt Meyer, sometime commander of the Leibstandarte's sister division, Twelfth SS Panzer Division "Hitler Jugend," to the traditional soldier's death by musketry.[85]

Not until 1:30 on the afternoon of the following Tuesday did the court reconvene. The judges had obviously found the task of assessing punishment more difficult than that of establishing guilt. There were some notable absences from the courtroom. Shumacker and Elowitz for the prosecution had been excused, as had Dwinnell and Sutton for the defense, the latter, sick in hospital. Dalbey deepened the already oppressive atmosphere of the courtroon by beginning with a response to the prisoners' request that shooting be substituted for hanging as the capital sentence. The court, he announced, had been directed by the commanding general, USFET, to impose the sentence required by regulations, namely hanging, but might make its own recommendation in the matter, which, Dalbey grimly informed the prisoners, it would do.[86] With an abrupt warning directed at the spectators' gallery to remain silent during sentencing, Dalbey began: "Valentin Bersin." Bersin rose from his place, strode before the bench and stood at rigid attention; to his left stood Everett, also at attention, as he would stand throughout the sentencing. "Valentin Bersin, the Court in closed session, at least two-thirds of the members present at the time the vote was taken concurring, sentences you to death by hanging at such time and place as higher authority may direct." For three-quarters of an hour, Dalbey droned alphabetically through the list. Forty-three Malmédy convicts, including Jochen Peiper, received death sentences; Sepp Dietrich was given a life sentence; Priess, twenty years; Kraemer, ten. Of those not sentenced to death, twenty-two were sentenced to life imprisonment, the remainder to prison terms of ten, fifteen, or twenty years. At 2:20 the court adjourned sine die.[87]

85. *Ibid.*, 000737 (3250).
86. *Ibid.*, 000738 (3251). The judges recommended that shooting be substituted for hanging. That recommendation was rejected by higher authority.
87. *Ibid.*, 000738-54 (3251-67).

On the following day, the seventy-three prisoners were placed in the custody of the commandant of Landsberg fortress, now a prison operated by the U.S. Army.[88] Some twenty years before, Landsberg had been the place of incarceration for Adolf Hitler, the unsuccessful putschist. It now seemed likely to be the place of death for two score members of his personal division.

88. *Ibid.*, 000757 (3270).

VII. CONFLICT AND CONTROVERSY

In its coverage of the Malmédy trial, the American press had expressed little doubt as to the criminal guilt of the German defendants. A few days after the trial had begun, the *St. Louis Star Times* wrote:

> . . . The brutality at Malmedy has its documentation. . . . Six of the American soldiers escaped the massacre . . . and they are telling their story in the trial of 74 of Germany's Elite Guard. These 74 will get their punishment . . . because the conscience of humanity has not quite been stilled. . . . The world reaches out for a new concept of international law. . . .[1]

The editorial revealed not only confusion about the facts of the case (many more than six Americans had survived the "massacre") but a measure of hypocrisy which, in retrospect, ill-became the destroyers of Hiroshima and Nagasaki. In addition, it reflected a less-than-clear conception of the legal significance of the Malmédy case, probably rooted in a failure to recognize the distinction between what was taking place in the courtroom at Dachau and, concurrently, in Nuremberg. Trying Nazi leaders for the planning and commission of crimes against humanity and peace was, indeed, reaching out "for a new concept of international law." Trying enemy soldiers for the killing of prisoners of war and Allied civilians was not. For many Americans, the Malmédy defendants and their trial

1. *St. Louis Star Times,* May 22, 1946, in "The Judicial Processes Concerning the Malmédy War Criminals. Digest of Editorial and Column Opinion, 22 May 1946–27 January 1949" (hereafter Digest), p. 1, NA, RG 319.

represented much more than that, as was indicated by the form in which the *Ohio State Journal* expressed its satisfaction with the findings of the Dachau court.

. . . In business-like and expeditious proceedings . . . a military court in Dachau has convicted 73 members of Hitler's elite SS. . . . There is not much that they can say in extenuation. . . . In a sense, more was on trial at Dachau. . . . The Nazi philosophy of ruthlessness . . . and the policy of frightfulness as an end in itself stood also at the bar of judgment and were found guilty.[2]

But the ring of finality contained in those words proved unjustified for two reasons. By theater directive, the Deputy Judge Advocate for War Crimes, Lt. Col. Clio Straight, was required to review each war crimes trial and prepare an opinion for the theater commander.[3] The Malmédy death sentences, therefore, could not be executed immediately. At the same time, Everett remained convinced that justice had not been done in the courtroom at Dachau. Letters to his family during and immediately after the trial reveal more than professional disappointment over a case going badly and ultimately lost; they carry a sense of deep depression and personal failure. On the day following sentencing, he wrote of his heart having been "crushed" by the outcome of the trial and of a head "whirling-splitting and hammered."[4]

Did he believe the Malmédy defendants to be innocent? Strictly speaking, no. He knew that atrocities had been committed by Kampfgruppe Peiper. The bodies uncovered at the Baugnez crossroads could not be argued away, and some defendants had admitted other crimes in their final courtroom statements. Moreover, Peiper, in candid letters written to Everett during the trial, had said little to counter a conclusion that his Kampfgruppe had not always scrupulously observed the "laws and usages of war," although he had attempted to place the conduct of his men within a conceptual

2. *Ohio State Journal*, July 16, 1946, *ibid*.
3. MMIH, p. 926.
4. Everett to family, July 17, 1946, EP.

framework which would evoke the American attorney's sympathy. His men, he wrote "are the products of total war, grown up in the streets of scattered towns without any education. The only thing [they] knew was to handle weapons for the Dream of Reich. They were young people with a hot heart and the desire to win or to die according to the word: right or wrong—my country!"[5] It may not have been coincidental that Peiper wrote this letter on July 4, supposing, perhaps, that Everett would more likely be impressed with the claim of patriotism as a mitigation on the great American national holiday. Peiper also wrote openly to Everett concerning his own attitudes. In spite of six bloody years in the field and several wounds, he recalled the war as "a proud and heroic time. Where we were standing was Germany and as far as my tank gun reached was my kingdom." Nor did he attempt to conceal his devotion to Adolf Hitler, regretting only that, at the end of the war "when the Fuehrer was needing his Leibstandarte the most, . . . fate had separated us from him. . . ." Depressed and apprehensive following the announcement of the mass verdict, Peiper mourned the passing of all that had given meaning to his life. "When seeing today the defendants in the dock, don't believe them to be the old combatgroup Peiper. All of my old friends and comrades have gone before! . . . The real outfit is waiting for me in Valhalla."[6] A Nazi Peiper had been (in spite of never having joined the Party) and a Nazi he remained, even while facing the gallows in an American military prison. However, from Everett's point of view, that was irrelevant. As one who was attracted to the military life and had been associated with the U.S. Army since World War I without ever having experienced combat, Everett admired (and perhaps envied) Peiper's spectacular battlefield record.[7] As a member of a prominent Atlanta family who had been raised a traditional "southern gentle-

---

5. Peiper to Everett, July 4, 1946, EP.
6. Peiper to Everett, July 14, 1946, EP.
7. Everett deposition of October 10, 1949, MMIH, pp. 1555-56.

man" Everett might well have felt a kinship with the punctilious and rigidly self-controlled SS officer who was able to
converse with him in cultivated and articulate English.

Other factors entered into Everett's refusal to accept the
outcome of the Malmédy trial. While not a racist, he shared
with many contemporaries a suspicion of Jews as a clannish
subculture with motives and ambitions not entirely in harmony with the best interests of the countries of which they
were citizens. This manifested itself in a distrustful attitude
toward the Jewish principals in the Malmédy investigation
and trial, particularly the law member of the court, Colonel
Rosenfeld, and in the assumption that Germans, SS men at
that, could not have received just treatment at their hands.[8]
In a nutshell, Everett believed that confessions had been ex-
torted and then legitimated in court by a collusive system
which had been weighted against his clients from the beginning.

But what of the offenses themselves, the commission of at
least some of which Everett could not deny? Here, he was
guilty of ambiguity. During the trial, he had contended that
those shootings which had taken place were unpremeditated
"heat of battle" cases in which the emotional momentum of
combat had carried some troopers involuntarily beyond the
confines of legality. Whether troops of the Waffen-SS might
have been more prone than others to lapses of this kind was a
question that he seems not to have considered. But in other
contexts, he bemoaned the confirmation by the Dachau court
of the "principle of condemning an eighteen or nineteen year
old boy who has never known anything else and who would
have been instantly shot if he refused to obey the order of his
superior officer."[9] Everett was further convinced that the
"crimes" for which his clients had been tried and condemned
had had their counterparts in the U.S. Army. One evening,
shortly after the trial, Everett encountered the president of

8. Everett to family, July 11, 1946, and undated fragment, EP.
9. Everett to family, July 17, 1946, EP.

the Malmédy court, Gen. Josiah Dalbey, in the officers' club at Dachau. Although lubricated by the cheer dispensed at the club, Dalbey seemed in full possession of his faculties. The ensuing conversation, as Everett recalled it, could only have confirmed the American attorney's views. Dalbey declared that the sentencing of the seventy-three defendants had been the most difficult assignment he had ever undertaken because, according to Everett, he knew that American soldiers had been guilty of similar offenses. Everett suggested, and thought Dalbey agreed, that the Malmédy case should never have come to trial.[10] Everett's unwillingness to accept the outcome of the Malmédy trial, thus, had manifold roots. But he would work for its revision with a fierce singleness of purpose which would dominate his life.

Everett was not alone in expressing doubt concerning the quality of justice dispensed at Dachau. Within a month following the end of the trial, the case was assigned for review to Maximilian Koessler, a civilian attorney employed by the War Crimes Branch, Judge Advocate General's Department (JAGD). Koessler, then in his late fifties, had been born a citizen of the Austro-Hungarian Empire but had immigrated to the United States after the Anschluss and had been admitted to the New York Bar.[11] Koessler's English was often tortured, but he set out to discharge his task with painstaking industry backed by excellent legal training and extensive practical experience in criminal law. He was pressured to complete the review expeditiously—the chief of the review section hoped all would be finished within three or four months—but, in fact, the case remained in Koessler's hands until February 1947. Even by then, Koessler had managed to complete the study of only fifteen of the seventy-three convictions.[12] He recommended the confirmation of guilty verdicts in twelve but concluded that the evidence against the remaining three, one of whom had been sentenced to death and two to life im-

10. Everett to family, n.d., EP.   11. MMIH, pp. 1365-66.
12. *Ibid.*, pp. 1338-44.

prisonment, had been insufficient. One of these convictions had been secured on the basis of a rather strained evidential construct, consisting of the sworn statement of another defendant who had observed machine-gun fire streaming from the tank behind his own into a group of American prisoners in Stoumont. The deponent had heard from yet another defendant that this was the tank of the company commander whose machine-gunner the defendant in question was. The latter, himself, had confessed to nothing. Another conviction had been secured by the vague and contradictory testimony of a witness who asserted that the defendant had emerged from the house near Stavelot with two jars of preserved fruit for which he was supposed to have declared that two civilians had had to "pay." This defendant, too, had made no confession. A sworn statement had been taken from the third defendant and was confirmed by other testimony to the effect that the defendant, under direct orders from his superior, had shot a male civilian claimed to be a guerrilla fighter in Wanne.[13] But in addition to strong reservations about the rectitude of these three convictions, Koessler was uneasy about several general characteristics of the trial. Not only had seventy-four men been tried simultaneously, but all sat in the dock for many days identified only by the numbered placards around their necks. That, Koessler concluded, had made it extremely difficult for the judges to distinguish one prisoner from another, with the probable result that the substantial evidence of guilt against some had tended to damage all. Koessler's suspicions were aroused by what seemed to be unnaturally similar wording shared by a number of the sworn statements, and he deemed the use of hoods, false witnesses, and mock trials, the employment of which the prosecution had freely admitted, to have been improper.[14]

13. *Ibid.*, pp. 1361-62; U.S. v. Bersin, 153/4/000501, 000578, 000582-83, 000602 (3017, 3094, 3098-99, 3118).
14. MMIH, pp. 1343, 1351, 1355.

Koessler had not performed the speedy review that had been expected of him, nor, perhaps, were his conclusions palatable to the JAGD. Lieutenant Colonel Straight, into whose hands Koessler's work was delivered, was clearly displeased for reasons which, three years later, he was able to describe only in vague and contradictory terms. In response to a question as to why he had been dissatisfied with Koessler's work, he responded awkwardly: "For the reason that I did not believe it accurately portrayed the record. It was not editorialized in such a manner that it facilitated my work or my superiors [*sic*], but it accurately portrayed what was in the record."[15] Straight's unenlightening attempt at clarification might have been due to badly strained nerves, the result of the preceding several years during which the conduct of the Malmédy investigation and trial had come under increasingly heavy fire. Or, perhaps, he was unable to recall the drift of Koessler's incomplete report; in fairness to Straight, it must be said that the Austrian emigré attorney was capable of exceedingly prolix language; moreover, two attorneys who had assisted Koessler had not agreed with his conclusions.[16] But it is difficult to rule out the possibility, even the likelihood, that an official of the JAGD would have taken exceedingly ill a report which in 1947 cast substantial doubt upon judicial proceedings on which the same department had lavished vast effort and which it had conducted, literally and figuratively, under the glare of spotlights less than a year earlier. To be sure, the exertions of defense attorneys and reviewers were as organic to the function of the JAGD as the endeavors of investigators and prosecutors. But apprehension, prosecution, and punishment of war criminals were the activities which in the immediate postwar period earned for army lawyers favorable publicity and public approbation.

The rejection of Koessler's incomplete review failed to still critical attention originating from outside the JAGD. Although

15. *Ibid.*, p. 1047.
16. *Ibid.*, p. 1341.

Everett worked in other cases tried before military government courts during the balance of 1946, he remained overwhelmingly engaged by the Malmédy trial and his determination that its verdict not be allowed to stand unchallenged. The Atlanta soldier-lawyer was torn between loyalty to the United States Army, which had played a significant role in his life and whose image he was reluctant to besmirch, and his conviction that his higher duty lay in the service of justice, which in his view had been ill served at Dachau. Although inclined to make public his negative assessment of the investigation and trial during his fit of depression which had followed sentencing of the defendants, he seems, in fact, to have remained silent while preparing a petition for review which he completed around the end of the year and submitted to the JAGD. By January 1947, however, the American press was receiving and publishing hints indicating that embarrassing questions were being asked about the Malmédy investigation and trial. The source of this information—whether Everett or "leaks" within the JAGD—is not clear, but by the end of the month the *New York Herald Tribune* was offering accounts of the more outrageous of the allegations concerning American pretrial interrogation methods. Thus, *Tribune* staffer Edwin Hartrich reported, Everett's petition suggested that some defendants had been beaten in order to force confessions.[17]

JAGD's reaction was the frequent reflex of the bureaucratic organism under attack: a cover of "official secrecy" was drawn over the now simmering Malmédy pot. Everett, however, could not be so easily silenced. Early in 1947 he and his wife and son (who had joined him in Germany after the Malmédy trial) returned to the United States, an event closely followed by his honorable discharge from the U.S. Army. Following more than six years of active duty, Everett's separation was nothing abnormal and does not seem to have been related to the activities which were disconcerting the JAGD.

17. *New York Herald Tribune*, January 22, 1947, Digest, p. 1., NA, RG 319.

In fact, his formal departure was delayed to permit the replacement at government expense of some of the sixteen teeth which he had lost during his period of active service. Once out of uniform, Everett felt able to work more openly for the trial revision which had become for him a moral imperative. On his way from New York to Atlanta in February, Everett paused for several days in Washington to pursue his obsession in the War Crimes Branch of the Office of the Judge Advocate General. There, he seems to have encountered polite indifference combined with an expression of extra-legal arbitrariness which harmonized well with Everett's own view of what had taken place the previous year at Schwäbisch Hall and Dachau. A war crimes suspect, he reported one colonel as having informed him, was simply without legal rights. That condition obtained from the moment suspicion of criminality fell upon him and persisted until his innocence had been demonstrated. The colonel's opinion was by no means shared by everyone in the War Crimes Branch, but the point of view had a familiar ring to one who had heard certain of the prosecution arguments in the courtroom at Dachau.[18] Everett's visit to Washington produced little, but he had already reached an important decision: if the army's review of the Malmédy case allowed its outcome to stand, he would attempt to appeal to the United States Supreme Court. A telegram to this effect was sent to the European Theater Judge Advocate, Colonel Micklewaite. In part, this was an expression of courtesy toward a man whom he respected, but there can be little doubt that Everett hoped that the threat implied by his stated intention would not pass unnoticed. In addition, Everett feared that if the review should confirm the verdicts and penalties, the death sentences might be carried out with such dispatch as to render an appeal to the Supreme Court pointless for a majority of the defendants. Had he been aware of the reception accorded Koessler's attempt at review his apprehensions might have been sharpened. Micklewaite, then

18. Everett to Mickelwaite, February 28, 1947, EP.

preparing for reassignment to the United States, replied with assurances that arrangements had been made by JAGD to allow sufficient delay between the completion of the review and execution of the sentences to permit Everett to perfect legal countermeasures.[19]

Everett expected that a final and, from the standpoint of JAGD, definitive review would be promptly produced and that he would be informed of the result, permitting him to react accordingly. As the first anniversary of the Malmédy verdicts approached without word from army legal authorities in Germany, Everett began to suspect treachery. In a letter whose threatening character was clearly evident, Everett informed Cecil Hubbert of the War Crimes Branch, JAGD in Washington, that his ambition was to force a retrial of the Malmédy case; if that could not be achieved, he suggested bitterly, the defendants should simply be kept in prison without the dishonest sanction of a farcical trial. "It is requested," he continued, "that you use your good offices to encourage such a course in order that it will not be necessary for me to make further attempts to correct wrongs. Newspapers and editors have been and still are hounding me for the inside story. I have kept faith and issued no statement due to my desire not to expose certain facts until definite word has been received as to the findings."[20]

It is not easy to gauge the effect of Everett's attempt at intimidation. He would not receive any communication from JAGD for nearly a year. On the other hand, the extreme caution with which the army proceeded in its review of the Malmédy case may have been, in part, a reflection of its reluctance to see Everett resort to the public media. Following Straight's withdrawal of the reviewing function from Koessler's hands, a small legal staff was established in the office of the Deputy Judge Advocate for War Crimes into whose hands the steadily warming potato was placed. On October 20,

19. Micklewaite to Everett, March 24, 1947, EP.
20. Everett to Hubbert, June 17, 1947, EP.

1947, the recommendations of this body, with Straight's revisions, were sent to the Theater Judge Advocate, an office occupied since April 1947 by Col. James L. Harbaugh, Jr.[21]

Straight and his staff, after having reviewed the Malmédy trial documentation, reached conclusions that were substantially different in some respects from those of the trial judges. Of the forty-three death sentences which had been assigned at Dachau, only twenty-five (including Peiper's) were recommended for confirmation. In the eighteen cases in which Straight did not believe the death penalty to be justified, a commutation to life imprisonment was suggested in seven instances and to terms of ten, fifteen, and twenty years in ten. In one instance in which a defendant had been sentenced to death, the staff found the evidence insufficient to sustain the verdict. Twenty-two life sentences had been imposed at Dachau. The Deputy Judge Advocate recommended that only five of these be confirmed, while urging that the remainder be reduced to sentences of ten and fifteen years' imprisonment. Reductions were recommended in most of the lighter sentences handed down in July 1946.[22]

On what basis had Straight made recommendations that were considerably milder than the Dachau judgments? Clearly, he had broken markedly with their findings in having disapproved the verdict of guilt against a defendant upon whom the supreme penalty had been imposed. That defendant, a former tank crewman in the First Company, First SS Panzer Regiment, had produced an enormously detailed sworn statement of six single-spaced typewritten pages in which he had described inter alia having fired a burst from one of his vehicle's machine guns into the prisoners at the Baugnez crossroads in response to a direct order from the tank commander. According to the statement, six American prisoners of war

21. MMIH, p. 927; "Report of Proceedings of Administration of Justice Review Board, Headquarters, European Command" (meeting of July 7, 1948), p. 23, NRC, Box 4-1/11.
22. Department of the Army, Tab A, Memo for File, Malmedy Case, NA, RG 319.

had been shot by crewmen of the same tank in Stavelot. The defendant denied having participated in this atrocity but was implicated in it by another defendant who swore to having heard the young tank crewman later declare, "Well, we bumped those fellows off and some of them had not been dead and they were moaning and groaning."[23] Reasons could no doubt be found to challenge the sufficiency of this evidence and the appropriateness of the death penalty. The soldier's sworn statement contained suspiciously minute detail concerning events which had taken place over a year before, including the movement of specific individuals over precise distances at closely spaced intervals of time.[24] Assuming that the defendant had participated in the crossroads shootings, his actions had almost certainly been carried out in obedience to orders, a factor which, along with his age at the time of the killings (nineteen), might have served to mitigate his degree of apparent guilt. And undeniably, the evidence pointing to his involvement in the Stavelot killings was thin. But viewed in the context of other decisions reached by Straight, the recommendation of disapproval in this case is difficult to understand. The evidence against the defendant, whatever its weaknesses, was substantially stronger than that against the noncommissioned officer of the Sixth Panzer Company who had been sentenced to death for having ostensibly killed two Belgian civilians for two jars of preserved fruits, a judgment that Maximilian Koessler had seriously questioned. Yet, Straight recommended that the death penalty be confirmed.[25]

While Straight had diverged from Koessler in the direction of the sternest punishment for the homicidal pilferer of fruit, their respective positions were nearly reversed on another case, that of an SPW driver of the Second Platoon, Third Panzer Pioneer Company, accused and convicted of having participated in the crossroads shootings and, two days later,

23. U.S. v. Bersin, 153/2/000311 (1421).
24. *Ibid.*, 5/000407-16.
25. Department of the Army, Tab A, NA, RG 319.

in the killing of prisoners of war in Stoumont. At Dachau, this defendant had been one of the forty-three condemned to death. Koessler had recommended the confirmation of that sentence. Straight, contrarily, suggested a reduction to fifteen years in prison. Evidence against the former SS man consisted of his own sworn statement and that of a codefendant. The defendant's statement was exhaustive, occupying more than fifteen single-spaced typewritten pages, describing a half dozen incidents involving the shooting of prisoners of war and implicating dozens of his comrades by name. Less voluminous was the codefendant's statement, although clear in its identification of the SPW driver as a participant in the shooting of American prisoners.[26]

While his suspicions might have been aroused by the remarkably verbose unburdening of guilt in which some of the defendants had engaged, the Deputy Judge Advocate did not base many of his recommendations on findings of evidential insufficiency. An exception to that generalization was the case of the trooper whose death sentence he recommended be disapproved. But that recommendation might have been the result of an error in research on the part of Straight or his staff, for in his report Straight noted mistakenly that the defendant's conviction had been supported by his sworn statement alone, uncorroborated by any other evidence.[27]

More important as a justification for commutation of sentences was the age of the convicts. In twenty-nine and possibly thirty of the thirty-six instances in which Straight recommended the reduction of death sentences or penalities of life imprisonment, the convicts had been under twenty years of age at the time of their alleged crimes; and in no case was a death sentence or a sentence of life imprisonment recommended for confirmation if the convict had been in his teens in December 1944. In that light, the marked differences be-

26. U.S. v. Bersin, 153/5/000465, 6/000419.
27. "Deputy Judge Advocate's Office, Review and Recommendations," October 20, 1947, pp. 210-11, NRC, Box 4-1/11.

tween certain of Koessler's recommendations and those of the Deputy Judge Advocate can be easily understood. The fruit thief whose conviction Koessler had found unconvincing but whose death sentence was upheld by the Deputy Judge Advocate had been in his early thirties at the time of the Ardennes offensive; the SPW driver whose death sentence Koessler had approved but for whom Straight urged a prison term of fifteen years had been nineteen years old in December 1944.[28]

Intellectually and substantively, the Deputy Judge Advocate's report was unsatisfying, its authors having performed violent verbal contortions to avoid seriously challenging the rectitude of the Malmédy investigation and trial. Except in the single instance where the verdict and death sentence had been found, with questionable justification, to have been insufficiently supported by evidence, the Deputy Judge Advocate recommended the approval of all findings of the Malmédy court, including all other death and all life sentences but then suggested numerous commutations on the basis of tender years and, in some cases, ostensible evidence of repentance. It might well be interpreted as indicative of uneasiness over the course and outcome of the investigation and trial combined with reluctance to concede the possibility of error.

Straight's desire to skirt the central issues associated with the Malmédy investigation and trial is perhaps understandable, given the fact that he had been an important figure in the War Crimes Branch since it had begun to operate shortly before the end of World War II. To have found substantive fault with the Malmédy proceedings would have been, in a sense, public self-criticism, an activity in which human beings normally engage only with the greatest reluctance. But the review function now ascended an additional step to the office of the Theater Judge Advocate who received Straight's recommendations. Unlike Straight, Col. James Harbaugh had had no previous direct involvement in war crimes work. He had

28. *Ibid.*, pp. 50-210; MMIH, pp. 1063-64.

served with the Army Air Force as a staff judge advocate in Europe during World War II but had been in the United States when the Malmédy case was under investigation and in court. In format, the review procedure at this level paralleled that which had taken place in Straight's office: one of several war crimes boards of review operating under Harbaugh was assigned to study the case and to prepare an advisory report for the guidance of the Judge Advocate. That Harbaugh considered this to be more than a routine matter was indicated by his appointment of Col. Howard F. Bresee, chief of his office's review branch, to the chair of the review board.[29] Ironically, Bresee had been the officer who, as a matter of form, had brought the charges of "violation of the laws and usages of war" against the defendants on April 11, 1946.[30]

The report completed on February 8, 1948, by this reviewing body was drastically different from Straight's effort of several months before and, in fact, was highly critical of it. Not only had the Deputy Judge Advocate's report misstated crucial testimony in its analysis, but it had failed to address itself to the central question of the techniques used in securing sworn statements from the Malmédy defendants. Bresee's war crimes board of review found "much evidence" of improper pretrial investigation, singling out "mock trials" in this regard and asserting that in some cases "confessions" had been the creation of the investigation team rather than statements of fact. Pointed criticism was leveled at numerous procedural rulings made by the bench during the trial, which seemed to limit the defense in its examination of witnesses while allowing the prosecution greater latitude in its endeavors.[31]

In fully twenty-nine of the seventy-three individual Malmédy cases, the War Crimes Board of Review found the evidence insufficient to sustain conviction and recommended

29. *Ibid.*, pp. 1145, 1164-65.
30. *Ibid.*, pp. 1572-73.
31. "War Crimes Board of Review and Recommendations in the Case of United States v. Valentin Bersin, et al.," February 8, 1948, pp. 9-14, NRC, Box 4-1/11.

disapproval of findings and sentence. Most notable in this category was the case of Sepp Dietrich, sometime member of Hitler's retinue, organizer and longtime leader of his Leib-standarte, and commander of the Sixth Panzer Army during the Ardennes offensive. Dietrich's role in the scenario of slaughter outlined by the prosecution had been as transmitter of the Führer's murderous intentions declaimed at Bad Nauheim to the military forces in the field; and for this, he had been sentenced to life imprisonment. Bresee's board was not persuaded by the evidence that had been developed against the fifty-four-year-old SS general. No proof that Dietrich had ordered prisoners or civilians to be shot had been offered, nor had Dietrich confessed to having issued orders of that nature. He had conceded in his sworn statement that he had issued orders to the Sixth Panzer Army reflecting the Führer's command that a "wave of fright and terror" should precede the attacking German forces; but that, the Bresee board report insisted, was hardly a "violation of the laws and usages of war." To create fright and terror in the mind of the enemy and thus break his will to resist must be the aim of any attacking army (that Dietrich had seemingly also admitted to having ordered that "no humane inhibitions" should be shown by his forces was ignored).[32]

Reductions of sentences were urged in most other cases; but in twelve instances, the Bresee board found the evidence sufficient to sustain verdicts of "guilty" and sentences of death. One of these was the case of Jochen Peiper. The board deemed the finding and penalty appropriate for reasons somewhat different from those advanced by the prosecution at Dachau. Peiper, the report declared, was criminally liable in that he had omitted giving his subordinates specific orders concerning the disposition of prisoners of war.[33] It had, therefore, been left to the discretion of soldiers of lesser rank whether to permit themselves to be burdened by prisoners,

32. *Ibid.*, pp. 31-33, 39-82.
33. *Ibid.*, pp. 74-75.

thus, possibly jeopardizing their missions, or to divest themselves of the encumbrances in the most direct and brutal way. Some had apparently chosen the latter course. The logic and consistency of the board's report were not at all points compelling. Peiper was also judged guilty of having transmitted the illegal army order that had played so central a role in the prosecution's courtroom presentation. But the same board had recommended disapproval of the conviction of Sepp Dietrich and his chief of staff, Fritz Kraemer, on the charge of having issued illegal orders. From whom, then, had the order criminally circulated by Peiper come? Yet, even in the absence of such an order, his willingness to permit prisoners of war to be killed seemed to be confirmed by his abandonment of the starved American at Petit Thier to a foreseeably terminal fate and by a possible tacit acquiescence in the shooting of two other prisoners.

All of the eleven other instances in which the Bresee board recommended the confirmation of the death sentence showed several characteristics: the prisoners had held command responsibilities as officers or high-level noncommissioned officers and all had been over twenty years of age at the time of having committed their alleged offenses. In every case, moreover, multiple elements of testimony attested to the actual ordering of killings by the accused, his participation in shootings or, at least, his obvious acquiescence in such atrocities.[34]

In spite of its agreement that major war crimes had been committed by Kampfgruppe Peiper, the War Crimes Board of Review, nevertheless, had left the overall penal judgment of the Dachau court a shambles. Almost three-quarters of the death sentences had been found inappropriate; the total number of life sentences had been reduced by over 60 percent, and, most significantly, in nearly 40 percent of the individual cases, the evidence had been judged inadequate to

---

34. Department of the Army, Tab A, NA, RG 319; "Memorandum for the Secretary of the Army. Subject: United States v. Valentin Bersin, et al. (Malmedy Case)," March 21, 1949, *passim*, NA, RG 319.

sustain conviction. Moreover, the board had openly accused the army investigators of conduct at best inept, at worst unprincipled, and the army judges of consistent bias to the advantage of the prosecution.

Had Willis Everett, now returned to civilian life but still profoundly involved in the Malmédy case, been aware of the board's report (as he was not), he would surely have been pleased, for the essence of his own condemnations of the investigation and trial was contained therein. The close agreement between Everett's views and the board's report was certainly not coincidental. And, arguably, it may not have been the product of rational minds reaching similar conclusions on the basis of like evidence. It was, perhaps, an index of the confusion that still reigned in the army's war crimes operation that to Colonel Bresee's board was initially assigned none other than Lt. Col. John S. Dwinnell, one of the most energetic and effective members of the defense team. Bresee quickly realized the error, and a replacement was found for Dwinnell; surprisingly, however, Harbaugh insisted that Dwinnell play a continuing, albeit less formal, role in the review process. Dwinnell became an advisor to the Bresee board and worked closely with it throughout its three-month deliberations.[35]

Harbaugh's judgment in this regard may well be questioned, for Dwinnell's assistance legitimately opened the board's recommendations to suspicion of prejudice in favor of the Malmédy convicts. Harbaugh would later explain that the assistance of someone with a working familiarity with the case was advisable to facilitate the work of the board, and this, no doubt, had been a factor.[36] The trial documentation was intricate and of considerable bulk. Over a year had elapsed since the conclusion of the trial, while ominous rumblings of dissent from Atlanta and elsewhere suggested that a prompt resolution of the Malmédy affair was highly desirable. But it

35. MMIH, p. 1165.
36. *Ibid.*

is likely, too, that Harbaugh was not loath to encourage the production of a trial analysis far more daring in its willingness to criticize army justice than the earlier Straight report had been; such a counterweight seemed called for both by political caution and judicial equity. He might have got more than he bargained for, however, as Dwinnell openly argued for the defense position during the board meetings.[37] These were skirmishes in which he clearly held the high ground due to his superior knowledge of the case, and his triumphs of persuasion were reflected in the board's recommendations.

Harbaugh pondered Bresee's conclusions for several weeks and did some reading of his own in the trial transcript in preparing a final set of recommendations for Gen. Lucius Clay, Chief of Military Government in the American Zone of Occupation. This was completed on March 8, 1948, and represented a cautious mean between the Straight and Bresee reports. At the same time, Harbaugh sought to bring to Clay's attention the grave nature of the Bresee report's criticisms while implicitly disclaiming responsibility for them. He noted that the War Crimes Board of Review chaired by Bresee had recommended disapproval of twenty-nine convictions, most for lack of credible evidence. Dwinnell's influence had been clearly reflected in the assertion that many of the sworn statements were worthless as the result of having been secured through promises of lighter punishment and that most had, in fact, been dictated by army interrogators; even had this not been the case, the Bresee report had noted a fundamental principle of Anglo-American law, that a confession is admissible only against the party making it, a point that had been advanced by the defense during the trial. Harbaugh did not overtly associate himself with the War Crimes Board of Review's conclusions and, in fact, expressed criticism of them.[38] Nevertheless, there was substantial agreement between his recommendations to Clay and those made to him

37. *Ibid.*, p. 447.
38. Harbaugh to Clay, March 8, 1948, NRC, Box 4-1/11, pp. 4-5.

by Bresee. To be sure, Harbaugh found only thirteen cases worthy of disapproval; he urged the confirmation of an equal number of death sentences, one more than had the Bresee board. Approval was recommended for Sepp Dietrich's life sentence, while ten years was suggested for Fritz Kraemer. In most other respects, the differences between the two sets of recommendations were slight.[39]

With the exception of a death sentence reduced to life imprisonment, Clay accepted Harbaugh's recommendations and formally confirmed the remaining sentences on March 20. Thirteen of the Malmédy seventy-three departed Landsberg; twelve faced the brief walk to its gallows, the hood, rope, the fatal jolt that would break the neck and sever the spinal cord.[40]

But not immediately. As Everett had been assured, an interval sufficient to permit appeal was to separate the confirmation of sentence from the scheduled executions of the death penalty. Although there was some delay between the completion of the review process and Everett's notification, the Atlanta attorney found himself with two months to develop legal action to save his clients.[41] As the opportunities for revision within the structure of military justice had been exhausted, Everett could only turn to the U.S. Supreme Court with a motion to file for a writ of habeas corpus which, if granted, could lead to a retrial of the remaining Malmédy prisoners. Previous experience in petitions of this nature was not encouraging. In the case of Japanese General Yamashita, a majority had ruled that the Court lacked the power to review the judicial proceedings of military courts, although Associate Justices Rutledge and Murphy had vigorously dissented. Nineteen days later on February 23, 1946, Yamashita had been hanged.[42]

Everett's effort, by necessity, was a shoestring undertaking.

39. Department of the Army, Tab A, NA, RG 319.
40. *Ibid.*
41. Young to Everett, March 23, 1948, EP.
42. Appleman, *Military Tribunals*, pp. 346-56; Reel, *Yamashita*, p. 239.

His legal training and experience were limited, and his efforts
to secure Dwinnell's temporary assignment to him as assistant
in the preparation of the Supreme Court brief were blocked
by the army, although his former co-worker was able to
render useful service during a short unofficial visit to New
York. An element of pettiness was evident in the army's
refusal to provide Everett with a copy of the trial transcript,
necessitating his working from memory to the detriment of
his brief.[43] Naiveté and desperation were reflected in an attempt to discuss the preparation of the petition with
Supreme Court Justice Frank Murphy, an obviously improper
approach which Murphy politely but firmly repulsed.[44] Yet,
by dint of furious labor, Dwinnell's assistance, and the secre-
tarial skills of his daughter, the petition was completed and
submitted to the Court on May 14, 1948.

An objective discussion of the facts of the Malmédy investigation and trial was not to be expected in a document of this
nature, nor was it to be found. Guilt and frustration, which
had grown within him over two years, together with the realization that twelve of his clients might stand on the gallows
within a week of the submission of his petition and place on
his conscience a burden that he feared he could not bear, led
Everett to combine sober legal argumentation with lurid allegations for which there was little foundation and to exagger-
ate those instances of impropriety for which some evidence
seemed to exist. Alongside reasoned challenges to the jurisdiction of the Malmédy court and the elaboration of a claim
that the defense had had inadequate time and facilities to
prepare its case stood hair-raising descriptions of beatings,
starvation, and other torments used routinely to compel prisoners to confess to crimes that they had not committed. Mock

43. Eberle (Acting Chief, Civil Affairs Division, War Department Special Staff)
to Everett, April 12, 1948, EP; Everett deposition, October 10, 1949, MMIH, p.
1569.
44. Everett to Murphy, April 21, 1948, EP; Murphy to Everett (telegram), April
22, 1948, EP.

trials, it appeared, had been the rule rather than the exception admitted by the prosecution and had been terrifying affairs in which "18 and 20-year-old plaintiffs" had been brow-beaten, confused by false witnesses, beguiled by prosecutors pretending to be their defense attorneys, and, if recalcitrant, led to believe they would be hanged within a day or two. In other situations, Everett's petition alleged, prisoners had been promised immunity or light sentences if they signed confessions implicating others. Much was made of the suicide of the prisoner Arvid Freimuth, who ostensibly had been heard to cry from his cell, "I cannot utter another lie!" shortly before having been found dead. Everett's contention, in sum, was that the Malmédy convicts had been incarcerated without legal justification.[45]

Although presenting a substantive critique of the Malmédy case, Everett, technically, was applying not for the writ of habeas corpus itself, which, if granted, would vacate the sentences of the remaining convicts, but for leave to file for such a petition. First, therefore, it was necessary for the Court to accept jurisdiction in the case. The decision could not have been closer. With Justice Robert Jackson disqualifying himself due to his earlier involvement in the Nuremberg trials, the Court divided four members to four on the question of jurisdiction. Chief Justice Vinson and Associate Justices Frankfurter, Burton, and Reed were of the opinion that the Court lacked jurisdiction while Associate Justices Black, Douglas, Murphy, and Rutledge expressed the contrary view and urged that the case "be set for argument forthwith."[46] The balance was much closer than in the earlier Yamashita case, but the outcome was the same. In the absence of a favorable majority the application for leave to file was denied.

45. *In the Supreme Court of the United States. Petition for Writ of Habeas Corpus,* pp. 2-12, EP.
46. *United States Supreme Court. Law. ed. Advance opinions,* Vol. 92 (1947-1948), No. 17, pp. 1051-52.

Although Everett toyed later and unrealistically with the idea of attempting an appeal to the International Court at the Hague, which would have been an impossibility in that only governments may plead before that bench, his juridical avenues—few and narrow to begin with—were exhausted; the influence that could be wielded by Everett as a member of a prominent Atlanta family was not. Everett saw to it that a copy of his petition reached the hands of his close friend, Georgia Congressman James C. Davis. Davis carried it to Senator Walter F. George of Georgia who, in turn, conveyed Everett's allegations directly to Secretary of the Army Kenneth C. Royall, leading, ultimately, to an interview between Everett and Royall.[47] The secretary, who until this point had remained ignorant of the charges and countercharges surrounding the Malmédy case, was sufficiently disturbed by the contents of Everett's petition to order an immediate stay of all executions pending further review of the case.[48]

Everett's Supreme Court petition and its immediate aftermath surfaced in the midst of growing general criticism and controversy surrounding all war crimes trials conducted in Germany by American military authorities. Sources and motives behind the outcry were various and included the high-minded objections of pacifists and civil libertarians as well as the perverse rantings of pro-Nazis and anti-Semites. In the American Zone of occupation in Germany, likewise, criticism came from German nationalists, many of them churchmen, who were not averse to applying to American justice the lofty standards that had been preached to them by their occupiers and mentors in the ways of democracy. Most notable in this category was the Auxiliary Bishop of Munich, Dr. Johannes Neuhäusler who eloquently conveyed his grave doubts concerning the Malmédy case to members of Congress, doubts based on information that he had received from the priest ministering to the Malmédy convicts in Landsberg

47. Everett to George, May 18, 1948, EP; Everett to Davis, May 20, 1948, EP.
48. MMIH, p. 4.

prison. Prisoners had told tales of having signed statements under extreme duress and, with the assistance of the priest, had made sworn depositions to that effect. Neuhäusler was obviously convinced and his convictions were given moral weight not only by the church he served but by the fact that the bishop had suffered four years of imprisonment at the hands of the Nazis in Dachau.[49] The motives of others were more open to suspicion. Dr. Rudolf Aschenauer, who coordinated legal efforts on behalf of the Malmédy defendants in Germany after the trial, was an old Nazi Party member who had also served as defense counsel in the trial of former SS-Obergruppenführer Otto Ohlendorf, sometime commander of Einsatzgruppe D and a man responsible for the deaths of many thousands of Jews. Aschenauer was to become increasingly active in right-wing extremist German politics and became the leading German spokesman for the Malmédy prisoners.[50] Unavoidably, the United States government was required to pay increasingly close attention to German public opinion. The Cold War was rapidly intensifying. In February 1948, the democratic coalition government of Czechoslovakia was overthrown by Russian-backed Communists. On March 19, the functioning of the Allied Control Commission was, for all intents, terminated by a Russian walkout. In June, the blockade of Berlin and the Allied airlift began. The western zones of Germany were poised on the brink of transition from defeated enemy to ally.

It was not only critics of the army's handling of the Malmédy case whose voices were heard. Members of the investigation and prosecution staff, including Ellis and Crawford, called for a definitive investigation which would clear them of the accusations heaped upon them by Everett.[51] Survivors of

49. Neuhäusler to Members of Congress, March 25, 1948, EP; cf. Guenter Lewy, *The Catholic Church and Nazi Germany* (New York, 1965), pp. 353-54, n. 47, p. 363, n. 7.

50. On Aschenauer, see Kurt Tauber, *Beyond Eagle and Swastika. German Nationalism since 1945* (Middletown, 1967), I, 714-15; II, 1125, n. 16; 1303-04, n. 65.

51. Ellis to Hubbert, May 25, 1948, NRC, Box 4-1/11; Crawford to Monroney, May 28, 1948, NRC, Box 4-1/11.

the massacre and relatives of those killed pressed for a resolution of the case which would permit justice to be done.[52] For the army, it was, to use the slang of a later era, a "no win" situation, since any conceivable compromise, quite apart from legal and moral factors, would be unacceptable to one group of partisans. Yet, inaction was the worst alternative, as it infuriated both sides. Political expedience on the international and domestic levels as well as concern for justice suggested, therefore, that the Malmédy investigation and trial be subjected once more to review.

On July 23, 1948, Secretary of the Army Royall established a three-man commission to investigate and review all the well over one hundred death sentences which had been handed down in the series of sixty-seven war crimes trials held at Dachau and subsequently sustained by review. The chairman of the committee was Gordon Simpson of the Texas Supreme Court. Joining Simpson were Judge LeRoy van Roden of the Orphan's Court of Delaware County, Pennsylvania, and, representing the army, Lt. Col. Charles W. Lawrence of the Judge Advocate General's Corps.[53] All three men had been involved in the administration of military justice and were familiar with the general procedures and issues in question. That fact brought with it, of course, the likelihood of acquaintance with other participants in war crimes work. Coincidentally, and there is no evidence to suggest that it was more than coincidence, van Roden was well known to Everett, the two, in fact, having lived for three months in the same hotel in Frankfurt during their tours of duty in Europe. Once having learned of van Roden's appointment to the investigatory commission (but after the Pennsylvania judge had left for Europe) Everett clearly made an effort to color his judgment of the Malmédy case through correspondence with van Roden's wife.[54] What impact, if any, this may have had upon

52. Paul C. Geisler to Rep. Richard M. Simpson, June 3, 1948, NRC, Box 4-1/11; Virgil P. Lary, Jr. to Secretary Royall, June 10, 1948, NRC, Box 4-1/11.
53. MMIH, pp. 4, 191.
54. Everett to Mrs. van Roden, August 4, 1948, EP.

him is uncertain, but van Roden's later widely publicized opinions were to have a significant impact on the development of the Malmédy affair as a public issue. Before the Simpson Commission had been appointed, yet another probe of the Malmédy case had begun. A year earlier, General Clay had ordered the establishment of an "Administration of Justice Review Board" to be composed of the Director of the Legal Division, Office of Military Government, the Judge Advocate of the European Command, and the Adviser for Governmental Affairs to the Military Governor. The function of the board as outlined by Clay was to periodically examine the administration of criminal justice in U.S. courts martial and military courts with the major focus on its handling of American citizens.[55] Nothing in the original order prevented it from examining the impact of American military justice on enemy nationals and, upon receipt of a cable from Royall ordering an investigation of the allegations contained in Everett's petition to the Supreme Court, Clay assigned the increasingly annoying case to the board.[56]

The two bodies conducted their assignments in manners dramatically different. Simpson, van Roden, and Lawrence spent less than two months selectively reading in the trial records and reviews, studying posttrial affidavits by prisoners and others, and allowing themselves to be petitioned by German critics of the trial. In view of the fact that this brief span of time was spent reviewing not only the Malmédy case but the records of over sixty other trials, the care with which the work was performed might legitimately be questioned. But if the Secretary of the Army wanted quick results, he got them in the form of a report dated September 14, 1948.[57]

General Clay's Administration of Justice Review Board, on the other hand, proceeded with considerable care throughout a series of sessions which spanned the period from July 1948

55. "General Orders Number 90," August 18, 1947, NRC, Box 4-1/11.
56. MMIH, p. 72.
57. *Ibid.*, pp. 190-219, 1196-97.

until February 1949, finally submitting a report dated the fourteenth of that month.[58] Not only was the trial documentation restudied, but evidence, both oral and written, was received from former members of the defense and investigation/prosecution staffs, and Lt. Col. Clio Straight was subjected to a particularly intense grilling. A certain reluctance to ask hard questions was evident on the part of the two military members, Col. John M. Raymond, Director of the Legal Division, U.S. Military Government and the chairman of the board; and the Judge Advocate for the European Command, Col. James L. Harbaugh, who had been deeply involved in earlier reviews and, therefore, may have been disinclined to produce evidence calling into question his earlier efforts. Lacking such inhibitions, however, was the civilian Adviser to the Military Governor for Military Government Affairs, the scholarly Harvard Professor of Government, Dr. Carl J. Friedrich, who reacted to much testimony with a healthy skepticism and asked the most significant questions yet posed concerning the investigative techniques used upon the Malmédy suspects, showing a sensitivity to the ease with which very young men raised in a totalitarian atmosphere and disoriented by defeat and capture might be manipulated and misled by their captors.[59] In the midst of the board's deliberation, Friedrich left military government and the Malmédy review, to the latter's detriment. Nevertheless, the Administration of Justice Review Board produced an analysis more searching in all particulars than that of the Simpson Commission and one, in general, less favorable in its implications to the prisoners.

Simpson, van Roden, and Lawrence expressed the by now customary reservations concerning certain of the ''tricks and ruses'' employed by the American investigators, in particular, the so-called ''mock trials.'' Nevertheless, they professed to

58. ''Headquarters European Command. Final Report of Administration of Justice Review Board,'' February 14, 1949, NRC, Box 4-1/11.
59. ''Report of Proceedings of Administration of Justice Review Board,'' pp. 14-17, 19, NRC, Box 4-1/11.

be satisfied that the twelve death sentences which had been confirmed had been assigned to men whose guilt had been adequately demonstrated. They doubted, however, that an American court martial would have imposed sentences sterner than life imprisonment upon Americans convicted of similar crimes. In view of what appeared to be improper investigative methods and an absence of even-handed objectivity in sentencing, therefore, the report recommended that all death sentences be commuted to life imprisonment.[60]

The Administration of Justice Review Board report was much more complex, both because the board, unlike the Simpson Commission, had devoted a much longer period of time to the Malmédy case alone and because it had been specifically intended to respond to the numerous allegations of Everett's Supreme Court petition. In general, the report rejected the more extreme of Everett's claims, particularly those involving pronounced physical brutality and outright dictation of statements, but conceded the existence of lesser improprieties: the use of mock trials, occasional physical force employed "in the heat of the moment," encouragement to prisoners to make statements by suggestions that the investigators were interested primarily in convicting the prisoner's superiors, and threats of reprisals against relatives (e.g., the withdrawal of ration cards) if the prisoners did not "talk."[61] Had Carl Friedrich still been a member of the board as it ended its deliberations, the report might have been more adventurous in its willingness to draw conclusions from these findings. As matters stood, Colonels Raymond and Harbaugh observed somewhat blandly "that the conditions obtaining at the prison and the methods employed in the interrogations had a definite psychological effect on the defendants and resulted in their being more amenable to giving statements."

60. "Memorandum for the Secretary of the Army," September 14, 1948, Appendix III, pp. 1-2, NA, RG 319.
61. "Administration of Justice Review Board in the Malmedy Case," February 14, 1949, "Conclusions," MMIH, p. 1204.

Their recommendations offered even less guidance, being limited to a suggestion that the report "be considered in connection with any further consideration of the Malmédy case."[62] At least as much as pusillanimity and loyalty to army comrades, the Administration of Justice Review Board report reflected simple confusion and an inability, three years after the fact, to reconcile widely differing and largely subjective elements of evidence. Affidavits from members of the investigative staff denied with varying degrees of eloquence and verbosity but with great fervor and indignation all charges of improper conduct.[63] On the other hand, affidavits from German citizens, neither SS men nor war crimes suspects, conveyed to the board quite a different picture. Dietrich Schnell, a young medical student who had been assigned to work in the prison hospital at Schwäbisch Hall, claimed to have observed the results of brutal treatment of the Malmédy suspects and claimed that an American sergeant whom he had known at "Hall" had several times declared that he could not bear to witness such brutality and wanted to be transferred.[64] Dr. Edward Knorr, a German dentist employed by the U.S. Army, asserted that he often treated the dental damage of prisoners caused by beatings and that cries of pain emanating from the prison could often be heard in the town.[65] These statements seemed to support affidavits produced by many of the Malmédy convicts which had been sworn in particularly large numbers in January and February 1948 and which, in badly broken English, claimed vicious beatings and inhuman deprivations at the hands of the American captors. Blows to the genitals were a frequently alleged abuse ("I was beaten in my most sensible point," declared one prisoner), while others claimed to have been

62. *Ibid.*, p. 1205.
63. Affidavit of Raphael Shumacker, October 14, 1948; Affidavit of H. Barney Crawford, November 9, 1948; Affidavit of Morris Elowitz, November 10, 1948; Affidavit of William R. Perl, November 15, 1948; NRC, Box 4-1/11.
64. Affidavit of Dietrich Schnell, January 10, 1948, NRC, Box 4-1/11.
65. Affidavit of Dr. Eduard Knorr, May 29, 1948, NRC, Box 4-1/11.

threatened with hanging during their interrogations. Still others asserted that they had been refused drinking water for long periods of time and had been compelled to slake their thirsts from the water closets. Many of these affidavits had been gathered and sent to General Clay by Josef Cardinal Frings, the Archbishop of Cologne, who possessed substantial anti-Nazi credentials.[66] Where then, did the truth lie? In the absence of genuinely disinterested witnesses or some method of objectively evaluating conflicting testimony, it was impossible to tell. Those who had reviewed the case had either become bogged down in its contradictory convolutions, as had Maximilian Koessler, or had seemingly abandoned themselves to their prejudices, not surprisingly, in 1947 and 1948, predominantly pro-U.S. Army and anti-German. A notable exception to the latter rule was Judge LeRoy van Roden, who although lending his name to the bland Simpson Commission Report, returned home to the United States to lend credence to the most extreme of the allegations made by Willis Everett and the German convicts. His efforts went far toward raising the Malmédy affair to the white-hot political temperature which it would attain in the first half of 1949.

66. Josef Cardinal Frings to Clay, November 27, 1948 (includes numerous affidavits), NRC, Box 4-1/11; Lewy, *Catholic Church*, pp. 234, 291-92.

VIII. McCARTHY AND FREEDOM

In contrast to what it had been in the summer of 1946, opinion expressed in print had changed radically by the spring of 1948. The *Chicago Tribune*, powerful voice of midwestern conservatism, turned frequently to the topic of Malmédy, condemning the Supreme Court in May for its rejection of Everett's petition and calling for a court martial of the army investigation/prosecution team. By October, Judge van Roden was uncritically spreading the more extreme of the antiprosecution allegations, which prompted the *Tribune* to write in tones of outraged hyperbole that "never has American justice sunk to the degradation depicted by Judge E. L. van Roden."[1] *The New York Times* was less inclined to condemn American military justice out of hand but, in writing of the Malmédy affair, warned that "a decent respect for the opinion of others demands that no final action be taken . . . until a complete and satisfying explanation is given."[2] Most honest in his recognition of the brutal realities of war, which formed a major component of the context in which the massacres had taken place, was Kenneth L. Dixon of the *Denver Post* who mused: ". . . When you think of the bodies of those kids . . . the fury of such postwar gentleness toward their executioners gets hot within you. Then you remember the chain reaction it set off, and how we took mighty few prisoners before the whole tale was told, and your conclu-

---

1. *Chicago Tribune*, October 13, 1948, Digest, p. 2, NA, RG 319.
2. *New York Times*, October 10, 1948, *ibid.*

sions become bitterly confused."[3] Awkwardly for the army, the Communist *Daily Worker* was one of the few publications to express unreserved confidence in the rectitude of the investigation and trial and opposition to a revision of its outcome.[4] The legislative branch of the United States government, among its several identities and functions, serves as a national tympanic membrane which reverberates to currents of opinion. To James Davis, who had early acted as Everett's spokesman in Washington, were added a handful of other congressmen and senators, primarily from the Midwest and South, who found occasion to ask critical questions of the army's conduct in the Malmédy affair.[5] Again, motives were mixed and certainly went beyond (or fell below) the simple but sublime conviction that justice must be done. A will to embarrass an administration of the rival political party was combined in some cases with a desire to please Germanophile constituents and even covert anti-Semitism. Then, too, increasing fear of the Soviet Union and the perspective of several years made the events of December 1944 seem less horrendous than they had earlier appeared.

General Lucius Clay, head of American Military Government, was not isolated from the uproar surrounding Malmédy.[6] The execution and incarceration of remaining German war criminals was his immediate responsibility, and it was he who could issue the orders which would send the twelve Malmédy convicts still under sentence of death on the brief walk to the gallows. It was Clay, too, who became the target of efforts on the part of Germans attempting to secure what they conceived to be justice for the Malmédy prisoners;

3. *Denver Post*, October 8, 1948, *ibid.*
4. *Daily Worker*, October 7, 1948, *ibid.*
5. Case to Royall (telegram), November 4, 1948, NRC, BOX 4-1/11; speech of Lawrence H. Smith, March 10, 1949, NA, RG 319; Royall to McCarthy, March 14, 1949, NA, RG 319; speech of John Rankin, *Congressional Record*, Vol. 93, Part 7, p. 9054. National Council for the Prevention of War, press releases of January 26-27, 1949, EP; George to Everett, January 3, 1949, EP; John Rankin, "Disgrace of German War Crime Trials," EP.
6. Davis to Clay (telegram), March 5, 1949, EP.

but rumblings from Capitol Hill were beginning to reach Frankfurt by the early months of 1949. In February, Clay received a cable from Senator William Langer, Republican of North Dakota, informing him of his (Langer's) introduction of Senate Resolution 39 calling for an investigation of American military justice in occupied Europe and urging that Clay suspend all executions until the completion of the review. The cable from Langer did not specifically mention the Malmédy case, although Clay assumed that that was at the focus of the senator's concern, for of all the cases reviewed by the Simpson Commission only Malmédy had been singled out as having been characterized by the employment of questionable methods.[7] Clay had no serious doubts that the Malmédy prisoners were guilty and that the twelve sentenced to death deserved to die. He further regarded the case as a political annoyance which he preferred to get out of the way with the greatest possible dispatch to avoid additional complications with German political authorities when military government came to an end. Although he had not completed his own review in the light of the Administration of Justice Review Board and the Simpson Commission reports, he seems to have doubted that these documents would contain information or insights sufficient to weaken his resolution, and on March 3 telephoned Assistant Secretary of the Army Tracy Voorhees in an effort to secure a cancellation of the stays of execution ordered by Royall the previous spring. But the political pot in Washington was boiling too vigorously to permit Clay's brutally direct solution. Royall ordered Clay on the same day to delay all executions associated with the Malmédy case until further notice.[8] Although Clay would proceed with his review of the Malmédy death sentences and reduce the total number to six, the possibility that anyone would hang for the crimes of Kampfgruppe Peiper was becoming increasingly remote.

7. Jean E. Smith, ed., *The Papers of General Lucius D. Clay, Germany, 1945-49* (Bloomington and London, 1974), II, 1012-13.
8. *Ibid.*, p. 1041.

Several organs of the legislative branch had begun to jostle one another for the opportunity to investigate the army's role in the Malmédy affair. Senator Pat McCarran, Chairman of the Senate Judiciary Committee, expressed some interest in conducting such a probe, as did Senator Clyde Hoey, Chairman of the Senate Investigations Subcommittee. One member in particular of that subcommittee, Senator Joseph McCarthy of Wisconsin, manifested a high degree of enthusiasm for the undertaking and addressed inquiries to the Department of the Army for additional information on the Malmédy investigation and trial, receiving a summary of Malmédy-related events from beginning to end. Secretary Royall was eager to cooperate and, through McCarthy, encouraged the subcommitee in its intentions; Malmédy was an uncomfortably hot item the discomfort of which the secretary was only too happy to share.[9]

Since the focus of the Malmédy controversy was the conduct of the U.S. Army, the Senate Armed Services Committee had a strong and, perhaps, preeminent claim to jurisdiction. Moreover, two members of that committee had personal grounds for interest in the Malmédy affair. Senator Raymond E. Baldwin of Connecticut was a member of the Bridgeport law firm with which Dwight Fanton, director of the earlier stages of the interrogation process, was associated. The two men had corresponded concerning the case since the previous summer, and Baldwin had written a letter in support of Fanton to Royall.[10] Senator Estes Kefauver of Tennessee, another committee member, had practiced law in the same firm with Raphael Shumacker, second in prominence to Ellis on the prosecution team; Kefauver openly proclaimed Shumacker "a friend of mine for whom I have the highest respect."[11] It was purely coincidental that these two senators, friends and

9. Royall to Truman, March 14, 1949, Harry S. Truman Library, Papers of Harry S. Truman, official file (hereafter TP); Royall to McCarthy, March 14, 1949, TP; Hoey to Truman (telegram), March 11, 1949, TP.

10. Fanton to Baldwin, July 13, 1948, NRC, Box 4-1/11; Baldwin to Royall, July 14, 1948, NRC, Box 4-1/11.

11. MMIH, p. 803.

associates of men whose conduct would unavoidably come under close scrutiny in the forthcoming Senate investigation, should have been members of the Senate Armed Services Committee; but that the committee chairman, Senator Millard Tydings, fought hard and successfully to acquire the investigation for the committee and that the three-man subcommittee appointed to conduct it was chaired by Baldwin and included Kefauver had little to do with chance. On March 29, 1949, pursuant to Baldwin's Senate Resolution 42, the subcommittee was appointed, including in its membership, besides Baldwin and Kefauver, Senator Lester C. Hunt of Wyoming (following the withdrawal of Senator Russell of Georgia). Its charge was a simple one—to investigate the numerous charges of misfeasance leveled against the army in the Malmédy case.[12]

Given the composition of the subcommittee, it might have been assumed that the investigation would move smoothly in directions favorable to the investigation/prosecution team. And so it would have, had not the subcommittee, in a gesture of compromise to the Senate Investigations Subcommittee, invited the participation of Joe McCarthy. From the opening session on Monday, April 18, in Senate Office Building, Room 212, until his dramatic withdrawal a month later, the flamboyant and unprincipled junior senator from Wisconsin dominated the proceedings.

On the national political scene McCarthy was still, relatively, a political unknown. His anti-Communist witch hunt was not to begin for almost a year. It would be a mistake or, at least, an oversimplification to attempt too close a correlation between McCarthy's role in the Malmédy Massacre Investigation Hearings and his later demagogic pursuit of "Communism in high places" which would make him the darling of the extreme right. Elements of the radical and anti-Semitic right both in the United States and Germany did provide

12. "Baldwin Named Head of Malmedy Inquiry," *Washington Post*, March 30, 1949; "Nazi Hoodwinked into Confession, He Now Claims," *Times Herald*, March 17, 1949; *Congressional Record*, Vol. 95, Part 1, 598-600.

him with encouragement and information. At least indirectly, he received material critical of the Malmédy proceedings from Rudolf Aschenauer and probably was stimulated in his condemnation of the army's conduct by wealthy, right-wing, pro-German figures in Wisconsin.[13] But he also received support from the National Council for the Prevention of War, an organization that had become deeply involved in the anti-Malmédy movement and whose membership included isolationists, conservatives, and Quaker, liberal, and left-wing pacifist groups, reflecting not only the complexity of opposition to the army's handling of the Malmédy case but also the complexity of an American political spectrum in flux following the end of World War II.[14] Both defy simplistic analysis. McCarthy was about to be found guilty by the Wisconsin Supreme Court of unethical conduct as attorney and judge and may well have been attempting to distract public attention from that impending blow.[15] He was an ideologically rootless opportunist, seeking publicity and approbation where he could find them. He found them in the Malmédy Massacre Investigation Hearings, but, thereby, he made those hearings more meaningful than they otherwise would have been.

Following an opening statement by Secretary Royall in which that harried public servant expressed his undoubtedly genuine delight at being able to share the Malmédy embarrassment with the United States Senate, the lines of future conflict were drawn. Baldwin's bias was made evident as he pontificated in response to Royall's summary of the Malmédy case and its numerous reviews:

> So, up until now, it is fair to say, is it not, Mr. Secretary, in an effort to lean over backward to be just and considerate to these

13. Tauber, *Eagle and Swastika*, II, 1305, n. 65; "One Man Mob," *New York Post*, September 13, 1951; "Win at Any Cost," *The Progressive*, Vol. 18, No. 4 (April 1954), p. 70.
14. See Finucane to Everett, May 2, 1949 (text and letterhead), EP.
15. Robert Griffith, *The Politics of Fear: Joseph McCarthy and the Senate* (Lexington, 1970), pp. 27-28.

people, not a single German who took part in the perpetration of the Malmedy Massacre, where some 250 [sic] of our boys were lined up and shot down, not a single German has yet been executed?[16]

As defender of army justice which had sought to punish the slaughterers of "American boys," Baldwin's role was a simple and politically safe one to play. McCarthy's, on the other hand, was far more hazardous. While acting as critic of the investigation and trial, he had to avoid giving the impression of being unpatriotic or willing to coddle German prisoners who were, in the minds of most Americans, brutes whose humanity was moot. McCarthy would attempt to neutralize these dangers by stressing his own (largely imaginary) war record in the Pacific and the ostensibly high level of military justice which had been dispensed in that theater while declaring at every opportunity that Germans genuinely guilty of murdering American prisoners of war should be hanged. Nor was McCarthy reluctant to evoke images of himself as a stern but upright judge in prewar Wisconsin. Within a few moments of the opening of the hearings, McCarthy was droning in his humorless monotone:

. . . Every member of the committee realizes the gruesomeness of the crime perpetrated over there. I think every member of our committee feels that when the guilty are found and properly tried, they should either be hung or whatever sentence happens to be meted out to them. . . . However, in view of the exceptionally good record over in the Pacific [critics of the Yamashita trial would have been startled] where every war criminal was tried honestly and fairly and executed as quickly as they were over in Europe—in all the unusual reports coming out of the European Theater, some of us were very much concerned in checking to see exactly what type of justice we are meting out in Germany. . . .[17]

That, of course, was empty wind, and McCarthy would ex-

16. MMIH, p. 5.
17. Ibid., p. 7.

pel great volumes of it during the hearings. He was also to reveal profound and grimly amusing confusion concerning the nature of the organization to which the Malmédy defendants had belonged and of Nazi Germany itself. In questioning John W. King, who had been a guard at Schwäbisch Hall, about conditions under which the SS suspects had lived at that facility, McCarthy desired to know whether the prisoners had had benefit of clergy: "Did you," he intoned, "ever see a priest or a minister or a rabbi in the Malmédy section of the prison?" It was not a slip of the tongue. King replied that he had not seen clergymen in that part of the prison. McCarthy reacted with indignation: "And you knew there was some sizable number of Protestants, Catholics, or Jewish boys. I understand then there was no chaplain assigned to these boys."[18]

Those with a penchant for psychoanalysis might find interesting McCarthy's extreme sensitivity to the question of his own war record and his fascination with the claims made by certain of the Malmédy convicts that they had received blows to the genitals. In the course of the stormy questioning of William R. Perl, the most important of the Malmédy interrogators, the meaning of the term "heat of combat" came under discussion. Perl innocently suggested that the Wisconsin senator did not fully understand its meaning. McCarthy exploded: "I am under no misconception as to the meaning of what 'in the heat of combat' is. You may be. I don't know whether you saw any combat or not; but don't tell me I don't know what the heat of combat is."[19] Injuries to private parts were seldom far from McCarthy's mind: "Teeth being kicked out, genitals being ruined, it is all in the affidavits"; "16-or-17-year-old boys, who were kicked in the testicles, crippled for life"; "if it is found that they have ruptured testicles and that sort of thing from being kicked"; "one of the witnesses testified that he was kicked in the genitals so badly that he

18. *Ibid.*, pp. 569-70.
19. *Ibid.*, p. 680.

was taken to the hospital in Stuttgart.''[20] It sometimes seemed that McCarthy believed the quality of postwar American military justice to hinge on the condition of the sexual organs of German prisoners.

Although conducting himself with greater dignity, Baldwin was also guilty of obscuring the fundamental issues. He insisted on calling before the subcommittee two survivors of the crossroads incident, Kenneth Ahrens and Virgil Lary, who described at some length the shootings of American prisoners and their own narrow escapes. But the crossroads killings were not at issue; no one denied that they had taken place. The likely purpose in calling for the testimony became clear, however, in the following exchange between Ahrens and Senator Hunt:

Senator Hunt: Mr. Chairman, I would like to ask the witness: As I understood your statement, during the killing the SS troops seemed to be in a hilarious mood and seemed to be enjoying their work?

Mr. Ahrens: Oh, yes; very much so.

Senator Hunt: Let me ask you if any of those SS troops were, during the trial, pushed up against the wall, would you consider that they were being mistreated, after what they did to your boys?

Mr. Ahrens: No; I certainly would not. I often wish I would have a chance to push them up against a wall.

Senator Hunt: Do you think that a trial of men of that type, that character, for committing acts such as they had committed, should be shown all of the rights that we expect today in a civil trial?

Mr. Ahrens: No; I don't.[21]

Hunt thereby revealed himself more closely akin to the root of the Malmédy problem than its solution.

20. *Ibid.,* pp. 217, 247, 367, 782.
21. *Ibid., p. 109.*

Nevertheless, in spite of the obscurantist conduct of the senators, additional light was shed on the Malmédy affair. McCarthy had been contacted by James J. Bailey, a court reporter by profession who had been employed by the army at Schwäbisch Hall from the end of December 1945 until early March 1946. Bailey might have been expected to possess knowledge that would go to the heart of the Malmédy controversy, for he had transcribed many of the sworn statements on which the prosecution case against the defendants had been largely based. Undoubtedly because he indicated that he had information detrimental to the army's image, Bailey was invited by McCarthy to testify. Bailey's testimony did not confirm claims of extreme physical violence which had been made subsequent to the trial by convicts and persons sympathetic to them but did indicate that the interrogation procedure had not always been the scene of calm propriety that the investigation/prosecution staff had indicated. Bailey had seen blood flow on only one occasion. That had occurred in the course of an interrogation when a hooded young prisoner, brought into the interrogation cell, collapsed in terror as the hood was jerked away, bloodying his nose on the floor.[22] Otherwise, Bailey testified, he had observed occasional scratches and bruises on the prisoners "but nothing serious" and had seen Perl slap men under interrogation. To McCarthy's probable satisfaction, Bailey claimed to have watched Perl "knee a couple of them in the groin." He had also seen an "oversized blackjack," probably a German *Gummiknüppel* or police rubber truncheon, on a table in the interrogation cell but had never seen it used. Emotional tension among the prisoners had apparently been high, for Bailey had seen some, at least, enter the interrogation "shakey and nervous." Bailey named Harry Thon and Frank Steiner as members of the interrogation team sometimes inclined to brutal conduct, but this seemed to consist more of rough language and a warped sense

22. *Ibid.*, pp. 158-59.

of humor than actual physical violence. Bailey made it clear that he believed that the behavior of at least Perl and Steiner had been linked to the fact that both were refugees from Nazi Germany and that Steiner had been convinced that his mother had been murdered by the Gestapo.[23]

All of this was of secondary importance, although obviously related to the question of the all-important sworn statements. Bailey asserted that "fifty percent" of the statements "were either made up by Perl or Thon, and they were altered, changed and deleted." Here, Bailey was claiming to know much more than he could know, for he had witnessed only a fraction of the interrogations and, moreover, knew no German. But he did have first-hand knowledge of his own function, which had been to take down, in shorthand, the translations into English of the original German sworn statements and then to type them. Perl, however, had been difficult to please and had repeatedly required amendments to the translations until they met his approval. It would have been most helpful if Bailey had been able to offer examples of the numerous alterations that Perl had supposedly required, but he did not and was not asked to do so.[24]

McCarthy exulted in what appeared to be clear evidence of forged confessions:

Senator McCarthy: In other words, there was some writing that would come from a cell in the accused's handwriting?
Mr. Bailey: That is right.

Senator McCarthy: And the interpreter would interpret in English?
Mr. Bailey: That is right.

Senator McCarthy: You would type it out and give it to Perl?
Mr. Bailey: That is right.

Senator McCarthy: And then he would change it?
Mr. Bailey: Never satisfied; he said this is not what, he would say, he would have to have.

23. *Ibid.*, pp. 153-90.
24. *Ibid.*, pp. 177-78.

Senator McCarthy: Typewritten in English?

Mr. Bailey: Typewriting it over a half dozen times to meet his satisfaction.

Senator McCarthy: You would typewrite it over and over until it met his satisfaction?

Mr. Bailey: That is right.

Senator McCarthy: Then, take it over to the man who could not read English and he would sign it?

Mr. Bailey: Only conclusion you could arrive at.[25]

In fact, Bailey's imagination had outstripped his memory. The "writing that would come from a cell in the accused's handwriting" was the completed sworn statement which the prisoner had already signed in the presence of witnesses. In no case was a prisoner required to sign a statement in English. And while in translating from one language to another there is always latitude for subjective judgment, there was no real possibility of gross changes of meaning from the German original to the English translation, for both were to be submitted in evidence.[26] Important deviations from what the prisoners had actually stated, if any, must have been introduced into the German original, but Bailey, in his inability to understand German, could not have identified these.

Bailey's testimony, therefore, lacked the significance that it appeared, on the surface, to have. Yet, testimony suggesting the existence at Schwäbisch Hall of an atmosphere in which duress might well have been a factor was offered by others. Kurt Teil, a refugee from Nazism, not himself involved in the Malmédy case but employed by the U.S. Army as an interpreter-investigator on cases which sometimes took him to Schwäbisch Hall, came away uneasy over what seemed to be taking place there. Thon, he recalled, seemed to advocate violent methods of interrogation, and Perl had a similar reputation. Teil had no direct knowledge of brutal conduct

25. *Ibid.*, p. 178.
26. See prosecution exhibits, U.S. v. Bersin, 153/5-6.

on the part of the two interrogators but remembered an incident that strengthened his suspicions. Early in 1946, he was taken on a tour by Thon of a block of cells occupied by Malmédy prisoners. Pausing at the peephole in the door of one cell, Thon summoned Teil to have a look. Inside, Teil testified, he saw a prisoner with a hood still over his head lying crumpled and motionless on the floor. In response to Teil's question as to what ailed the man, Thon replied, "He just got out of interrogation and probably got roughed up a bit."[27] Teil had no doubt, however, that instances of physical duress were the exception rather than the rule and emphasized that Ellis had repeatedly stressed the importance of avoiding violence.[28] He might have added, however, that Ellis had not assumed control of the Schwäbisch Hall operation until March 1946.

Notable by his absence from the hearings was Willis Everett, who had been hospitalized in March with a massive heart attack, attributable in large measure to his compulsive involvement in the Malmédy case over a period of three years.[29] Three other members of the defense staff testified in tones less strident and, therefore, probably more convincing than Everett would have done.

During the trial, Everett had been somewhat critical of the courtroom conduct of defense attorney Herbert Strong. Whatever his shortcomings might have been at that time, he was an effective witness in the Senate hearings, not only because he had obviously given the problem of defending the Malmédy seventy-four careful retrospective thought but because he, himself, had been a refugee from the Hitler terror and was a Jew. His criticisms of the army's conduct of the investigation and trial of the SS prisoners could not, therefore, be brushed off as camouflaged pro-Nazism or anti-Semitism. Strong impressed the senators and audience by recalling that he had participated in several war crimes trials

27. MMIH, pp. 546-48.   28. *Ibid.*, p. 549.
29. Everett to McCarthy, May 11, 1949, EP.

but had not heard the same degree of reservation concerning the justice of those proceedings as he had about the Malmédy case.[30] He apparently believed that some truth, at least, adhered to the defendants' claims of having been subjected to physical violence. Francis Flanigan of the Subcommittee on Investigations, who acted as McCarthy's staff assistant, quite reasonably asked why the defense had not attempted to verify the claims of physical abuse through medical examination. Strong replied that by the time the defense learned of these complaints (in April 1946), they were already at least a month to six weeks old and were not of a nature that would have left long-term evidence.[31] Obviously, Strong had not been left with the impression that anyone had been "crippled for life," but he leveled some serious charges against the prosecution staff, accusing them of obstructing the calling of defense witnesses and attempting to intimidate those that were secured. He was convinced, too, that the law member of the court, Colonel Rosenfeld, had been prejudiced against the defense, having ruled too often against it when the law was on its side.[32] As Everett was willing to do in his calmer moments, Strong admitted that he thought some of the Malmédy defendants were guilty but that in many cases guilt had not been proven beyond a reasonable doubt.[33]

John Dwinnell's testimony agreed with Strong's in most respects. He, too, believed that the Malmédy prisoners had been subjected to some degree of physical duress and that the defense had worked under unnecessary disabilities imposed upon it by the court, so much so that he had developed a "defeatist attitude." He did not doubt that SS troopers had committed war crimes during the offensive but had substantial reservations about the picture that had been painted by the prosecution. Obviously, American prisoners had been killed at the crossroads, but Dwinnell was not convinced that the persons whom he had defended were guilty of that crime.

30. MMIH, p. 572.   31. Ibid., pp. 576-78.
32. Ibid., pp. 580-84.   33. Ibid., pp. 595-96.

Nor was he convinced that American soldiers shot elsewhere had not been killed in combat or that the Belgian civilians killed had not been guerrilla fighters or, at least, mistaken for guerrillas.[34] Granger Sutton, who testified briefly, agreed with Strong and Dwinnell that physical duress had probably been applied to the SS defendants although he, like they, had seen no direct physical evidence of it.[35]

These witnesses gave testimony to which considerable weight must adhere. They had been thoughtful in their responses to questions and moderate in the criticisms that they had leveled at army investigative and trial procedures, charges that grew out of their own experiences with the events under examination. It was noteworthy that the testimony of the three was far from being in agreement with the extreme accusations replete with savagery resulting in broken jaws, dislodged teeth, and "ruptured" testicles.

The two men most responsible for circulating these lurid assertions were Judge LeRoy van Roden of the Simpson Commission and James Finucane, Secretary of the National Council for the Prevention of War. If it is true that first impressions are the strongest, then it is significant to note that van Roden claimed to have first learned of the Malmédy Massacre while serving as an intelligence officer with an American combat unit during the Ardennes offensive. He had been present during the oral reports of an exhausted young lieutenant who (this was van Roden's impression) had been a witness to the crossroads incident and who had described the massacre as a confused situation in which the efforts of some American prisoners to escape had resulted in a mass shooting by "trigger-happy" German soldiers.[36] This image of the Malmédy Massacre had remained with van Roden, and to it had undoubtedly been added opinions critical of the army's subsequent investigation and trial heard during his association with Everett in postwar Germany. It seems likely, too, that

34. *Ibid.*, pp. 434-36.   35. *Ibid.*, pp. 1169-80.
36. *Ibid.*, p. 232.

van Roden harbored anti-Semitic feelings and came to view war crimes trials in general as, at least in part, a Jewish effort to wreak vengeance on Germany which had resulted in numerous injustices.[37] He had, therefore, been predisposed to accept rather uncritically extreme allegations of American brutality not only in the Malmédy case but in the numerous Dachau proceedings which he, along with Simpson and Lawrence, had been directed by Royall to investigate. His views had been repressed by his more moderate colleagues in the official commission report but burst forth in public statements after his return to the United States. Finucane had sought out van Roden, listened to a speech dealing with American judicial abuses in Germany which the judge had delivered to a Rotary Club meeting near Philadelphia and, with van Roden's agreement, cast it in the form of a sensationalistic and lurid article which he had sold to *The Progressive* magazine. The article had received wide circulation, was read into the Congressional Record and clearly was the source of McCarthy's conviction that American investigators had been preoccupied with the destruction of German genitalia.[38]

Both men were called upon to testify before Baldwin's subcommittee. Van Roden was fearful and penitent, seeking to dissociate himself from *The Progressive* article which had appeared in February 1949 under his name. He sought to fob off responsibility for the article on Finucane, who, he claimed, had taken unjustified liberties with what had been said in the Rotary Club speech. Ultimately, van Roden sought the refuge of the official report which bore his signature, reaffirming that no evidence of "general or systematic use" of improper methods to secure prosecution evidence had been found. The Pennsylvania judge came off as a rather imprudent man whose prejudices and desire for publicity had progressively

37. On van Roden, see *Proceedings and Debates of the 81st Congress, 1st Session, Appendix*, A 4375-76.
38. *Congressional Record*, Vol. 95, *Appendix*, A 1365-66; MMIH, pp. 303-04. Van Roden's accusations echoed even in Harvard's hallowed halls. See Ted Lewis, Jr., "War Trial: Malmedy," *The Harvard Advocate*, 132, No. 6 (April, 1949), 23.

alienated him from reality and finally brought him to public embarrassment.[39]

Finucane was a man of a different stripe. A journalist before the war, he had registered with Selective Service as a conscientious objector and had spent thirty-three months in a government work camp. Unable, finally, to tolerate the physical and psychological stress of camp life, he had volunteered for active military service and had been inducted and trained in time to see action in Europe during the last months of the war. Finucane had suffered, both in the labor camp and in the army.[40] He had been required to take basic training twice. But he had probably suffered more as a result of having compromised his pacifist principles. Well might he view himself as a victim of injustice inflicted upon him by the American military system, a perception that likely gave him a sense of kinship with the Malmédy convicts, at least as their plight and sufferings had been portrayed by their defenders in Germany and the United States. Finucane's pacifist beliefs also played a role in his approach to the Malmédy case. World War II itself had been the surpassing crime; Malmédy had been an insignificant component of that greater crime and a minor matter even in comparison to Allied crimes perpetrated at Dresden, Hiroshima, and Nagasaki.[41] Ideology, personal experience, and a sensitivity to hypocrisy had combined to make James Finucane a passionate advocate of freedom for the Malmédy prisoners and a willing and uncritical conduit for propaganda from Rudolf Aschenauer and others.[42]

McCarthy was unable to appreciate or understand Finucane's principles and had in any event already withdrawn from the hearings by the time Finucane was called to testify. Baldwin and Hunt found the principles politically unpalatable and his assertions factually suspect. He was subjected to a vigorous questioning by Baldwin and Col. J. M. Chambers of the Armed Services Committee staff. Nothing more was es-

39. MMIH, pp. 304-16. 40. *Ibid.*, pp. 985-86.
41. *Ibid.*, p. 958. 42. *Ibid.*, pp. 1027, 1459.

tablished thereby than that Finucane's conviction that the Malmédy trial had been a judicial travesty was unshakable.

Members of the prosecution and investigative staffs painted the Malmédy investigation and trial in strikingly different colors from those of trial critics; that, to be sure, was revealed under the benevolent gaze of Baldwin and exposed to the vituperation of Joe McCarthy. But McCarthy could also engage in reasoned and illuminating disputation, as he did with Dwight Fanton, Ellis's predecessor as leader of the investigation team at Schwäbisch Hall. McCarthy raised the significant question concerning whether the Malmédy suspects had been under the protection of the Geneva Convention of 1929. At Dachau, the prosecution had advocated the Kafkaesque argument that the defendants had forfeited all claim to prisoner-of-war status at the time of having committed their criminal acts. Fanton had not been involved in the actual prosecution of the case, nor did he advance that argument; yet, McCarthy skillfully led him onto logical ice virtually as thin:

Senator McCarthy: Anyone that didn't violate the rules of the Geneva Convention, that followed the rules insofar as land warfare was concerned, he was not a war criminal?

Major Fanton: That would be right.

Senator McCarthy: So, when you say "war criminal," you refer to a man who violated the rules of the Geneva Convention?

Major Fanton: War crimes suspect, one suspected of such a violation.

Senator McCarthy: After you suspected them of having violated the Geneva Convention rules, then they were moved to Schwabisch Hall?

Major Fanton: That is right.

Senator McCarthy: Then you say you no longer followed the rules of the Geneva Convention insofar as those men were concerned?

Major Fanton: With the exception that we did, insofar as possible, follow them, we could not for instance—could not let them exercise, in answer to your question; we didn't humiliate them, or assign them to dangerous missions, of course it wasn't wartime, and I assume other things of that nature, but to my knowledge, none of that was done.

I remember Peiper had a cell in the hospital ward. He was given reading material. I myself gave him some stuff to read, as I recall. He was well treated, insofar as it was consistent with our interrogation and with the job we had to do.

Senator McCarthy: In otherwords, if you felt that following the Geneva Convention rules was inconsistent with your interrogation, you felt justified in violating the rules yourself, is that right?

Major Fanton: I don't like the word "violation" but I suppose that is a correct statement, because I felt about it this way: I don't think the rules apply, I may be wrong, and if I am I am willing to stand on that. I don't think they do—

Senator McCarthy: You don't think the rules apply after you suspect the man of having violated the rules?

Major Fanton: That is right. Of course, I am assuming you do so on reasonable grounds. . . .[43]

Heard against the background of McCarthy's own later blatant disregard for individual rights and due process, these words ring discordantly. Nevertheless, the Wisconsin senator had laid bare one of the most significant issues involved in the Malmédy case. Fanton was undoubtedly speaking honestly when he implied that, to his knowledge, the Malmédy suspects had not been ill treated. But he had also conceded that he had not been aware of everything that might have taken place in Schwäbisch Hall.[44] If the suspects had been regarded as being outside the protection of law, then a great deal could have taken place which, in calmer times, might appear reprehensible.

Perhaps out of deference to Baldwin, McCarthy treated Fanton rather gently and dealt with Shumacker, Kefauver's friend, with some restraint. He handled Col. Burton Ellis less

43. *Ibid.,* pp. 482-83.
44. *Ibid.,* p. 525.

considerately. Ellis was naturally intent upon refuting the charges of misfeasance which had been directed at him and his team, particularly by Everett. In support of his position, he submitted an affidavit sworn by Lt. Col. Charles J. Perry. Perry had not participated in the Malmédy investigation and trial but had occasion to interview Peiper and one of his subordinate officers in February 1947 at Landsberg Prison. According to Perry, both men had denied maltreatment at the hands of the Americans, and Peiper's subordinate had opined that claims to that effect by other convicts had been simply a crude stratagem concocted by the defense to attempt to neutralize damaging confessions which had been voluntarily given. Both men purportedly expressed their kindly feelings and high regard for Colonel Ellis and his associates, recognizing that, in prosecuting the Malmédy defendants, they had only been doing their military duty.[45] Ellis added a bit of humor while buttressing his defense of the investigation / prosecution team by submitting a piece of doggerel written to him during the trial by the same officer who had been interviewed, along with Peiper, by Perry. The verse had been written in mocking response to testimony by a defendant who had claimed to have been imprisoned in a cell whose walls had been pitted with apparent bullet holes to which bits of flesh still seemed to adhere:

> Sir, do you know Schwabisch-Hall?
> With bullet-holes in the wall
> With pieces of flesh
> The latter still fresh
> O, yes; you were on the ball!

The author of this humbly begs not to introduce the Limerick in evidence.[46]

The credibility of this affidavit might well have been challenged. It conflicted emphatically with statements that the

45. *Ibid.*, pp. 1233-35.
46. *Ibid.*, p. 1235.

two Germans had made previous to February 1947 and would make subsequently.[47] It is at least conceivable that men under death sentences which they had every reason to believe would be executed in the near future would clutch at the straw of attempting to ingratiate themselves with their captors, perhaps hoping to establish for themselves value as witnesses willing to testify to the probity of American investigative methods, thus staving off the noose. The fact that Ellis had clearly requested the affidavits by Perry is further grounds for skepticism, while the verse is, literally, gallows humor, by itself signifying nothing but the sangfroid and linguistic ability of its author.

In any event, McCarthy was more interested in the "mock trials," which had considerably greater dramatic appeal, and which gave him a better opportunity to demonstrate his ostensible concern for high standards of justice. Ellis, as an active officer in the Judge Advocate General's Corps and the man under whose general authority "mock trials" had taken place, defended them as legitimate ruses and thereby opened himself to what McCarthy was pleased to call "vigorous" cross-examination, extending to insulting inferences of professional incompetence.[48] Little additional light was shed on the investigation although Senator Hunt, in an effort to rescue Ellis from McCarthy's clutches, elicited from Ellis the important information that the investigation/prosecution team had felt under intense pressure from American public opinion to bring the case to trial (and, presumably, to secure convictions).[49]

Tension peaked and decorum reached its nadir with the appearance of William R. Perl, the most active of the interrogators at Schwäbisch Hall and the man against whom a majority of the charges of brutality had been lodged. In his

---

47. That these statements were made to Perry was denied by both prisoners in affidavits dated November 8 and 9, 1949, and witnessed by Karl Erman, Protestant chaplain at Landsberg Prison, EP.
48. MMIH, p. 45.
49. *Ibid.*, p. 67.

physical make-up—short, balding, and rather plump with a face that often wore an amiable smile—Perl seemed an unlikely strong-arm man. He also bore substantial academic credentials, having been trained both in psychology and the law, a person apparently admirably qualified for the job of investigator in a case such as Malmédy, particularly inasmuch as he spoke fluent German.[50] It was clear from the testimony of other members of the investigation/prosecution team that Perl had been the emotional and intellectual dynamo within the investigation effort at Schwäbisch Hall.

Other aspects of Perl's background were such as to encourage suspicion of investigatory misconduct. Born in Prague and educated in Vienna, Perl had established a highly successful law practice within one of the largest law firms in the Austrian capital. An active Zionist, he had assisted in the emigration of many central European Jews to Palestine. Following his own emigration to the United States, Perl was inducted into the U.S. Army and assigned to intelligence duties involving the interrogation of German prisoners of war for military information. This work took Perl to England and, eventually, to the fighting front on the Continent. At the end of the war, Perl was transferred to war crimes investigation work for which, with his training in law, he seemed even better qualified than for military intelligence. His new superiors in the army's War Crimes Branch might have questioned whether a Jew who had suffered personally as a result of Nazi aggression and who was acutely conscious of the torments of the Jewish people at the hands of the Nazis was temperamentally suited to the investigation of German war crimes, particularly those involving SS men.[51] Under different circumstances, such questions might have been raised. In 1945, with wartime passions still high and the need for German-speaking personnel desperate, they were not.

Everything about Perl seemed to invite attack by McCarthy.

50. *Ibid.*, pp. 609-10.
51. *Ibid.*, pp. 609-13; interview with William R. Perl., Dec. 16, 1977.

Perl described with pride his wartime achievements as an army interrogator; he had, on occasion, worked under enemy fire for which he had received two battle stars.[52] This could only arouse envy within McCarthy for whom a combat record (his own was largely a work of self-composed fiction) had great political and psychic significance.[53] Perl was an intellectual, multilingual, comfortable with complex abstractions, whereas McCarthy craved the simple and concrete. Physically, Perl was small, a factor that encouraged aggression from the insecure, burly, and bullying Wisconsin senator. He was foreign born, spoke with an accent, and was a Jew. To the extent that McCarthy, in his assaults on the army's conduct of the Malmédy investigation and trial, was catering to anti-Semitic and isolationist sentiment in his home state, Perl was an ideal target. Finally, Perl was extraordinarily verbose in his responses to questions, a quality that infuriated McCarthy who was determined to use the hearings as a stage for his own political advancement.

The image of the Malmédy investigation which Perl sought to convey was one of a carefully calculated and psychologically sophisticated campaign directed toward breaking down the defenses of men presumed to share a high degree of group loyalty and individual toughness. It was a campaign which, ultimately, was spectacularly successful. Defenses crumbled, confessions were made, truth was made manifest. Physical violence would have been beneath practitioners of such subtle stratagems and had not been utilized.[54] What came to be known as "mock trials" had been used in a few instances but had been legitimate and not very effective interrogative devices meant to simulate not a trial in the strict sense but the pretrial investigative hearing before a judge common to Continental judicial procedure with which the suspects, presumably, had been familiar.[55]

52. *Ibid.,* p. 613.
53. Griffith, *Politics of Fear,* p. 5.
54. MMIH, pp. 613-29, 659-791, 1125-43.
55. *Ibid.,* pp. 725-26.

Yet, Perl was not always able to sustain the demeanor of dispassionate investigator, even three years after the event. When challenged by McCarthy on his denial of an allegation that he had deceived a defendant with the aid of his "word of honor," Perl exploded. "It is absolutely untrue! It is a lie! . . . I would have found it beneath my dignity to give one of those men my word of honor as an American officer. . . ."[56] And Perl's emphatic denials that physical force had been employed were called into question when, under heated questioning by McCarthy, he complained of "noise, noise raised about this case where 700 Americans were murdered and it is a question of 1 or 2 Germans getting slapped."[57]

It was over the credibility of Perl's testimony that McCarthy precipitated the crisis that led to his withdrawal from the Senate hearings. McCarthy bluntly and repeatedly accused Perl of perjury before the subcommittee and asked that he submit to a lie detector examination in the most provocative and insulting terms: "I wonder, Mr. Perl, if you would be willing to submit to the Kieler lie-detector test. There is no physical punishment involved, no kicking in the groin or anything like that. I wonder if you would be willing?" Although expressing reservations about the reliability of such a procedure, Perl agreed to submit, and it was not long before the proposal had been expanded to include similar examinations of the other Malmédy interrogators and the German convicts who had claimed mistreatment.[58]

Baldwin was wary and noncommittal. The ramifications of any response to the proposal were likely to be to McCarthy's benefit and to do nothing to enhance the reputation of the subcommittee's investigation (which, of course, is precisely why the Wisconsin senator had thrown the nettle onto the floor). Should the proposal be rejected, McCarthy could dramatically brand the investigation a "whitewash." If an attempt should be made to implement it, the investigation would be much protracted, allowing McCarthy additional time to strut upon the stage, while the results of the electronic examination would be sufficiently ambiguous as to resolve nothing. Hence Baldwin temporized, declaring the proposal a matter that would have to be discussed by the subcommittee and the full Senate Armed Services Committee. The nettle's spikes immediately began to draw blood as McCarthy launched into a tirade accusing the Senate Armed Services Committee of an intent to suppress the bitter truth concerning the Malmédy affair and Baldwin of attempting to shield his friend and professional associate, Dwight Fanton.[59] Of course, the accusations were not entirely without foundation, but if these kernels of truth had not existed as a base from which an attack on the Senate hearings could be launched, McCarthy, we may suspect, would have found other grounds.

McCarthy laid his trap on Friday, May 13. On the following Thursday, Baldwin lumbered into it. The Senate Armed Services Committee had given the subcommittee the power of veto over McCarthy's proposal. Baldwin and Kefauver, with Hunt absent, had vetoed it, because, Baldwin explained, it would constitute a ''marked departure from congressional procedures in the past'' and would present logistical difficulties. The junior senator from Wisconsin savored the moment. Hunt had not participated in the decision?

Senator Baldwin: Senator Hunt was out of town.

Senator McCarthy: Not Hunt.

Senator Baldwin: Senator Kefauver did. I spoke to him about it before the meeting this morning of the Armed Services Committee, and at the meeting itself. He expressed himself as being firmly in opposition to it.[60]

It had been Baldwin and Kefauver, then, senators with close personal ties to two principals on the investigation/prosecution team, who had elected to exclude the lie detector. Whatever their motives might have been, there was no question as

59. *Ibid.*, pp. 632-39.
60. *Ibid.*, pp. 793-94.

to the interpretation that McCarthy would publicly assign to their decision. He would, McCarthy ominously informed the subcommittee, have a public statement to make the following day.

On the morning of Friday, May 20, McCarthy had, in fact, two statements to air; one, an address to the Chair, and the other, a release to the press. On balance, McCarthy had thus far played a constructive role in the Malmédy hearings. To be sure, he had been insulting, was inclined to go off on inconsequential tangents, and sometimes displayed a shocking ignorance of fundamental aspects of the case. But he had also posed important questions which others were reluctant to ask. This was now overshadowed by the ill-considered and outrageous verbal shot from the hip as he announced his withdrawal from the Senate hearings. His address to Baldwin was salted with lurid references to men screaming and signing confessions under torture and, laughably, "brutalities greater than any we have ever accused either the Russians or Hitler Germany of employing." McCarthy's release to the press was even more unrestrained, directly accusing the U.S. Army of employing "Gestapo and OGPU tactics," stating as fact certain unproven accusations and claiming enormities which even the convicts, themselves, had not alleged. By attempting to suppress these "facts," the subcommittee was not only "impugning the fair name of the millions of men and women who served with valor and distinction in the armed services," but also "sabotaging our efforts under the European Recovery Act." Should the subcommittee's effort to "whitewash" the army's conduct in the Malmédy case succeed, McCarthy concluded, "the United States can never protest the use of these methods by totalitarian countries."[61]

Baldwin's response was understandably bitter and, although more moderate in its language, also prone to distortion and innuendo. That McCarthy had seemed more willing to believe the affidavits of "German SS troops" guilty of

61. *Ibid.*, pp. 838-39.

murder than the "sworn testimony of American officers and military personnel," suggesting the irrational but emotionally acceptable premise (in 1949) that the one category of human beings was inherently more credible than the other, was a point made by Baldwin with some persistence. But McCarthy managed to secure the last word. Declaring the hearings a "shameful farce" which Baldwin would come to "bitterly regret," he stalked out of Senate Office Building, Room 212.[62]

The hearings continued on a more decorous level but without producing evidence capable of resolving the essential questions surrounding the Malmédy case. Ambiguity was piled on ambiguity. Dr. Max Karan, a German-speaking American physician, briefly in charge of the dispensary established for the Malmédy suspects, testified that he had seen no physical evidence of brutality during his one-month tenure nor had any prisoner complained of mistreatment, and he expressed certainty that if physically damaging treatment had been meted out to the prisoners during that period, he would have learned of it, presumably from the prisoners, as those responsible for the maltreatment would have been unlikely to noise it abroad. But was that a safe assumption? Seemingly not, for Karan himself admitted that only from the American staff had he learned of a bread and water regimen imposed for a couple of meals upon the prisoners as punishment for illicit efforts at communication.[63] Karan's apparent assurance that physical violence had not been employed was rendered even more questionable by his recollection of conversations in the prison staff mess during which Perl spoke in admiring tones of the violent methods presumably employed by the Soviet secret police to extract confessions. Other interrogators, Karan remembered, expressed the view that since the prisoners were "unquestionably" guilty, any methods might be legitimately used to encourage talkativeness. Karan

62. *Ibid.*, pp. 843-44.
63. *Ibid.*, pp. 844-47.

had also come away from Schwäbisch Hall with the impression that prisoners under interrogation had been threatened with summary execution if they refused to tell the "truth."[64] That was a potentially significant recollection from an apparently unbiased witness. McCarthy, had he still been part of the hearings, would have pounced eagerly upon it. At the very least, it was a statement whose basis should have been carefully probed. Baldwin, however, hastened on to less sensitive matters.[65]

Dr. John Ricker had been Karan's successor as director of the dispensary, serving from January until March 1946. He, too, denied having seen evidence of brutality but admitted that he examined only those prisoners who voiced complaints. Sadly, Ricker's memory failed him when he was queried on the contents of the post-trial affidavit of one of the convicts which included the claim that the deponent had received medical treatment for blows to the genital area.

Mr. Chambers: Here is a man who says he was admitted to the hospital where he was operated on as a result of having been kicked in the genitals. Now you testified that there was never any kicking in the genitals that you know of around there, and nobody got medical care for it. Now, what have you to say on this?

Dr. Ricker: I remember the name and I remember that we took him to the hospital, but I do not remember what the reason was.[66]

Ricker was not questioned as to why, after the passage of more than three years, he could remember having taken one of a great number of prisoners to the hospital but not the man's complaint; he was gently assisted around that incongruity into calmer waters.[67]

Herbert K. Sloan had played a marginal role in the army's war crimes project having acted as "rat catcher"—sallying

64. *Ibid.*, pp. 854, 857.   65. *Ibid.*, p. 857.
66. *Ibid.*, p. 878.   67. *Ibid.*, pp. 878-79.

forth from time to time to apprehend suspects and delivering them to interrogation centers. In that capacity, he had acquired a familiarity with the interrogation program at Schwäbisch Hall involving the Malmédy case. In general, he attested to the decent treatment accorded the prisoners but testified that it was generally known among those associated with war crimes work that things were "a little rough" at Schwäbisch Hall.[68] This, of course, was a classic example of hearsay evidence of a vague and inconclusive nature. And Paul C. Guth, who had assisted in the War Crimes Branch's pretrial investigation of the earliest allegations of brutality, testified that he had found no evidence of physical duress but offered interesting recollections of a conversation conducted with Peiper at Dachau (Peiper, it should be noted, has denied that this conversation took place).[69] Shortly after the end of the war, Guth had interrogated Peiper at Freising for military information unrelated to the Malmédy case; the atmosphere had been relaxed and the SS officer and the Vienna-born American interrogator had got along well. At Dachau, Peiper spoke to Guth in contemptuous terms of the conduct of his men during the investigation. They had betrayed their officers and comrades in a desperate effort to save their own necks, Guth recalled Peiper's having said, but were now advancing claims of duress. "You know how much those are worth."[70]

In fact, what they were worth was far from clear. The same might have been said of the testimony offered before the Senate subcommittee. It continued to accumulate in inconclusive fashion until June 6. The hearings then recessed until early September when they were resumed in Munich.

A trip to Germany (although it was combined with a junket to the Interparliamentary Congress meeting in Stockholm) gave the impression of an investigation that was leaving no

68. *Ibid.*, p. 902.   69. Peiper affidavit, November 8, 1949, EP.
70. MMIH, p. 946.

stone unturned. Still in Germany were important participants in the Malmédy investigation and trial: the law member of the Malmédy court, Col. A. H. Rosenfeld; army interrogators; the German defense attorneys and, of course, the defendants themselves in addition to other German nationals who claimed to have significant knowledge of the case. But it was more of the same. Participants in the investigation denied all wrongdoing, albeit, with minor but sometimes suggestive exceptions. A former interrogator admitted that at least on one occasion a suspect had been threatened with the withholding of ration cards from his parents. Once more, American personnel who had been in contact with the proceedings at Schwäbisch Hall testified to having heard rumors of brutality but admitted to having seen little or nothing to confirm those rumors.[71]

While in Germany, the subcommittee had its first opportunity to question a witness who had had an important function in the trial but who, unlike the prosecution and defense staffs, had been duty-bound to observe the courtroom proceedings with impartiality. As law member of the Malmédy court, Colonel Rosenfeld had wielded great power, interpreting the law and making frequent procedural rulings for a bench whose members were combat soldiers inexpert in such matters. His conduct had been second—a distant second, to be sure—to the methods used to secure sworn statements as a focus of criticism. The defense had been particularly incensed by Rosenfeld's limitation of their freedom to challenge the credibility of prosecution witnesses. Rosenfeld maintained at Munich, not entirely convincingly, that had the defense made clear its intentions, he would have permitted such challenges.[72] Admittedly, the defense was often maladroit, but its aim should have been obvious to Rosenfeld when, for example, it attempted to challenge the credibility of a witness

71. *Ibid.*, pp. 1319, 1132-33.
72. *Ibid.*, p. 1377.

whose testimony supported the prosecution's contention that Peiper had issued illegal orders. Following the witness's direct examination at Dachau, Strong had asked, "Now, how often would you say you were approximately interrogated at Schwabisch Hall?" The prosecution had offered an objection which had been sustained by Rosenfeld. Strong had tried once more, "Isn't it a fact that you, during the time you were in Schwabisch Hall, signed a statement for the prosecution in question-and-answer form, consisting of approximately 20 pages?" Again, the prosecution had objected and Rosenfeld had thundered, "That is not cross-examination. This is the last time the court will notify you."[73] Rosenfeld tried hard to impress the senators at Munich with his evenhandedness at Dachau three years earlier, but it was an impression he found difficult to sustain. He expressed personal admiration for Peiper as a soldier but lashed out furiously at Hal McCown whose testimony at Dachau had badly undermined an important facet of the prosecution case. It was a highly emotional Rosenfeld who recalled that dramatic element of the trial:

> I did not like McCown's testimony. That wasn't a question of a lawyer sitting on a bench evaluating his testimony. That was a question of one soldier who had been in combat evaluating another soldier who had been in combat. I just didn't like the manner in which he presented his testimony. I didn't like the manner in which he took the stand. I didn't like the manner, his manner on the stand, and no other member of the court—I should say this—strike that—all the other members of the court agreed with me unanimously. McCown—I don't know; I don't know whether McCown was telling the truth or not. I can't go behind it, but—and I am glad to say for the record—after 3½ years, I personally doubt the veracity of his testimony. . . .
>
> Now, McCown and Peiper were entirely too friendly those nights they spent together. Peiper, with 600 [*sic*] of his men, was able to escape the trap when he was completely surrounded, and when he escaped McCown was with him; and then McCown

73. U.S. v. Bersin, 153/1/000220-21 (215-16).

simply said—and I think I am almost stating the exact words he said—it is in the record that, when they got to a certain stage in their march out of La Gleize, McCown simply walked off and Peiper went in another direction with his some 600 men. I have no faith—and I am glad to say at this time I didn't have one bit of faith in the testimony as given by the then Major McCown.[74]

In fact, McCown had explained in some detail how he had managed to escape into the surrounding woods during the confusion of a firefight between Peiper's column and an American outpost. But Rosenfeld's sensitivity and highly subjective reaction to McCown's testimony over three years after it had been given did not suggest a man likely to have always responded objectively to the events unfolding in the Dachau courtroom during the spring and summer of 1946.

More than any other aspect of the Malmédy case, the senators were interested in the subject of physical brutality. German witnesses questioned during the subcommittee's brief European trip were unanimous in insisting on the reality of physical duress. The attorneys Leer and Aschenauer professed to have been convinced by their clients that violence had played a major role in the American interrogation procedure.[75] This seemed only partly to be confirmed by the testimony of former inmates of Schwäbisch Hall. One, an ex-defendant and former adjutant of one of Peiper's battalions, did not himself claim to have been subjected to physical violence during interrogation. But he testified to having undergone a "softening-up" procedure over a two-week period which ultimately led to his signing an incriminating statement. He had been prevented from sleeping by guards who had turned on the lights in his cell "every five or ten minutes" and then interrogated for "six or eight hours" at a stretch. On one occasion, he claimed, he had been confronted by a haggard

74. MMIH, p. 1429.
75. *Ibid.*, pp. 1432-68.

comrade and told by Perl that unless he attested to the existence of superior orders encouraging the shooting of prisoners of war, his comrade would be summarily executed. He, himself, had been threatened with "secret liquidation." Ultimately, the witness informed subcommittee staffer Chambers, he could tolerate no more and informed Perl that he was willing to sign a statement dictated to him. Chambers was sufficiently impressed by this testimony as to compliment the witness on having spoken "frankly and fully."[76]

Other witnesses were less convincing. A former suspect against whom charges had not been brought claimed to have been subjected to brutalities including kicks to a wounded leg, beating, and partial strangulation as well as threats of death. Yet, while he testified to having informed defense counsel of these occurrences, the evidence, in fact, had not been introduced in court.[77] Another witness, who told a hair-raising tale of matches having been driven under his fingernails, stabbings, and hangings, proved, by his own admission, to be an habitual although resourceful liar.[78]

The German phase of the investigation led ultimately to Landsberg, where the fifty-nine remaining Malmédy convicts had completed their third year of imprisonment. Six still wore the red jackets of prisoners under sentence of death. Only Senator Hunt made the trip to the old fortress prison and ventured nothing more than the most superficial questioning of eight prisoners. Hunt was primarily interested in claims of physical violence employed in interrogation, heard some testimony to that effect, and clearly disbelieved it.[79]

Even as Hunt undertook his brief and trivial effort, the most serious attempt yet to determine whether or not the prisoners had been beaten was in progress. During the first ten days of September, an American team of two physicians and one dentist made a careful physical examination of all fifty-nine remaining prisoners. But the results were inconclu-

76. *Ibid.*, pp. 1469-99.   77. *Ibid.*, pp. 1508-10.
78. *Ibid.*, pp. 1513-23.   79. *Ibid.*, pp. 1630-39.

sive. Forty-eight of the prisoners contended that they had been beaten in the prison at Schwäbisch Hall, but only eleven asserted that they still bore physical evidence of that maltreatment in the form of scars and missing teeth. Of these, the examiners found ten instances of trauma which might have been produced by beatings of the sort alleged, although it was possible to speak with certainty only of effect and not of cause. None of these traumas was incapacitating and on that basis and in view of the fact that physical signs of abuse could be produced by only a small fraction of the prisoners, the examiners concluded that the evidence of maltreatment was "relatively minimal." Indeed it was, but it must be recalled that the examinations took place over three years after the alleged instances of abuse and that while some wounds inflicted at the time might have left permanent scars, lesser although still painful injuries could have healed without a trace. Yet, the examiners could report only on what they had seen and did so honestly.[80]

Baldwin's subcommittee completed its charge under Senate Resolution 42 with a report completed on October 13, 1949. The report reflected the limitations in scope of the Senate inquiry as well as the prejudices of the subcommittee membership. On the basis of the medical examinations at Landsberg, the allegation that physical maltreatment had played a role in the securing of sworn statements was summarily rejected as being without foundation.[81] The issue of "tricks and ruses" was subjected to somewhat greater scrutiny. That mock trials had been employed, albeit in a handful of cases, could not be denied and was condemned in the report, less, however, as an illegitimate stratagem than as an unnecessary complication of the investigative process which could be misinterpreted or misrepresented by critics.[82] Some

80. See "Summary Report on the Medical Examination of the Malmedy Prisoners," *ibid.*, pp. 1616-18.
81. *Malmedy Massacre Investigation. Report of Subcommittee on Armed Services, United States Senate* (Washington, 1949), p. 16.
82. *Ibid.*, pp. 7-8.

interesting and significant presuppositions lay behind this and other assessments by the subcommittee of investigative methods employed in 1945 to 1946. The German defendants, in the subcommittee's view, had been in some sense abnormal human beings, a condition that had both necessitated and, by implication, justified interrogative techniques the legitimacy of which, under other circumstances, might have been questionable. For example, the senators conceded that the threat of ration cards being withheld from families on the outside had, on occasion, been used against suspects; they could scarcely have done otherwise in that one of the interrogators questioned by the subcommittee had testified to the use of that tactic. Astoundingly, the subcommittee report did not condemn the use of so cruelly coercive a stratagem but merely expressed doubt that such threats could have had much effect on the "type of individual under interrogation."[83] In general, the subcommittee found little fault with the investigative methods employed at Schwäbisch Hall; the subjects, after all, had been "hardened, experienced members of the SS who had been through many campaigns and were used to worse procedure."[84] That facile but illogical rationalization reflected the approach that the subcommittee had taken toward the Malmédy affair since April.

Beyond expressing the vague opinion that the investigation would have been "better handled" if personnel trained for such work had been available to conduct it and noting that the use of interrogators who were not native born Americans had aggravated the "natural resentment that exists within a conquered country" (which was hardly the point), the subcommittee found little grounds for substantive criticism.[85] And since it had found little about the investigation and trial to condemn, the subcommittee naturally looked askance at those who had reached different conclusions. Mention of McCarthy's name was scrupulously avoided, and it was some-

83. *Ibid.*, pp. 17-18. 84. *Ibid.*, p. 19.
85. *Ibid.*, p. 32.

what condescendingly conceded that defense counsel and clergy in their continued efforts on behalf of the Malmédy convicts were only doing their professional and spiritual duty;[86] but the subcommittee hinted darkly (and without evidence) at the long arm of the Kremlin manipulating the controversy to discredit American occupation policies and to harness German nationalism to its nefarious purposes.[87] That, one cannot forbear to observe, is deliciously ironic in view of the use to which McCarthy was soon to put the "Communist menace" and the frequency with which he would affix the brand of Communist dupe to others.

The Senate investigation of the Malmédy Massacre trial had been sound and fury signifying, if not quite nothing, then certainly very little. In spite of the indulgent tone in which the subcommittee rendered its judgments on the investigation and trial, critics had not been stilled, and, if anything, the Senate inquiry lent additional currency to the doubts of these critics. It had been in late March and early April 1949 that General Clay had announced the commutation of six of the remaining twelve death sentences to life imprisonment, justifying his action with a tortured logic that reflected the contradictory evidence as well as the political pressures surrounding the case. In explaining the commutation of the sentence of a former SS-Hauptscharführer (master sergeant) of the First SS Panzer Regiment found guilty of shooting American prisoners at Ligneauville, Clay observed that the bulk of the evidence on which the prisoner had been convicted consisted of sworn statements later repudiated as having been made under duress. These were obviously claims made in self-interest, but, as Clay was forced to concede, the Simpson Commission and the Administration of Justice Review Board reports had afforded general support to such claims. It is odd, therefore, that Clay should have stoutly maintained his belief in the guilt of the prisoner but in the

86. *Ibid.*
87. *Ibid.*, p. 33.

light of that confidence, odder still that he should have commuted his sentence.[88] Essentially the same bewildering argument accompanied announcement of the five other commutations. Little distinguished these cases from the remaining six (including Peiper's) in which Clay confirmed the death sentences except that in the latter the proportion of unrepudiated to repudiated testimony was more even.[89]

While the Senate subcommittee had been conducting its hearings, a fundamental change had taken place in the status of the western zones of Germany. In May, the German "Basic Law" was approved by the Western Allies as the legal foundation for a German Federal Republic. This was not yet full sovereignty. Military government came to an end, but the occupying powers reserved for themselves broad areas of authority, including continued custody of convicted war criminals.[90] Yet, a new day was clearly dawning, and the constraints upon criticism of the occupying powers which had existed under military government were relaxed.

While attorneys such as Eugen Leer continued to assemble exculpatory evidence in support of their clients, others, most notably the Munich lawyer and right-wing political activist Rudolf Aschenauer carried on the campaign against the Malmédy judgments on a broader front. As executive secretary of a "Prisoners' Aid Society" with links to both the Roman Catholic and Evangelical Churches in Bavaria, Aschenauer published attacks on Allied war crimes trials in general and the Malmédy trial in particular. These were translated into English and distributed by the Washington-based National Council for the Prevention of War.[91] Somewhat later Dietrich Ziemssen, former chief of staff of the First SS Panzer Division

88. Attachment to letter of Royall to Truman, March 22, 1949, TP.

89. *Ibid.*; attachment to letter of Royall to Truman of March 25, 1949, TP; Clay press releases of March 17–April 8, 1949, in MMIH, pp. 1602-15.

90. Alfred Grosser, *Germany in Our Time. A Political History of the Postwar Years*, trans. Paul Stephenson (New York, 1971), pp. 71-74.

91. See Leer's "Statement to the Report of the Commander-in-Chief General Lucius D. Clay to the Army Department from 8 April 1949, EUCOM Release No. 197," October 14, 1949, EP; Dr. Rudolf Aschenauer, *Review of the War Crimes Trials?* (Nuernberg, 1950), and Aschenauer's *Truth or "Clever Strategy" in the*

and defense witness at the Malmédy trial, entered the fray with a pamphlet which, in execrable translation, found its way into right-wing book stores in the United States.[92] As a member of the "Committee for the Preservation of Rights of the Sentenced in the Malmédy Case," Ziemmsen aided in the distribution in the United States of yet another of Aschenauer's works, a sixteen page pamphlet entitled *Seven Years After the Malmédy Trial* which strongly made an argument hinted at in early literature: that the Malmédy affair had injured American prestige in Germany, a factor which, Ziemssen noted, should be of concern to Americans "interested in winning Germany's World War II Generation over to the American Side." American readers were treated to versified propaganda of lamentable crudity:

> Statesmanship and Common Sense—
> Wanted on your side of fence—
>
> Will result in many friends—
> On the German Side of fence—
>
> If the Diplomats can't act
> Should not CONGRESS know the fact:
>
> THE MALMÉDY CASE NEEDS YOUR ATTENTION!

And on the same level:

> Get those Germans out of jail!
> Let revenge of Haters fail!
> Justice be your strategy.
> Solve the Case of Malmédy![93]

Mass circulation newspapers focused on the Malmédy trial, both reflecting interest among the German public in the case and stimulating it. In January and February 1951, the Hamburg weekly tabloid *Die Strasse* (The Street) ran a series of articles entitled "Gerechtigkeit für die Rotjacken" (Justice for

---

Case of Malmedy? (Nuernberg, 1950); press release of National Council for Prevention of War, June 11, 1950, EP.

92. Dietrich Ziemssen, *The Malmedy Trial* (Munich, 1952).

93. Dr. Rudolf Aschenauer, *Seven Years After the Malmedy Trial. An Unsolved Problem Endangering U.S. Prestige in Europe* (Miesbach, 1953), pp. 1, 13.

the Red Jackets) which combined the most extreme of the accusations leveled against the American investigators with
heart-wrenching photographs of Peiper's wife and three
blond children. "Millions Intercede for Peiper" began one
installment in the series.[94] Peiper and his fellow prisoners
became folk heroes. Absolved of all wrongdoing in the minds
of most Germans, they were viewed as brave soldiers victimized by circumstance and the vengeful wrath of the conquer-
ors. Through no culpability of their own, they were nevertheless being made to suffer. This goes far toward explaining intense public interest in their plight, for in a somewhat more
attenuated sense, many Germans viewed themselves, surrounded by material hardship and the opprobrium of much
of the rest of the world, as in the same situation. *Die Strasse's*
series produced an avalanche of reader response, of which the
following excerpt of a letter from a reader in Dieringhausen is
typical:

> . . . If Eisenhower wants German soldiers, he should first re-
> spond as a soldier and human being to the Landsberg case, for
> Peiper and his men are our comrades. If the noose should be put
> around their necks, hate would be sown, and [the] words "grass
> grows over battlefields but never over gallows" would become
> the watchword for those whom the Western Powers want to
> make their hirelings.[95]

In a similar vein wrote a reader from Detmold: "We have a
great need of personalities like Colonel Peiper at the present
time, and no Allied powers should demand of us participation in a plan of defense while such an injustice exists."[96]

Letters such as these reflected an issue of increasing sensitivity to the United States government. Although there had
been almost universal agreement among the Allies during
and immediately after the war that Germany should be per-
manently disarmed, that resolve was now fast crumbling.

94. *Die Strasse,* February 4, 1951, p. 9, and January 28, 1951, p. 1.
95. *Die Strasse,* February 4, 1951, p. 13.
96. *Ibid.*

Cold war had become hot in Korea, and the former Allies, with the exception of France, were coming rapidly to accept the idea of a rearmed Federal Republic as ally. Not surprisingly, in view of its preponderant share of the burden of defending the "Free World," the United States was most anxious that the Federal Republic should eventually contribute her substantial military potential to Western defense. But there was little popular enthusiasm for rearmament in the Republic.[97] That condition, to be sure, was rooted in factors that transcended the Malmédy case, but the prisoners of Landsberg, especially those under sentence of death, unquestionably stood as an issue complicating an already tense political situation.

It could not have escaped the attention of the Office of the U.S. High Commissioner and the U.S. Army in Germany that Willis M. Everett, Jr. had become a figure widely admired among the German people. To some Germans, he had come to represent the good and genuine American as opposed to the vengeful "new" Americans increasingly seen as the authors of the Malmédy injustice, a contrast that sometimes only thinly concealed anti-Semitic feelings.[98] The fate of the Malmédy convicts was out of Everett's hands, but continuing doubts concerning the case, which the Senate investigation had failed to resolve, coupled with the political flammability of the affair in a country seen increasingly as ally rather than conquered enemy, resulted in far more courteous responses to Everett's ceaseless inquiries. With the end of military government had come the establishment of a European Command War Crimes Modification Board headquartered, along with the U.S. Army in Europe, in Heidelberg.[99] The board worked closely with the office of the Judge Advocate, European Command, in an ongoing review of war crimes cases. That the

97. Grosser, *Germany*, pp. 221-27.

98. "Gott Sei Dank," *Die Strasse*, February 11, 1951, p. 13; see reference to the "showtrial of the avenging angels" in *Die Strasse*, January 21, 1951, p. 8.

99. Office of the U.S. High Commissioner for Germany, *6th Quarterly Report on Germany*, p. 50.

wind now blew from quite a different direction was clearly indicated by a letter dated January 23, 1951, from the Chief, War Crimes Section, JAGD, Lt. Col. T. L. Borom, to Everett. With the bonhomie of one deep southerner far from home addressing another, Borom informed Everett that approximately 80 percent of the cases now reviewed were being recommended by him for remission or drastic reduction and that, in most cases, these recommendations were being followed by the board. The Malmédy death sentences had been under review since the previous fall, and Borom looked forward to an early decision with optimism.[100]

Borom's optimism was not misplaced. Eight days later Gen. Thomas T. Handy, Commander-in-Chief, European Command, announced in Heidelberg the extension of clemency to eleven German prisoners under death sentence in Landsberg Prison, among them the six remaining Malmédy condemned. Their sentences were now commuted to life imprisonment. But Handy scrupulously avoided any suggestion that commutation was the result of doubtful guilt or questionable investigative or trial procedures. All were declared to have been proven guilty of the crimes of which they had been accused, with Peiper singled out as bearer of the greatest share of responsibility. Why then commutation? Handy was forthright in admitting that he had been deluged with petitions for clemency, but he could hardly justify altering the decision of a U.S. Military Government court on the grounds that many Germans had disagreed with it. Rather, Handy alluded to the fact that the killings had taken place in a fluid and confused combat situation in which Germany was desperately attempting to turn the tide of war.[101] In effect, the U.S. Army advanced the argument of military necessity as a mitigating factor in a case involving the murder of its own men.

Understandably, Handy's decision produced jubilation

100. Borom to Everett, January 23, 1951, EP.
101. "Text of Headquarters European Command Press Release 31 January 1951," EP.

within the camp of Malmédy critics and convicts. In rare good humor, Peiper wrote to Everett:

We have received a great victory and next to God it is you [from] whom our blessings flow. In all the long and dark years you have been the beacon flame for the forlorn souls of the Malmédy boys, the voice and the conscience of the good America, and yours is the present success against all the well known overwhelming odds. May I therefore, Colonel, express the everlasting gratitude of the red-jacket team (retired) as well as of all the families concerned.[102]

Satisfaction over the commutations was far from universal. A resolution was introduced before the House of Representatives calling for an investigation of Handy's revision of the Malmédy death sentences. Post No. 1544, Veterans of Foreign Wars of Milford, Massachusetts, adopted a motion urging the removal of High Commissioner John J. McCloy. With unconscious irony, a New York couple wrote to President Truman condemning the commutations and, in the same letter, decrying the bias of Southern courts in the trial of blacks.[103] The *New York Times* conceded the possibility of a difference between Peiper and "those cold-blooded brutes who experimented on the helpless bodies of human beings in the concentration camps," but found the commutations a "compromise between justice and expediency."[104] The *Times* was correct but neglected to note that justice had also compromised with expediency in 1945 and 1946.

But these reactions were now largely irrelevant. Peiper's high spirits had been based not only on the certain knowledge that he would not face the gallows but also on the realization that powerful currents were flowing which would ultimately set him and his comrades free. Among those who had criticized

102. Peiper to Everett, February 6, 1951, EP.
103. William D. Hassett, Secretary to the President, to the Acting Secretary of State, February 27, 1951, TP; Richard and Sophie Berliner to Truman, February 18, 1951, TP.
104. "Compromise at Frankfurt," *New York Times,* February 2, 1951, p. 22.

General Handy's revision, but in a different sense, were politically influential Germans. Dr. Carlo Schmid, Social Democratic professor who had played an important role in the formation of the West German state, expressed regret that Handy had not gone farther in his review of the Malmédy case. Dr. Gerhard Seelos, deputy of the Bavarian Party, waxed indignant over the general's assurance that the guilt of the Malmédy convicts had been proven beyond doubt.[105] As the Federal Republic of Germany moved closer to full sovereignty and partnership in the European Defense Community, the ability of Germans to determine the fate of convicted German war criminals increased and ultimately became decisive. Following the termination of the High Commissions for Germany, actual custody of the prisoners passed into German hands while power of review and recommendation was vested in a mixed board composed of three Germans and one representative each from the United States, the United Kingdom, and France. The Board, while forbidden to challenge the guilt of prisoners, was empowered to make recommendations for clemency and parole.[106] In 1954, Peiper's life sentence was reduced to thirty-five years. By the summer of 1956, only three Malmédy prisoners remained in Landsberg. Sepp Dietrich had been released on parole the previous year, to the accompaniment of cries of outrage from American veterans groups. Finally, shortly before Christmas 1956, Jochen Peiper, the last Malmédy prisoner, walked free from Landsberg Prison.[107]

105. *New York Times,* February 1, 1951, pp. 1, 7.
106. Office of the U.S. High Commissioner for Germany, *Report on Germany* (September 21, 1949–July 31, 1952), pp. 102, 104.
107. "List of Evidence Submitted in the Case of Accused No. 42, Peiper, Joachim, Ex-Colonel," p. 1, EP; "Briefly Noted," *The American Legion Magazine,* January 1956, p. 31; "1946 Dachau-Landsberg 1956" (leaflet signed Dietrich Ziemssen, Brackenheim), EP; "Pech für ihn," *Der Spiegel,* July 19, 1976, p. 57.

IX. HINDSIGHT AND HISTORY

As a legal process and as a political cause célèbre, the Malmédy case ended in 1956. It has survived as an historical problem, prodded occasionally by popular writers but never confronted seriously. What actually took place at the crossroads and why did it occur? How credible are the claims of other atrocities committed during those chaotic and terrifying December days? What transpired behind the walls of the prison at Schwäbisch Hall, and how closely did the Dachau trial approach the ideal of justice?

Let us begin with the crossroads killings, the Malmédy Massacre in strict definition. More than seventy bodies were recovered, photographed, and autopsied. No weapons were found with the corpses, and some bodies had been frozen with arms raised in the universally recognized attitude of surrender. These had been prisoners of war and no one, including the German convicts and their supporters, has ever sought to claim otherwise. Had the American prisoners of war, or some of them, attempted to escape thereby prompting their German guards to open fire? Survivors testified that there had been no such attempt. The escape scenario was suggested years later by some German critics of the trial and hinted at by van Roden during the Senate hearings, but the most that can be said in its support is that some testimony by survivors is not inconsistent with the possibility that Germans at the crossroads might have mistakenly believed that an escape attempt was taking place. There was considerable "shifting and jostling" among the prisoners before the shooting began. Although Virgil Lary testified that the order "Stand fast!" had been shouted after the first prisoner had been shot by a pistol-wielding German, another survivor recalled that the command had come *before* the shot was fired.[1] Conceivably, the shout could have caused a nervous young SS trooper to fire his pistol, resulting in panic in the American ranks and the opening of massed automatic-weapons fire by the Germans. But this scenario is difficult to reconcile with certain facts. Several armored vehicles had been assembled along the road with their guns trained on the prisoners. It seems unlikely that potential firepower of that magnitude would have been gathered unless it had been decided to shoot the Americans. But the most telling circumstance militating against the escape hypothesis is that none of the defendants or the defense witnesses attempted to argue that the prisoners had been shot while trying to escape. That it occurred to no one indicates its remoteness from the actual events.

Could the Americans assembled at the crossroads have been mistaken for combatants? That, too, was alleged by German critics of the trial long after the fact and circulated in the United States by the right-wing writer Freda Utley.[2] According to this scenario, the prisoners, after having surrendered, were left unguarded in the pasture, were mistaken for combatants by succeeding elements of Kampfgruppe Peiper roaring down the road, and were taken under fire. This is even less likely than the

1. See Chapter V; MMIH, p. 1032. Five years before his death, Peiper suggested the following scenario for the crossroads killings: An SPW and a Panther had both halted at the crossroads for repairs shortly after the American prisoners had been assembled in the adjacent field. The crews of the disabled vehicles constituted the primary overseers of the prisoners. These Germans were most concerned with restoring their vehicles to road-worthiness and were increasingly fearful of being left behind in enemy territory. One German fired into the group of prisoners with his pistol. Why, Peiper did not know but opined that he might have detected movement among some of the prisoners which he interpreted as an escape attempt. Panic broke out among the Americans, the frightened Germans opened fire with the machine guns of their armored vehicles. While not an impossibility, this scenario is difficult to reconcile with eyewitness evidence. Peiper, "Kommentar," pp. 5-7.

2. *Die Strasse,* January 21, 1951, p. 8; Freda Utley, "Malmedy and McCarthy," *The American Mercury,* November 1954, p. 57.

"escape scenario." To be sure, Peiper spoke vaguely at the trial of having been informed on December 18, 1944, one day after the crossroads killings, that a "mix-up" had taken place the day before. But none of the eye-witnesses, either American or German, reported anything remotely resembling such a "mix-up." The American survivors testified unequivocally that the German fire had come from armored vehicles *parked* along the road, not traveling upon it; and it is clear, further, that at no time were the prisoners unguarded. The range at which the shooting had taken place, moreover, was short—so short that the prisoners could not have been mistaken for combatants. The "mix-up scenario" only becomes remotely credible when applied to the later raking by passing German vehicles of the bodies, living and dead, lying in the pasture. But neither allegation of attempted escape or mix-up, even if true, could excuse the fact that subsequent to the mowing-down of the prisoners, groups of SS troopers walked through the field shooting those Americans showing signs of life.

It appears certain, then, that the crossroads killings were, collectively, a deliberate violation of the "laws and usages of war." Why had the violation taken place and who was responsible for having initiated it? According to the prosecution argument, none other than Adolf Hitler stood behind the Malmédy Massacre. In his addresses to his commanders at Bad Nauheim, Hitler had, supposedly, called upon them to shed all humane inhibitions and to spread before their advancing forces a "wave of fright and terror." The essence of Hitler's wishes was reflected in orders issued to units in the field which included the specific requirement that prisoners of war be shot where the prevailing combat situation seemed to require it. There is absolutely no documentary evidence to support this facet of the prosecution case. Only a fragment of Hitler's Bad Nauheim speech survives, and it contains no language remotely similar to that alleged by the prosecution.[3]

3. *Hitlers Lagebesprechungen: Die Protokollfragmente seiner militärischen Konferenzen, 1942-45,* ed. Helmut Heiber (Stuttgart, 1962), pp. 713-24.

No copies of lower-level orders encouraging the shooting of prisoners of war could be introduced into evidence, nor have they since been uncovered. The prosecution's star witness on this point testified only that the regimental order urged that no "mercy" or "mildness" be shown the enemy, qualities seldom characteristic of modern mechanized warfare. Long before the Bad Nauheim speech, orders in great profusion had been drafted stressing the necessity for speed and the need to find capable commanders to lead the advance units to the Meuse, daring commanders (such as Peiper) who had to be impressed with the decisive significance of their assignments. But there was no overt suggestion that prisoners were to be shot.[4] It is conceivable that, if such orders had been issued, copies thereof might have been subsequently destroyed—conceivable, but doubtful that not a single copy of the order would have survived. Perhaps the order was transmitted only verbally? The prosecution did not make that assertion except in the context of the pre-attack "pep talks" given at the very lowest unit levels. The evidence for this was ambiguous. A prosecution witness testified that his company commander had issued verbal orders to take no prisoners. Under cross-examination, the witness explained that the order was understood to mean that surrendered Americans were to be left behind to be picked up by following infantry units.[5] If clear orders to shoot prisoners were given, we would have to conclude that the order was one of the most widely flouted in the history of the German military, for thousands of American soldiers were captured during the Battle of the Bulge and survived the experience. The purely morale-directed Order of the Day drafted by the Commander-in-Chief West, Field Marshal Gerd von Rundstedt, read simply:

> Soldiers of the Western Front! Your great hour has struck! Powerful attack armies are today moving against the Anglo-

4. See Jodl to OB West, November 25, 1944, T–311/18/7020392-97.
5. U.S. v. Bersin, 153/1/000292-99 (279-86).

Americans. More I need not say to you. You all sense it. *Everything hinges on this (Es geht ums Ganze)*! Carry within you the holy obligation to give everything and to perform superhumanly for our Fatherland and our Führer.[6]

But, it could be argued, the SS units involved in the offensive might have been given special orders not issued to army contingents or, alternatively, those SS units might have interpreted the concept of superhuman performance in a particularly sinister way. Perhaps. But the same objections noted above would have to be raised. No copies of such an order have survived (and it should be observed that far more damning documents related to SS atrocities have come down to us in substantial quantities). If verbally transmitted or tacitly understood, it was poorly obeyed. Kampfgruppe Peiper took and sent to the rear many prisoners in addition to those held and released in La Gleize where, it could be persuasively advanced, the close proximity of the encircling American troops would have strongly discouraged the killing of prisoners.

Did not the prosecution assert only that orders existed to the effect that prisoners should be shot where the existing military situation required it? True, but if literally interpreted, such orders would have had little meaning. The question of whether or not to take prisoners would then have been simply left to the discretion of the local commander where, in practice, it has always been in combat situations. Facts and common sense therefore render unlikely the existence of the murderous orders attested to in many of the sworn statements, although they do not exclude the possibility of unlawful verbal directives by junior officers.

One passage of a sworn statement bearing on this issue has the clear ring of truth. In his statement of March 11, 1946, Peiper, in describing the December 14 conference with his immediate subordinates, declared, "At this meeting, I did not mention anything [to the effect] that prisoners of war

6. *Entwurf* (n.d.), T–311/18/7020616.

should be shot when local conditions of combat should so require it because all those present were experienced officers to whom this was obvious."[7] It certainly would have been obvious to Waffen-SS officers, schooled in the ideal of *Härte*, veterans of combat on the Eastern Front, and impressed with the critical nature of their objective, that prisoners could be sacrificed to operational requirements. Certainty concerning the events at the crossroads will never be achieved, but it is likely that the story told repeatedly to American investigators in the early stages of the Malmédy probe (and disbelieved by the Americans) was true. The commander of the "point" elements, SS-Sturmbannführer Walther Pringel, was a commander who had passed most of his adult life in the SS, had attended Junkerschule Braunschweig, was *gottgläubig*, and a Party member.[8] Clearly, Pringel was a Waffen-SS "core type." His brand of leadership was to be demonstrated on the morning of December 19, 1944, at Stoumont, when Pringel would threaten with destruction any of his battalion's tanks (and their crews) which retreated so much as a meter. That this was the kind of spirit esteemed in the Waffen-SS is reflected by the fact that the incident was featured prominently in the recommendation for the award of the Oak Leaves to the Knight's Cross which Peiper subsequently wrote for Pringel (he received them).[9] It is reasonable to conjecture that on that December afternoon at the crossroads Pringel concluded that one hundred or so American prisoners were too many to be conveniently dealt with by a unit needing every ounce of manpower and second of time to attain its objectives. To detach sufficient men to guard them would be awkward for a unit already weak in infantry. To leave them without guard would be dangerous. They might rearm themselves and, taking cover in the nearby woods, cause considerable difficulty for the Kampfgruppe's vehicles as they passed

7. U.S. v. Bersin, 153/1/000169 (164).
8. "Lebenslauf," BDC/MDF.
9. "Vorschlag Nr. 42 für die Verleihung des Eichenlaubes zum Ritterkreuz des Eisernenkreuzes," p. 2, BDC.

along the road. Taking them along was an obvious impossibility. Therefore, they were shot; even then the Germans'
haste was so great that a sloppy job was made of it, for a good
many of the Americans survived. Peiper was near the point
and could have had a part in the decision to shoot the prisoners but probably did not. He denied having had any knowledge of the killings until the following day and was probably
telling the truth, for Peiper was remarkably forthright in admitting his role in other incidents detrimental to his image
during the trial. The crossroads killings were the product of a
set of military circumstances which would have created strong
pressures for the shooting of prisoners in any army. Troops of
the Waffen-SS in December 1944, given their combat traditions and the attitudinal bent of their young company and
field-grade officers, were not likely to have resisted those
pressures very vigorously.

An intriguing possibility is suggested by the testimony of
Virgil Lary and Kenneth Kingston, two of the massacre survivors. As the group of prisoners of which the two men were a
part marched toward the crossroads pasture, they were approached by a German officer who declared that he needed
drivers for the abandoned American vehicles. This could well
have been Pringel, who spoke English[10] and who might have
been planning to load the Americans into their own trucks
and send them back toward German lines as was done in
other instances. The Americans ignored him, which could
have contributed to the criminal decision to shoot the pris-
soners. Pringel was killed in Hungary in 1945 and could not
be examined on his role in the massacre.

When we turn to the many other murders alleged by the
prosecution, it is much more difficult to make informed con-
jectures since, in many cases, no evidence beyond the questionable sworn statements was available. Almost without exception, no bodies could be connected with the alleged

10. U.S. v. Bersin, 152/1/000425-26, 000460 (412-13, 447); "Personalangaben," p. 2, BDC.

crimes. They might have existed, only to have been swept up as part of the grisly detritus of battle, without having been associated with the march of Kampfgruppe Peiper. That is a possibility; it is not evidence.

There is, of course, some evidence beyond the sworn statements pointing to the shooting of prisoners of war at locales other than the crossroads. A German prosecution witness and an American survivor both testified to incidents in which small groups of Americans were shot down by machine-gun fire from a tank after having apparently been invited to surrender. These incidents may be one and the same, although one witness placed it in Büllingen and the other in Honsfeld.[11] Other evidence independent of the sworn statements is either of questionable reliability or in that indistinct area between clearly legitimate acts of war and obvious criminality which unavoidably exists in the confusion, rage, and terror of combat. An American private whose experience was used as evidence against the Malmédy defendants described an incident (probably in Honsfeld) in which he and approximately twenty other men found themselves in a house surrounded by SS troopers. A dozen Americans attempted to surrender and marched out of the house under a white flag. They were cut down by German fire. An SS man then entered the house, apparently ascertained that the remaining Americans were offering no resistance and called to his comrades outside to cease their fire. The Americans were then taken from the house, added to a batch of two hundred or so other captured GIs and marched to the rear.[12] Regrettable scenes such as this were probably repeated thousands of times on all sides during World War II and are difficult to accept as clear evidence of criminal intent. The testimony of two German prosecution witnesses pointed toward the cold-blooded killing of six to ten American prisoners of war outside Stavelot. But neither witness had seen them killed or had viewed

11. U.S. v. Bersin, 153/1/000934-35, 000977-79 (907-08, 950-52).
12. *Ibid.*, 000918-22 (891-95).

the bodies. One had watched them being marched off and had then heard bursts of machine-pistol fire. Another had later heard from a comrade that they had been killed.[13] Other acts of criminal brutality rest on firmer ground. That the frozen and starved American prisoner was given a "mercy" death at Petit Thier is very likely. Substantial evidence points to the murder of a shot-down American pilot in the woods near Büllingen. Several defendants, it will be recalled, had admitted specific crimes in their final pleas following conviction. These included the shooting of an American jeep driver at Cheneux (after he had collided with a German SPW), the shooting of an American on the La Gleize-Stoumont Road (ostensibly on Peiper's orders), and the killing of Belgian civilians at Wanne. The fact remains, however, that the prosecution had evidence outside the sworn statements for only a handful of the hundreds of murders of prisoners, other than the crossroads group, which it claimed itself able to prove, and some of that evidence was diaphanous. Nowhere had the prosecution fallen so far short of demonstrating wrongdoing than at La Gleize, where it had been alleged that 175 to 311 prisoners of war had been murdered. The defense had been able to offer substantial evidence that American prisoners held in that town had been well treated while, beyond the sworn statements, the prosecution could present little more than misapplied accounts of corpses gathered at the crossroads. Colonel Ellis has since admitted uncertainty concerning this aspect of the prosecution case.[14]

Besides the killing of American prisoners of war, the Malmédy defendants had been accused and found guilty of the murder of unarmed Belgian civilians. Here, a somewhat higher proportion of the prosecution evidence was independent of the controversial sworn statements. More than half a dozen Belgian witnesses gave testimony confirming that

13. *Ibid.*, 001067-76, 001084-93 (1036-45, 1053-62).
14. Interview with Burton F. Ellis, May 15, 1976.

troops of Kampfgruppe Peiper had shot some Belgian civilians (the prosecution claimed approximately ninety), most in and around Stavelot. A list of ninety-three civilians, some of them young children, all supposedly killed by SS troops, was compiled in cooperation with the Red Cross of Stavelot and presented in evidence.[15] But, while witnesses had claimed to have observed the killing of some of these civilians by SS troops, it is by no means certain that all had met their deaths in that way. By the testimony of one of the prosecution's own witnesses, the Belgian Maquis had been active in the area. Peiper had claimed to have seen civilians firing on the troops. Conceivably, therefore, some of the civilians might have been legitimately killed in combat. Through their inculcation with the doctrine of *Härte* and their bitter experiences on the Eastern Front, many of Peiper's troops were primed to react ruthlessly to the slightest signs of civilian resistance. Belgian civilians were certainly killed, some murdered in cold blood, some perhaps killed as the result of having engaged in combat. The proportions of the two categories of victims cannot be established with any assurance nor can the total number actually killed by Peiper's men. Some Belgian civilians had been killed accidently during the heavy fighting of late December 1944 and could easily have been included in the totals imputed to SS frightfulness.

That Kampfgruppe Peiper killed prisoners of war and Belgian civilians is therefore established by evidence other than confessions. The circumstances under which the killings took place are often unclear. Numbers are problematical; the prosecution itself spoke in very uncertain numerical terms. It was the critical function of the sworn statements or confessions secured from the defendants to demonstrate the criminal nature of the killings and to identify individual perpetrators. The character of the sworn statements was the crux of the Malmédy case as it unfolded in the Dachau courtroom

15. Exhibit P-85, U.S. v. Bersin, Exhibits, 153/6/000004-10.

in 1946. It was the prime focus of post-trial criticism of the army's handling of the Malmédy case. It is also of central concern to the historian in his effort at dispassionate judgment of the Malmédy affair.

Extreme positions of the opposing sides in the Malmédy controversy must be rejected. The sworn statements, in general, were neither purely voluntary "uninfluenced by force, threats, duress or promises of any kind," as the prosecution maintained, nor were they the products of torture and "Gestapo tactics" as asserted by the trial's most vigorous critics. Truth, as it usually does, lies somewhere between the claims of partisanship; in some sense, it also lies beyond them.

Had the prisoners been beaten as part of the interrogation process? On this question, there are strong mutually contradictory claims. The interrogation/prosecution team vigorously denied it; many of the convicts claimed that they had been thus abused. Both parties would have had good reason to lie: the interrogators, to cover up the beatings if they had actually taken place; the convicts, to attempt to neutralize damning confessions. Obviously, the stakes were higher for the latter. Many Germans other than the convicts claimed knowledge of brutal interrogation methods. Their motives for lying, if lie they did, are less clear. The convicts would have had nothing to lose by lying, but what would others have had to gain? It is conceivable that some former SS men might have lied out of a sense of loyalty to their comrades languishing in prison and facing the gallows. Personal bonds forged in battle are exceedingly strong. Others might have been suborned to perjury by friends and relatives of the accused, right-wing political activists using appeals to patriotism and urging continued resistance to "the enemy." Much of this testimony was extremely flimsy and some of it was unquestionably false. But Americans also claimed to possess evidence of brutality, although this was primarily hearsay rather than direct observation. Nevertheless, one American present at Schwäbisch Hall said he had seen a prisoner crumpled on the floor of his cell and had been told by an interrogator that he had probably been "roughed up" during interrogation. Another testified to having seen a prisoner kneed in the groin while being questioned. Why should these Americans have lied? One may have had anti-Semitic feelings and was clearly antipathetic to a Jewish member of the interrogation staff, but when viewed against the background of widespread allegations of brutality, this testimony cannot be dismissed out of hand. The Malmédy convicts were given thorough medical examinations over three years after the alleged brutalities had been inflicted. The results were inconclusive. Obviously, they had not suffered serious permanent injury, but most of the brutalities alleged were not of a kind that would have produced long-term damage. One possible source of evidence which has heretofore been overlooked is the photographs of the defendants taken before and at the beginning of the trial for evidential and publicity purposes. These do not seem to be the faces of men subjected to serious physical abuse. One must finally conclude, therefore, that while there may have been isolated instances of physical violence in the interrogation procedure, there is insufficient evidence to support the conclusion that physical violence was employed by the American interrogation team as a matter of policy or that the sworn statements were the products of physical duress. It seems likely that violence, although still sporadic, came more frequently from the guards at the prison. These men were not under the control of the war crimes team and for a time included Polish refugees whose resentment of Germans in general and SS men in particular was understandably intense.[16] Thus, Peiper claimed to have been struck in the face while, with hood over his head, he waited in a corridor to be interrogated. Dietrich attested to having been kicked while being led to interrogation; others testified to random cruelties such as being pushed down flights of stairs.[17] These acts, and it is not unlikely that they occurred, had no direct

16. MMIH, p. 323.
17. *Ibid.*, pp. 1632-34; U.S. v. Bersin, 153/3/000114 (1893).

relevance to the interrogation procedure but might have contributed to a generalized atmosphere of intimidation surrounding it.

Many other forms of coercion were alleged, including inadequate food, threats of summary execution, interruption of sleep, deprivation of blankets, extremes of temperatures in cells, and threats against families. The first of these allegations can be ruled out. As their photographs indicate, the defendants had been adequately fed. On the other hand, it was admitted by a member of the interrogation team that at least one prisoner was told that ration cards would be withheld from his family if he were not cooperative. It is impossible to pass conclusive judgment on other allegations of duress. Some defendants claimed that such things happened. All members of the interrogation/prosecution staff denied them. It is not inconceivable that, in the course of hundreds of interrogations, dire threats might have been made. And in those few cases in which the "mock trial" approach was used, a confused and frightened prisoner might well have assumed, even if he had not been explicitly told, that his time of final judgment to be followed by swift punishment was at hand.

The American investigators admitted using psychological "ruses and stratagems" and were indeed proud of some of them. "Mock trials" were the most widely discussed of these, although employed in only a handful of cases. Prisoners were often led to believe that interrogators posessed information from other accused implicating them when, in fact, they did not. Occasionally, a recalcitrant subject would be confronted by another prisoner who would make accusations against him. In some instances, interrogators would pretend to grade answers given by subjects according to a system of plusses and minuses, the purpose apparently having been to create anxiety within the subject. "Stool pigeons" were occasionally introduced into prisoners' cells. Prisoners were generally kept in solitary confinement until they "confessed."[18] Most of

18. *Malmedy Massacre Investigation. Report of Subcommittee*, pp. 18-19.

these methods, in a time of cruder police techniques, were not unknown in domestic criminalogical work.

Reviews of the investigation and trial, including the Senate probe, limited themselves in evaluating the sworn statements to the narrow question of duress, with overwhelming attention lavished on a determination of the incidence of physical brutality. The implication of the final review—that conducted by the Senate— was clear. If it were concluded, as indeed it was, that physical abuse had been, at worst, infrequent, and if, with rare exceptions, "ruses and stratagems" employed had been similar to those often used in ordinary criminal investigation, then the sworn statements were authentic, the prosecution case overwhelming, and the verdicts just. That was an exceedingly superficial view. One of the few who recognized its limitations was Jochen Peiper. Peiper expressed an important insight on September 6, 1949, in the following exchange with Senator Hunt in Landsberg Prison:

Peiper: I believe that this investigation here that is based on marks and scars which are still to be seen resulting from treatment at Schwabisch Hall cannot settle the question why these violences made these so-called confessions and what happened at Malmedy Crossroads. I believe that the background is a psychological one and therefore I should be very thankful if you could spare a few minutes to give a clear account of this.

Senator Hunt: Our only object as set out in the preliminary statement is to check on actions of brutalities in Schwabisch Hall.

Peiper: Yes sir; but ill-treatment and ill-treatment has a difference. It is not necessary to treat a man with violence to get a confession from him, but to treat him with psychological tricks is for some men more effective. There are other possibilities especially after a complete break-down of a nation and a lost war. That is the story of Schwabisch Hall, the lost war and the hopeless situation of men who came from the front and who had been heroes of the country and who were now subject to Polish guards. Prisoners who had but one duty, that is to keep their face as former officers and to make the best of a bad business by their attitude and by covering their subordinates. That is the problem of Schwabisch Hall and not the beatings. Therefore, I wanted to point out that the looking for scars is not the problem. The problem is very different.

Senator Hunt: We understand that. This is one of the avenues we are using. We have volumes in our files on the other aspects.[19]

But did Hunt and his colleagues really understand? There is little evidence of it.

What Peiper was alluding to was the total experience which the Malmédy prisoners had undergone since May 1945 (in some cases, earlier, since a few had been captured during the Ardennes offensive). Captured, they had felt the despair and helplessness common to those who realize that their fate is beyond their personal control. This could only have been compounded by the knowledge that Germany had surrendered unconditionally, had ceased to exist, in fact, as a political entity. No hope of freedom through eventual German victory was supportable. Nor was this simply a matter of deprivation of physical freedom. The prisoners had been raised in a totalitarian society which had nurtured feelings of group omnipotence; they had been members of a rigidly disciplined segment of that totalitarian society which, in combination with the experience of comradeship in battle, had dominated their lives. Most of that collapsed with surrender and defeat. For a time, a remnant of the old relationship survived in prisoner-of-war camps and interrogation centers. Then came Schwäbisch Hall and solitary confinement.

To a human being enjoying freedom and normal human activity, the notion of confessing falsely to a hideous crime is alien. Yet, it is a phenomenon far from rare. During the witch crazes of the fifteenth through seventeenth centuries many innocent women confessed in great detail to dealings with the devil and described the characteristics of their imps and familiars down to names and feeding habits. This they did in the full knowledge that the consequences would likely

19. MMIH, p. 1637.

be death. More recently in the Soviet Union and other countries sharing the Communist brand of totalitarianism, we have witnessed men and women admitting to crimes having little if any basis in fact. Physical torture has sometimes been employed in extracting false confessions, but it is not a necessary component of the process, as Aleksandr Solzhenitsyn, who writes from personal experience, has most recently pointed out.[20]

William Walters Sargant, in his study of the psychology of religious conversion experiences and political "brain washing," provides insights that are directly applicable to the question of the Malmédy confessions. Prolonged anxiety and tension, he explains, can produce a state of mind in which the subject is highly vulnerable to suggestion and loses the ability to discriminate between reality and fiction. In that condition, the subject will not infrequently accept the picture of events presented over time by his examiner and "confess."[21] This is a phenomenon that can be created intentionally to elicit false confessions for purposes of political propaganda in totalitarian states. But it can also take place without the conscious desire of the interrogator. As an example, Sargant describes a notorious English murder case of 1950 in which a suspect confessed to having strangled his wife and daughter, later denied his confession but was nevertheless convicted and hanged. Evidence subsequently uncovered demonstrated the near certainty of his innocence. A study of police records in any modern society would reveal similar instances of false confession.[22] An important part of this phenomenon is the attitude of the examiner. He tends to suspect the guilt of the subject and often suggests to him hypothetical circumstances surrounding the crime. Not only may the fearful and confused suspect come to accept, at least temporarily, the reality

20. G. John Rogge, *Why Men Confess* (New York, 1971), pp. 55-56, 197; William W. Sargant, *Battle for the Mind* (New York, 1957), pp. 198-200; Aleksandr I. Solzhenitsyn, *The Gulag Archipelago, 1918–1956. An Experiment in Literary Investigation*, trans. Thomas P. Whitney (New York, 1973), p. 117.
21. Sargant, *Battle for the Mind*, pp. 190-91, 210.
22. *Ibid.*, pp. 200-08.

of what the interrogator has suggested to him, but the examiner, often himself under considerable tension and suffering anxiety (his superiors expect him to "crack" the case, for example), becomes the victim of auto-suggestion and comes to believe the reality of his hypotheses. When the suspect "spontaneously" confesses, the examiner is left with no doubt as to his guilt.[23] This sequence of events is, of course, paradigmatic; the point is not that all criminal confessions are false but that they may be false, even in the absence of obvious duress. Demands for corroborating evidence and a willingness to doubt truthfulness of confessions should logically increase in direct proportion to the intensity and duration of anxiety and tension suffered by the suspect.

The likelihood that the phenomena described by Sargant were involved in at least some of the Malmédy "confessions" is very great. Months of imprisonment, part of it in solitary confinement where imagination was given full play, would in itself have produced high levels of anxiety for most prisoners. Some defendants claimed to have heard cries of pain from neighboring cells. Whether the cries were real or imaginary is, in this context, immaterial; the fears of those who claimed to have heard them were, no doubt, genuine. Levels of anxiety must have increased tremendously immediately before interrogation sessions, when prisoners were led, hooded, stumbling, and sometimes falling, to the examination cell. On occasion, they were made to wait outside the cell before being taken in for questioning, still hooded and prey to their own imaginations and the resentment of passing guards. Mock trials, in which the subjects found themselves confronted by a row of uniformed Americans seated behind a table adorned with candles and a crucifix, were certainly calculated to heighten anxiety still further. The effect naturally varied from man to man, but it must be recalled that some defendants were very young and no doubt highly impressionable. Americans on duty at Schwäbisch Hall bore witness to the

23. *Ibid.*, p. 191.

mental state produced in some of the prisoners. One described a young prisoner brought into a cell in which a mock trial had been staged. When the hood was jerked from his head and he was left to survey the solemn scene before him, the prisoner fainted. An American guard spoke in compassionate tones of the terrified weeping of a teen-aged prisoner who had been awaiting interrogation in solitary confinement for several weeks.[24] One suspect hung himself. It is probably no coincidence that the longest and most highly detailed sworn statements were given by the younger prisoners.

Tension and anxiety were produced in many other ways—mysterious notations made during interrogation, the attitude of the interrogator, which varied between extreme hostility and friendliness, an occasional shove or the presence of a weapon, although it might never be used, all had their effect. The vulnerability to suggestion created by prolonged anxiety was heightened in a number of ways. Once prisoners had made sworn statements satisfactory to the interrogators, they were generally released from solitary confinement. Confession, therefore, produced relief from what was, for many prisoners, the greatest torment of incarceration. It must be recalled, too, that the sworn statements were generally dictated to the prisoners by the examiners on the basis of interrogation notes. To be sure, the prisoners were invited to make corrections before signing, but the opportunities for suggestion were obviously tremendous. Assurances that others had already confessed increased suggestibility. The apparent dangers of confession would have seemed diminished if a prisoner were told, as some seemingly were, that the interrogators were not really interested in him (he, they knew, had been following orders) but only in his superiors. Whether or not prisoners were promised lighter sentences in return for confessions is not clear. Some prisoners claimed that this was so; the prosecution/interrogation staff denied it. It is undeniable, however, that some suspects were used as prosecution

24. MMIH, pp. 119, 121, 159.

witnesses and thereby avoided being assigned seats in the defendants' dock. In effect, they had turned "state's evidence," a device that generally (and rightfully) excites suspicion. Major Dwight Fanton, under whose direction the Schwäbisch Hall interrogations had begun, can be faulted for ambiguity in the question of what inducement to confession might be dangled under the prisoners' noses. In his SOP (Standard Operating Procedure) No. 4, Fanton declared, "Any ruse or deception may be used in the course of the interrogation, but threats, duress in any form, physical violence, or promises of immunity or mitigation of punishment, should be scrupulously avoided." But in the succeeding paragraph appeared the following:

> Where a prisoner being interrogated in a crime is implicated in that crime, it is permissible to tell him that he will be recommended as a witness, if such statement to the prisoner will cause him to tell a full or more complete story so that he will be of more value to the case as a witness than as a defendant.[25]

Both through encouragement to use "any ruse or deception" and through imprecision, the interrogators enjoyed wide freedom in the methods adopted to secure sworn statements. In addition, even though Fanton and, later, Ellis occasionally observed interrogations, they understood no German and, therefore, could not know what was passing between the prisoners and their examiners.

Did not the interrogation/prosecution staff realize that their methods risked eliciting statements rather remote from reality? There is no evidence to suggest that they did. In part this was the product of a simplistic view of human psychology but, in fairness, it must be pointed out that many of the insights noted in this chapter received wide circulation only following Western knowledge of and experience with Communist "brain-washing," particularly during the Korean War. Beyond that, the interrogation/prosecution team

25. SOP No. 4, February 7, 1946, *ibid.*, p. 1229.

shared the belief that they were not dealing with ordinary men. The suspects, they believed, were tough and fanatical SS men possessing characteristics both super- and sub-human. Clearly, radical methods were necessary to extract the "truth" from such beings. Moreover, the very fact of membership in the SS must have carried with it a strong presumption of guilt, particularly among the refugee and Jewish members of the interrogation / prosecution staff. It was easy to assume that the prisoners must be guilty of something. The task at hand, therefore, could be conceived as one of simply maneuvering them into admitting it.

This analysis does not imply that the sworn statements were entirely false. Many—probably all—contained partial truths. Some may have been entirely factual. War crimes had been committed and Waffen-SS troopers of Kampfgruppe Peiper had committed them. But the circumstances under which the statements were elicited must produce very grave doubts as to the overall truthfulness of this block of evidence without which the Malmédy case would probably never have come to trial.

Of course, it was not the interrogation / prosecution team that found the defendants guilty on the basis of highly questionable evidence; that was the responsibility of officers of the U.S. Army who sat in judgment in Dachau. Under the loose rules of evidence obtaining in war crimes trials, the sworn statements were admissible, and the cumulative effect of confession after confession had been tremendous. The discrimination of the law member, Col. A. H. Rosenfeld, might have been colored by the fact that he had participated in the Mauthausen Concentration Camp trial, where evidence of SS frightfulness had been most persuasive. But that is probably less important than the rough and ready spirit of "justice" that characterized American attitudes toward war crimes trials. In his influential book *War Criminals: Their Prosecution and Punishment* published in 1944, Sheldon Glueck of the Harvard School of Law warned against permitting "outworn but still sacrosanct legal technicalities" to hinder the punishment of war criminals and urged, instead, a simple untechnical procedure comprehensible to the "common man" and anchored in his "grass roots" sense of justice.[26] That the "technicalities" referred to scornfully by Glueck are the essential defenses of individual rights under Anglo-American law and that demands for simple justice anchored in "grass roots" sensibilities were similar to the arguments used by Nazi jurists in their destruction of due process in Germany were facts easily overlooked in 1944. A similar spirit of expediency is present in a memorandum written for President Truman in June 1945. There, Mr. Justice Robert H. Jackson defended the view (and, in fact, took responsibility for its implementation) that prisoners of war must be denied the protection of international conventions if suspected of war crimes.[27] To a large extent, therefore, both the prosecution team and the bench were simply reflecting powerful currents of opinion present within the American public and government. In its simplest terms, the argument was that sterile procedural rules should not be permitted to stand in the way of justice. But the rules were not sterile; they were, in fact, the guarantors of justice. Their partial suspension produced something less than justice in the Malmédy case.

Although he was not a legal scholar, Everett sensed this. But under the evidential rules in effect at Dachau, he could not succeed in excluding the sworn statements. He was probably dimly aware of the psychological pressures operating on the prisoners which might have produced false confessions but did not fully understand them. Even if he had, such a defense would have fallen on uncomprehending and unsympathetic ears in 1946. In its brief pretrial investigation of alleged irregularities, the Judge Advocate's Office made clear that it would seriously consider only physical violence as duress. The investigating officer, Lt. Col. Edwin Carpenter,

26. Glueck, *War Criminals*, pp. 5, 120.
27. Report of Jackson to Truman, June 7, 1945, p. 3, TP.

recommended that four prisoners who claimed to have been struck be eliminated from the trial.[28] The implications for both defendants and defense counsel were obvious: only the assertion of violence stood a chance of neutralizing the sworn statements, and once these statements had produced convictions and forty-three death sentences, such assertions became the proverbial straws clutched at by drowning men, transformed through calculation and desperate imagination into timbers which ultimately bore the convicts to freedom.

American machinery of military justice moved deliberately and was sufficiently sensitive to criticism so that rather than risk hanging innocent men, it hanged no one. Willis Everett sacrificed health and fortune in his struggle for what he conceived to be justice for his "Malmédy boys." Given the unpopularity of that cause, that was devotion to principle of the highest order. These are morally satisfying aspects of the Malmédy affair. But there are few others. Burton Ellis did his duty in an atmosphere approaching hysteria with personnel ill-suited to the task assigned him and according to legal standards which had received the highest sanction. His career and reputation suffered when those standards rightly came under attack. American soldiers who had surrendered and were entitled to decent treatment had been killed. Nothing done in the courtroom could restore them to life, but the controversy over what took place in Dachau and, earlier, in Schwäbisch Hall denied the dead full juridical resolution of their case.

And what of the Malmédy defendants themselves? All suffered. Some doubtless suffered beyond their due. With the exception of one who died a natural death (if death in prison can ever be considered fully "natural") in Landsberg, all were released. Most sank into welcome anonymity. Two could not. Sepp Dietrich was tried by a West German court for his part in the Nazi "Blood Purge" of 1934 and returned briefly to prison. The last years of his life were spent peacefully as

28. MMIH, p. 895; U.S. v. Bersin, 153/1/000006 (1).

one of the most senior veterans of the Waffen-SS, much revered by his former comrades. Jochen Peiper retained his physical freedom but found neither anonymity nor peace. Peiper's is a disturbing presence, for it resists easy categorization. He had been a model SS officer and a favorite of Heinrich Himmler. His enthusiasm for Nazism and its Führer cannot be seriously doubted. In prison, he mourned his separation from Hitler during the cataclysmic last days of the Third Reich. He could hardly have been unaware of the genocidal policies which it was among the functions of the SS to execute and had, in fact, witnessed a gassing experiment upon a human subject. That he was a ruthless combat leader in the "best" traditions of the Waffen-SS is beyond question. With piercing eyes, aquiline nose, and mouth whose corners sometimes turned down in a hint of cruelty, he lacked only blond hair to match the Hollywood physical stereotype of the SS officer. One of the first Americans to question Peiper after his capture found him "very arrogant," a "typical SS man." Yet, few who came into contact with Peiper failed to sense that there was more to this man than arrogance and ruthlessness. That he sought to maximize his own responsibility in order to reduce the apparent culpability of his men is clear. Far from arrogant, he was characteristically courteous, and the high level of his intelligence was effectively conveyed to Americans through his fluency in English. Burton Ellis has recalled after thirty years the dignity with which Peiper bore himself in very difficult circumstances. He revealed human fears and anxieties. In prison, he agonized over the means by which his wife and children would support themselves; the threat of death weighed heavily upon him. Nevertheless, Peiper was able to contemplate his plight with detachment and occasional flashes of good humor. Of his imprisonment he wrote,

> The transition from resentful Achilles to Don Quixote to, finally, Diogenes was not an entirely painless metamorphosis. But if

one does not take oneself too seriously, things here are little different from the outside. Nothing that happens to oneself is unbearable. I have seen too much of life not to be able to laugh at it; for the thinking man, it is comedy. . . . Cogito!

He twitted those on the outside who offered him encouragement: "Head high!—Stiff upper lip! Don't let your courage slip!—etc. (just like in the old days when the brass would encourage you from the rear by phone to attack)."[29]

But wit is morally neutral. Few would deny that Peiper bore responsibility for the battlefield conduct of his troops and shared guilt for their crimes. Some might argue that he was not adequately punished. Nevertheless, he suffered substantial punishment: over ten years in prison, approximately half of it under sentence of death in solitary confinement. Americans have not seen fit to punish their own war criminals with equal severity for comparable crimes, a matter that did not escape Peiper's attention after the Vietnam War and should not escape ours.

Peiper returned at the end of 1956 to an "outside world" quite different from the one he had known, but he seemed able to integrate himself into it. Ironically, he was employed by the Porsche Motor Company (whose tanks Peiper once used to devastating effect) as (double irony!) manager in charge of American sales. Memories of the bleak period from May 1945 to December 1956 were, of course, unpleasant to him, and it was only with some reluctance that he kept alive a personal relationship with Everett, the American to whom he owed so much.[30] Fonder were the memories of conquest and glory. Peiper was an active member of the Waffen-SS veterans' association (HIAG) within whose ranks pale reflections of the old battlefield comradeship, memories of postwar hardship, and a suspiciously intense nationalism were (and are) kept

29. "Der Mensch. Jochen Peiper im Spiegel seiner Briefe," *Der Freiwillige*, September 1976, pp. 11-12.
30. See Peiper to Everett, December 13, 1959, EP.

alive. He neither sought to escape his past nor could he, and his past ultimately destroyed him.

Peiper's name and purported deeds were kept in public view by the postwar avalanche of popular World War II literature. In 1964, he came under investigation for his role in the death of over thirty civilians in the Piedmontese town of Boves in September 1943 while the Panzergrenadier battalion which Peiper then commanded had been engaged in antipartisan operations. Innocent lives, no doubt, had been lost, the victims of Waffen-SS *Härte* and of the confusing nature of guerrilla warfare. A lengthy inquiry produced insufficient grounds for indictment. Labor protests, in part by Italian "guest workers," cost Peiper his job with Porsche and a succeeding position at the Volkswagen firm in Wolfsburg. The comfortable "bourgeois existence" which Peiper had achieved since 1956 was destroyed.[31] But he again showed remarkable resilience. Feeling in some sense that his countrymen had betrayed him, he took up residence in the tiny village of Traves in eastern France. With the assistance of a local artisan, he built a comfortable house in a wooded setting near the River Saône. For four years he led a modest but, seemingly, happy life, supporting himself and his family as a translator of books. As he passed his sixtieth year, Peiper seemed finally to have found peace. That illusion vanished in the summer of 1976. Following the publication of a sensational article on the notorious resident of Traves in the French Communist newspaper *L'Humanité* and a two-week campaign of threats and harrassment, Peiper was killed in a fire-bomb attack on his house.[32]

Was it just retribution for unexpiated crimes or the politically instigated murder of an old soldier who, whatever his

31. Peiper to author in undated letter of spring, 1976; Michèle Cotta, "L'énigme Peiper," *L'Express,* No. 1306 (19-25 Juillet, 1976), p. 28.

32. *Ibid.,* pp. 28-29; "Qui protège les criminels de guerre?" *L'Humanité,* June 22, 1976, p. 7.

sins, had borne a heavy punishment with dignity and deserved to end his years in tranquility? Answers to the question will not be unanimous. It is clear, however, that at Traves as in Dachau, Peiper was condemned at least as much for what he symbolized as for his actual misdeeds. That may be deplored, but it was perhaps inevitable. In some sense, Peiper was one more victim of the crossroads of death. May he be the last.

SELECTED BIBLIOGRAPHY

UNPUBLISHED DOCUMENTARY SOURCES

The U.S. National Archives, Modern Military Branch
Foreign Military Studies Collection, Manuscripts A-924, C-004, D-154, D-178, ETHINT 10, 11.
Miscellaneous SS Records: Einwandererzentralstelle, Waffen-SS, and SS Oberabschnitte, Microcopy No. T-354, rolls 366, 407, 408, 615, 624, 625.
Records of German Field Commands—Army Groups, Microcopy No. T-311, rolls 18, 276.
Records of the Reich Leader of the SS and Chief of the German Police, Microcopy No. T-175, rolls 33, 90, 96, 204.
U.S. Army, Office of Legislative Liaison, Record Group 319.
U.S. v. Bersin, et al., Record Group No. 153, rolls 1-6.
National Record Center
Military Government, Box 4-1/11 (Malmedy).
Harry S. Truman Library
Papers of Harry S. Truman, Official File.
Berlin Document Center
SS Biographical Records
U.S. Army Film Depository
Malmedy Trial Films
Private Holdings
The Papers of Willis M. Everett, Jr.
Jochen Peiper, "Kommentar zum Buch *Massacre at Malmedy* von Charles Whiting" (unpublished manuscript).

PUBLISHED DOCUMENTARY SOURCES

Malmedy Massacre Investigation. Hearings Before a Subcommittee of the Committee on Armed Services, United States Senate, Eighty-First Congress, First Session, Pursuant to S. Res. 42. Washington D.C.: U.S. Government Printing Office, 1949. (Referred to in this book as MMIH.)

SECONDARY SOURCES

Ackermann, Josef. *Himmler als Ideologe.* Göttingen: Musterschmidt Verlag, 1970.

Appleman, John Alan. *Military Tribunals and International Crimes.* Westport: Greenwood Press, 1971.

Buchheim, Hans, et al. *Anatomie des SS Staates.* 2 vols. Munich: Deutscher Taschenbuch Verlag, 1967.

Cole, Hugh M. *The Ardennes: Battle of the Bulge (U.S. Army in World War II).* Washington, D.C.: U.S. Government Printing Office, 1965.

Eisenhower, John S. D. *The Bitter Woods.* New York: Putnam, 1969.

Glueck, Sheldon. *War Criminals. Their Prosecution and Punishment.* New York: Knopf, 1944.

Griffith, Robert. *The Politics of Fear: Joseph McCarthy and the Senate.* Lexington: University of Kentucky Press, 1970.

Hausser, Paul. *Soldaten wie andere auch. Der Weg der Waffen-SS.* Osnabrück: Munin Verlag, 1966.

Höhne, Heinz. *Der Orden unter dem Totenkopf. Die Geschichte der SS.* Gütersloh: Sigbert Mohn Verlag, 1967.

International Military Tribunal. *Nazi Conspiracy and Aggression. Opinion and Judgement.* Washington, D.C.: U.S. Government Office, 1947.

Klietmann, K.-G. *Die Waffen-SS. Eine Dokumentation.* Osnabrück: Verlag "Der Freiwillige," 1965.

Lehmann, Rudolf. *Die Leibstandarte.* Vol. I. Osnabrück: Munin Verlag, 1977.

Reel, A. Frank. *The Case of General Yamashita.* Chicago: University of Chicago Press, 1949.

Sargant, William Walters. *Battle for the Mind.* Westport: Greenwood Press, 1975.

Stein, George H. *The Waffen-SS. Hitler's Elite Guard at War, 1939-1945.* Ithaca: Syracuse University Press, 1966.

Sydnor, Charles W. *Soldiers of Destruction. The SS Death's Head Division, 1933-1945.* Princeton: Princeton University Press, 1977.

Tauber, Kurt P. *Beyond Eagle and Swastika: German Nationalism since 1945.* 2 vols. Middletown: Wesleyan University Press, 1967.

Waite, Robert G. L. *Vanguard of Nazism: The Free Corps Movement in Postwar Germany 1918-1923.* New York: Norton, 1969.

Weingartner, James J. *Hitler's Guard. The Story of the Leibstandarte SS Adolf Hitler, 1933-1945.* Carbondale: Southern Illinois University Press, 1974.

INDEX

Administration of Justice Review Board, 191–94, 198, 231
Ahrens, Kenneth, 204
Allied Control Commission, 189
Amblève River, 54, 55, 56, 58, 65
Andre, Achille, testimony of, 113
Anti-Semitism, 188, 197, 200, 208, 211, 218, 235, 250
Antwerp, 41
Ardennes offensive, 41–64 *passim. See also* Battle of the Bulge
Aschenauer, Rudolf: and McCarthy, 201; and Finucane, 212; *Seven Years After the Malmedy Trial* (pamphlet), 233; mentioned, 189, 227, 232
Atrocities: and Waffen-SS, 16; and German Army, 16–17; and Red Army, 17, 30; Germans in Russia, 30
Austria, 72
Auxiliary police, 6

Bad Nauheim, military conference at, 44, 45, 92, 102, 103, 123, 181, 241
Bailey, James J., testimony of, 205–07
Baldwin, Senator Raymond: statement of, 201–02; and lie detector, 219–20; mentioned, 199, 200, 204, 212, 221, 229
Baltic area, 31
Baltus, Armand, affidavit of, 145–46
Basic Law (West Germany), 232
Bastogne, 62
Bataan, 1
Battle of the Bulge, 1. *See* Ardennes offensive
Baugnez, descriptions of killings at, 69–70, 80–81, 82, 84–85, 104–09, 110, 204

Bavarian Army, Sepp Dietrich and, 11, 29
Bavarian Party, 238
Bergeval, 62
Berlin: blockade and airlift, 189; War Academy, 33
Bersin, Valentin, 97, 100
Black, Supreme Court Justice Hugo, 187
Blanche Fontaine, 62
Blankenheim Forest, 44, 45
Blockian, Father Louis, affidavit of, 145
Blood Purge, Sepp Dietrich and, 29, 260
Bonn, 43
Boraston, Lt. Col. J. H., 68
Borom, Lt. Col. T. L., 236
Boves, German attack on, 25, 263
Brain washing, 257
von Brandis Free Corps, 31
Bresee, Col. Howard F., 180–85 *passim*
Bullange. *See* Büllingen
Büllingen: Peiper refuels near, 50; purported killings, at, 83, 87, 102, 111–12, 144, 246, 247; purported civilian resistance at, 138; prisoners taken at, 140
Bund Oberland, Sepp Dietrich and, 11, 29
Burton, Supreme Court Justice Harold, 187
Butgenbach, 70
Byrne, First Lt. Robert, 96

Canadian Army, 36, 37, 163
Capitol Hill, 198
Carpenter, Lt. Col. Edwin, 117, 260
Chambers, Col. J. M., 212, 228
Cheneux: prosecution charges and, 103;

267

killing admitted at, 162; killing at, 247; mentioned, 57, 59, 60
Chicago Tribune, 196
Chrisenger, Capt., 128
Civilians, reflections on killing of, 247–48. *See also* Guerrillas; Maqis
Clay, General Lucius: accepts Harbaugh's recommendations, 185; commutes death sentences, 231–32; mentioned, 184, 191, 195, 197, 198
Clevinger, Staff Sgt. George, 71
Cold War, 189
Colinet, Antoine, testimony of, 114
Cologne, 195
Commissar Order, 16
Committee for the Preservation of Rights of the Sentenced in the Malmédy Case, 233
Concentration camps, 6, 8, 8*n*. See also *names of camps*
Confessions: admissibility of, 184; in petition for writ of habeas corpus, 186; psychology of, 253–58. *See also* Sworn statements
Congressional Record, 211
Crawford, Lt. Col. Homer B., 76, 96, 111–12, 189
Crossroads, killings at, 102, 239–41. *See also* Baugnez, descriptions of killings at
Czechoslovakia, 189

Dachau: SS training installation at, 13, 22; defendant imprisoned in concentration camp at, 37; liberation of concentration camp at, 95; Malmédy Massacre trial at, 97–164 *passim*; concentration camp case, 101; Neuhäusler imprisoned by Nazis in, 189; investigations of war crimes trials at, 190
Daily Worker, 197
Dalbey, Brig. Gen. Josiah T.: announces verdict, 161; sentences convicts, 164; conversation with Everett, 170; mentioned, 99, 100, 121, 123, 130, 139, 143
Daub, Cpl. Carl, 106
Davis, Congressman James C., 188, 197
Delcourt, Henri, testimony of, 113
Demelhuber, Karl-Maria, 12
Demyansk, 32

Denver Post, 196
Detmold, 234
Dieringhausen, 234
Dietrich, SS-Oberstgruppenführer Sepp: and creation of Leibstandarte, 6; personal qualities of, 11; and Goebbels' propaganda, 18; career of, 29–30; prisoner, 73; and prosecution charges, 102; sentence of, 164; sentence of reconfirmed, 185; release of, 238; mentioned, 9, 14, 20, 21, 26, 31, 33, 40, 42, 63, 92, 93, 97, 100, 123, 131, 154, 160, 181, 182, 250, 260
Dittmann, SS-Unterstrumführer Dr. Willibald, 61
Dixon, Kenneth L., 196
Dluski, Sgt. John M., and Honsfeld killings, 111
Dobyns, Samuel, testimony of, 109
Don River, 23
Douglas, Supreme Court Justice William, 187
Dresden, 212
Dwinnell, Lt. Col. John S.: cross-examines Kirschbaum, 119–20; examines McCown, 126; summarizes evidence, 155–57; appointed to War Crimes Board of Review, 183; testimony of, 209–10; mentioned, 130, 132, 164, 184, 186

Eastern Front, Waffen-SS combat methods and, 17–18
Eiche, Theodor, 12, 32
Einsatzgruppe D, 189
Eisenhower, Gen. Dwight, 234
Elias, Jean, testimony of, 115
Ellis, Lt. Col. Burton F.: assumes leadership of investigation, 81; cross-examines Peiper, 135–39; questioned by McCarthy, 214–16; mentioned, 76, 93, 96, 103, 117, 121, 129, 140, 143, 146, 160, 189, 199, 208, 213, 214, 257, 260
Elowitz, Morris: testimony of, 146; mentioned, 76, 96, 164
Engel, Gen. Gerhardt: testimony of, 123; mentioned, 47
Engelsdorf. *See* Baugnez
Epirus Army, 30

Eupen, 68
European Recovery Act, 221
Euskirchen, 43
Evangelical Church, 232
Everett, Col. Willis M., Jr.: appointed to Malmédy case, 96; summarizes evidence, 158–60; at sentencing, 164; and Jews, 169; attitude toward trial, 167–70; leaves Germany, 173–74; loyalty to U.S. Army, 173; files for writ of habeas corpus, 185–87; and Peiper, 262; mentioned 117, 125, 142, 143, 146, 173, 183, 189, 191, 193, 195, 197, 208, 209, 215, 235, 236, 237, 238, 259, 260
Evidence, rules of, 98–99

Fanton, Major Dwight: assigned to Malmédy case, 72; interviews Peiper, 74; assembles investigators, 74; and McCarthy, 213–14; mentioned, 76, 199, 220, 257
Final pleas of defendants, 161–63
Finucane, James, 210, 211, 212–13
Flanigan, Francis, 209
Fort Benning, Ga., 125
Fort Meade, Md., 148
France: defendants and fighting in, 22, 26, 35; government of withdraws defendant from trial, 160; mentioned, 23
Frankfurter, Supreme Court Justice Felix, 187
Free Corps: and SS ideology, 9; Sepp Dietrich and, 30; spirit of, 31
Freimuth, Arvid: suicide of, 118; in petition for habeas corpus, 187
Freising, 73, 224
Friedrich, Carl J., 192, 193
Frings, Josef Cardinal, 195
Froide Cour, 60

Geneva Convention of 1929: defendants' status under, 98, 213–14; and sworn statements, 121–22: American violations of, 126, 129; mentioned, 71, 137, 150
Genghis Khan, 150 and 150n, 153
George, Senator Walter F., 188
German Army: and Waffen-SS, 15; and atrocities, 16–17

German Army units (arranged numerically): First Panzer Corps, 33; Fifth Panzer Army, 41; Sixth Panzer Army, 21, 30, 34, 41, 42, 92–93, 97, 102, 123, 124, 154, 181; Twelfth Volksgrenadier Division, 47, 49, 123; Thirteenth Panzer Division, 33; Fortyeighth Panzer Corps, 24; 150th Panzer Brigade, 45, 132–33
Germany, Federal Republic of, 232, 238
German Legion, 31
Gestapo, 14, 206, 221
Glueck, Sheldon, 258
Goebbels, Paul Joseph, 18
Gottgläubig, significance of in SS, 38–39
Graves Registration, 66
Gregoire, Maria, 145
Gregoire, Regina, 114, 115
Guerrillas: and Waffen-SS combat methods, 18; in Italy, 25; German fear of Belgian, 47; in Büllingen, 50; in Stavelot, 54–55; and German orders, 123, 124; mentioned, 210
Guth, Paul C., 224

Habeas corpus, motion for filed, 185–87
Hague Convention: and military necessity, 157; mentioned, 150
Handy, Gen. Thomas T., 236, 238
Harbaugh, Col. James M., 176, 179, 180, 183, 184, 185, 192, 193
Härte: component of SS ideology, 10; Heydrich embodiment of, 14; defendant judged to possess, 28; mentioned, 15, 43, 244, 263
Hartrich, Edwin, 173
Harvard School of Law, 258
Hausser, Paul, 11–12
Heidelberg, 235
Heppenbach, alleged atrocity at, 71
Hepscheid, 50
Heydrich, Reinhard, 14
HIAG (Hilfsgemeinschaft auf Gegenseitigkeit der Soldaten der ehemaligen Waffen-SS), 262
High Commissions for Germany, 238
Himmler, Heinrich: and SS-Verfügungstruppe, 6; and SS ideology, 7, 8, 11; aims for SS Cavalry, 21; and Peiper, 22, 23, 137; and Dietrich, 29; and

Priess, 32; mentioned, 2, 3, 19, 34, 39, 261
Hiroshima, 166, 212
Hitler, Adolf: and SS Verfügungstruppe, 6; and appointment to German Chancellorship, 6; and Dietrich, 11, 29, 30; and Peiper, 22, 168; and Ardennes offensive, 44, 92, 241; and prosecution charges, 102; at Landsberg, 165; mentioned, 3, 5, 28, 29, 45, 151, 181
Hitler Youth: Peiper's membership in, 21; significance of membership in, 38
Hoey, Senator Clyde, 199
Honsfeld: killings at, 83, 110–11, 246; fighting in, 50; prosecution charges and, 102; prisoners directed to, 140
Hoods, use of in interrogations, 118
Hubbert, Cecil, 175
L'Humanité, 263
Hungary, 72, 245
Hunt, Senator Lester, 200, 204, 216, 220, 228, 252–53
Hunter, Col. Rosser M., 65–66
Huy, 43, 53, 55

International Court of Justice, 188
International Military Tribunal: and SS criminality, 8; and SS Cavalry, 21
Interparliamentary Congress, 224
Iron Cross, defendants win various grades of, 22, 24, 25, 26, 28, 32, 33, 62, 244
Iron Division, 31

Jackson, Supreme Court Justice Robert, 187, 259
JAGD (Judge Advocate General's Department), 170, 172, 173, 174–75, 236
Jonsten, Anton, 144
Junkerschulen. See SS

Kampfgruppe Peiper. See Waffen-SS
Karan, Dr. Max, 222–23
Kefauver, Senator Estes, 199, 200, 220
Kharkov, 36
King, John W., 203
Kingston, Kenneth, testimony of, 245

Kirschbaum, Joseph: cross-examination of, 119–20; testimony of, 146
Knorr, Dr. Edward, 194
Koessler, Maximilian: trial analysis of, 170–72; mentioned, 174, 175, 177, 178, 179, 195
Korea, 235
Korean War, 257
Kraemer, SS-Oberführer Fritz: career of, 33–34; prepares for Ardennes offensive, 43; and orders, 92; testimony of, 123–24; sentence of, 164; sentence of reviewed, 185; mentioned, 40, 93, 97, 131, 160, 182
Kremlin, 231

La Gleize: Peiper falls back to, 60; purported kilings at, 83, 86, 89, 126–27, 144–46, 147–49; and prosecution charges, 103; Americans prisoners in, 128, 129, 140
Landsberg Prison, 165, 185, 188–89, 215, 228, 229, 234, 235, 236, 238, 252, 260
Langer, Senator William, 198
Lanzerath, 49
Lary, Virgil P.: testimony of, 104–09, 245; mentioned, 204, 240
Law No. 10 of Allied Control Council, 152–53
Lawrence, Lt. Col. Charles W., 190, 191, 211
Leer, Dr. Eugen, 227
Leibstandarte SS Adolf Hitler. See Waffen-SS units
Leiling, Dr. Otto, 114, 115
Lester, Cpl. Raymond, 105
Lie detector, 219–220
Lienne River, 57
Ligneauville: alleged atrocity at, 71; and prosecution charges, 102; mentioned, 53, 54, 56, 231
Llandovery Castle case, 153
Losheim, 47, 49
Low Countries, 22
Lublin, 34, 35
Luftwaffe: defendants transferred from, 28, 36; paratroopers of in Kampfgruppe Peiper, 45
Lutre Bois, 103

MacDonald, Lt. Col. B. J. S., 68
Maidenek, extermination camp at, 35
Malmédy, 51, 56, 63, 70, 109
Malmedy Massacre Investigation Hearings, 200–31
von Manstein, Field Marshal Erich, 32
von Manteuffel, General Hasso, 41
Maquis, 115, 248
Mauthausen, concentration camp at, 101, 258
McCarran, Senator Pat, 199
McCarthy, Senator Joseph: invited to join senate investigation, 200; sources of support for, 200–01; in Malmedy Massacre Investigation Hearings, 202–22; mentioned, 3, 199, 230, 231
McCloy, John S., 237
McCown, Major (later Lt. Col.) Hal D.: capture of, 60, 125; escape of, 61–62; background, 125; testimony of, 125–29; Rosenfeld on, 226–27; mentioned, 140, 145
Meuse River, 41, 42–43
Meyer, SS-Oberführer Kurt, 163
Micklewaite, Col. Claude, 96, 117, 174
Milford, Massachusetts, 237
Military Government Courts, conduct of, 116
Military necessity: as defense, 156–57; and Hague Convention, 157; mentioned, 153–54
"Mock trials": criticism of, 180; noted in petition for habeas corpus, 186–87; Perl explains, 219; mentioned, 117, 119, 171, 216, 229, 251
Moderscheid, 50, 51, 68
Mohnke, SS-Oberführer Wilhelm, 44, 45, 61, 62, 64, 73n, 132
Morris, T/5 Charles L., on Honsfeld killings, 110–11
Msha River, 24
Murphy, Supreme Court Justice Frank: and Yamashita case, 185; approached by Everett, 186; mentioned, 187

Nagasaki, 166, 212
Narvid, Capt. Benjamin, 100–101
National Council for the Prevention of War, 201, 210, 232
Nazi Party: Organization Book of, 5;

defendants members of, 26, 28, 29, 31, 34, 35, 37, 38; Aschenauer member of, 189; mentioned, 6, 168
Neuhäusler, Bishop Johannes, 188–89
New York Bar, 170
New York Herald Tribune, 173
The New York Times, 196, 237
Nietzsche, Friedrich, 9
Normandy, 35, 36
Nuremberg Trial, 151, 166, 187

Ohlendorf, SS-Obergruppenführer Otto, 189
Oranienburg, defendant guard in concentration camp at, 37
Order Police, 14
Otto, Lt. Col. Martin H., 72

Paine, Tom, 159–60
Pearl Harbor, 1
Peiper, Jochen: youth and career of, 20–26; and Ardennes offensive, 41–64 passim; capture of, 72; interviewed, 74; and Petit Thier incident, 79; evidence against, 88, 89; sworn statement of, 89–91; and battlefield conduct, 91, 92; testimony of, 129–40 passim; thoughts of during trial, 167–68; review of conviction and sentence of, 181–82; freeing of, 238; speculation of on "massacre," 240n; verbal exchange with Hunt, 252–53; last years and death of, 261–63; mentioned, 40, 80, 100, 104, 214, 224, 232, 234, 236, 237, 243, 245, 250
Peiper, Waldemar, 21
Pekartschina, Peiper's attack on, 24–25
Perl, First Lt. William R.: cross-examination of, 118–19; Peiper interrogated by, 130–32; testimony of, 146, 147, 218–19; and McCarthy, 203: background of, 216–18; mentioned 76, 77, 78, 96n, 141, 205, 206, 207, 222, 228
Perry, Lt. Col. Charles J., 215, 216
Petit Thier: atrocity at, 79, 135, 182, 247; and prosecution charges, 103: mentioned, 62, 131
Pfeffer-Wildenbruch, Karl, 12
Polish refugees, 250

Porsche Motor Company, 262
Priess, SS-Gruppenführer Hermann: life and career of, 30–33; and orders received, 92–93; sentence of, 164; mentioned, 20, 40, 47, 62, 97, 131
Prisoners' Aid Society, 232
The Progressive, 211
Prokhorovka, 36

Quakers, 201

Raymond, Col. John M., 192, 193
Red Army: and German atrocities, 16; and treatment of Germans, 17; mentioned, 72
Red Cross, 248
Reed, Supreme Court Justice Stanley, 187
Reichsführer SS. *See* Himmler, Heinrich
Reichssicherheitshauptamt, 14
Reviews of trial, 170–72, 176–85
Ricker, Dr. John, 223
Riga, 31
Roman Catholic Church, 232
Rosenfeld, Col. Abraham H.: rules on severance, 101; testimony of, 225–27; mentioned, 99, 100, 104, 114, 123, 140, 149, 169, 209, 258
Royall, Secretary of the Army Kenneth C.: establishes commissions, 190; statement of, 201; mentioned, 188, 191, 198, 199, 211
Rulien, Miles, 144
von Rundstedt, Field Marshal Gerd, 242
Russell, Senator Richard, 200
Rutledge, Supreme Court Justice Wiley: and Yamashita case, 160, 185; mentioned, 187

SA, purge of, 6
Sachsenhausen, defendant prisoner in concentration camp at, 37
St. Edouard's Sanitorium, 59
St. Louis Star Times, 166
St. Vith, 51, 71
Salm River, 55, 62
Saône River, 263
Sargant, William Walters, 254, 255
Schenk, Capt. Edward W., 70
Schmid, Carlo, 238

Schnell, Dietrich, 194
"Schnell procedure." *See* "Mock trials"
Schörner, Gen. Ferdinand, 32
Schwäbisch Hall, prison at: suspects imprisoned in, 77; interrogation techniques in, 117, 141, 146; suicide in, 118; purported conditions at, 194, 207–08, 224, 227–28, 229, 252–53
Security and Intelligence Corps, 149
Seelos, Gerhard, 238
Selective Service, 212
Senate Resolution 39, 198
Senate Resolution 42, 200, 229
Sentences: defense requests shooting, 163–64; hanging imposed, 164n; reviews of, 176, 178–79, 181–82, 185, 236
Severance, defense motion for, 100–01
SHAEF (Supreme Headquarters, Allied Expeditionary Force): receives word of massacre, 65; court of inquiry of, 68–72 *passim*
Shumacker, Capt. Raphael: argues against severance, 101; explains use of hoods, 118; cross-examines Ziemssen, 124–25; testimony of, 146; case summary by, 150ff; mentioned, 76, 96, 142, 164, 199, 214
Siebenbürgen, 80
Signal Corps, 66
Simpson Commission: deliberations and report of, 191–93; mentioned, 195, 198, 231
Simpson, Judge Gordon, 190, 191, 211
Skorzeny, SS-Sturmbannführer Otto, 45, 133
Sloan, Herbert, 223–24
Social Darwinism, 10, 25
Social Democratic Party, 238
SOP No. 4, 257
Soviet Union, 197, 254
Sporrenberg, Lt. Gen. of Police, 34
SS: motives for joining, 28; defendants join, 29, 31, 36, 37, 76; attitudes of, 243; investigators' attitudes towards, 258
SS Cavalry, 31
SS Junkerschulen: curriculuml of, 13; example of at Bad Tölz, 13, 26, 78; at Braunschweig, 13, 244; at Klagen-

furt, 13; at Prague, 13; role of, 14; human product of, 14–15; defendants attend, 22, 26, 28: mentioned, 27
SS Political Alert Units, 6, 26, 32
SS Totenkopfverbände: defendants members of, 27, 37; religion in, 39
SS Verfügungstruppe: role of, 6–7; ideology of, 7–11; Hausser inspector of, 11–12; officer corps of, 11–15; Dietrich and, 29; motives for joining, 39. *See also* Waffen-SS
Stalinism, 17
Stars and Stripes, 73
Stavelot: taken by Peiper, 54; recaptured by Americans, 58; purported killings at, 87, 102, 113–15, 171, 177; purported civilian resistance at, 134
Stegle, T/5 "Johnie," 111
Steiner, SS-Obergruppenführer Felix, 12
Steiner, Frank, 205, 206
Steyr, 72
"Stool pigeons," 251
Stoumont: purported killings at, 103, 142, 171, 178; purported civilian resistance at, 134; mentioned, 58
Straight, Lt. Col. Clio: and Koessler's review, 172; mentioned, 167, 175–80 *passim*, 184, 192
Die Strasse, 233–34
Streckenbach, Bruno, 16
Strong, Herbert, 97, 130, 208–09, 226
Superior orders, as defense, 153–54, 157–58, 162. *See also* Law No. 10 of Allied Control Council; *Llandovery Castle* case
Sutton, Lt. Col. Granger: cross-examines Perl, 118–19; summarizes evidence, 158; testimony of, 210; mentioned, 97, 155, 164
Sworn statements: texts of, 77–78, 84–85, 86, 89–91; and instructions on prisoners of war, 87–88; and hatred of Americans, 88; importance of, 93–94, 116; defense efforts to exclude and discredit, 116, 118–20, 121–22, 158; Shumacker defends, 152, 154; Bailey; on, 206–07; reflections on character of, 249–58
Switzerland, 63

Technical Manual for Legal and Prison Officers, 98–99
Teil, Kurt, 207–08
Thon, Harry: testimony of, 146; mentioned, 76, 205, 206, 207, 208
Traves, 263, 264
Treaty of Versailles, 33
Trois Ponts: American defense of, 55–56; and prosecution charges, 103
Truman, President Harry, 237, 259
Tydings, Senator Millard, 200

Ukraine, 37, 46
U.S. Army units (arranged numerically): First Army, 65–68 *passim*, 71; Third Army, 17; Third Infantry Division, 99; Fourth Corps, 96; Seventh Armored Division, 53; Ninth Armored Division, 53; Twelfth Army Group, 65; Eighteenth Airborne Corps, 59; Thirtieth Infantry Division, 57, 58, 59, 66; Forty-fifth Infantry Division, 95; Eighty-second Airborne Division, 128; Ninety-ninth Infantry Division, 47, 109; 285th Field Artillery Observation Battalion, 51, 67, 104
U.S. Congress, 188
USFET (U.S. Forces, European Theater), 72, 75, 76, 122, 164
U.S. House of Representatives, 237
U.S. Senate: Armed Services Committee of, 199, 200, 220; Investigations Subcommittee of, 199, 200; Judiciary Committee of, 199
U.S. Supreme Court: and Yamashita case, 122, 185; and Malmédy case, 185–87; mentioned, 174, 188, 191, 193, 196
Utley, Freda, 240

van Roden, Judge Leroy: testimony of, 210–12; mentioned, 190, 191, 195, 196
Vernichtung, meaning of, 63–64
Veterans of Foreign Wars, 237
Veucy, 57
Vietnam War, 262
Vinson, Supreme Court Chief Justice Frederick, 187
Volkswagen Company, 263

Voorhees, Lt. Col. John S., 68
Voorhees, Asst. Secretary of the Army
Tracy, 198

Waffen-SS: origins and development
of, 5–7; German Army and, 15–16;
reputation of, 16–18 *passim*, 24, 83,
93, 134–35, 141; ideology and attitudes of, 7–11, 22, 38, 53, 123, 169,
244, 245, 263; manpower needs of,
28, 37
Waffen-SS units (arranged numerically): First SS Panzer Corps, 31, 33,
34; First SS Panzer Division "Leibstandarte SS Adolf Hitler," 2–3, 6,
23, 25, 42; Second SS Panzer Division
"Das Reich," 34; Third SS Panzer
Division "Totenkopf," 32, 34, 37;
Sixth SS Panzer Army, 72; Twelfth SS
Panzer Division "Hitler Jugend," 50;
Kampfgruppe Peiper, 41–64 *passim*,
67, 73–74, 91, 102, 131, 132
Wahler, Lt. Wilbert: cross-examines
Dobyns, 109; and cross-examination
procedures, 143; mentioned, 101
Walki, 24
Walters, Frank: summarizes evidence,
157–58; mentioned, 155
Wanne: and prosecution charges, 103;

killings at, 162, 171, 247; mentioned,
62
War Crimes Board of Review, 180, 182,
184
War Crimes Modification Board, 235
*War Criminals: Their Prosecution
and Punishment*, 258
War Department, 2
Werbomont, 125
Wheaton's *International Law*, 156
Wisconsin, 199, 201
World War I, 9
Wounds, suffered by massacre victims,
66
Wünsche, Max, 23

Yale Law School, 72
Yamashita, Gen. Tomoyuki, 74, 160,
185, 187

Zach, S. Sgt. Henry Roy, testimony of,
68–70
Zhitomir, 24
Ziemssen, SS-Obersturmbannführer
Dietrich: testimony of, 124–25; post-
trial activities of, 232–33; mentioned,
44
Zuffenhausen, 75, 130, 135, 147

Design: Dave Pauly
Composition: Freedmen's Organization
Lithography: Thomson-Shore, Inc.
Binder: Thomson-Shore, Inc.
Text: Compugraphic Garamond 11/13
Display: Beton Extra Bold and Stymie Bold
Paper: #50 Bookmark
Binding: Kivar 9 Kidskin, Mandarin Red

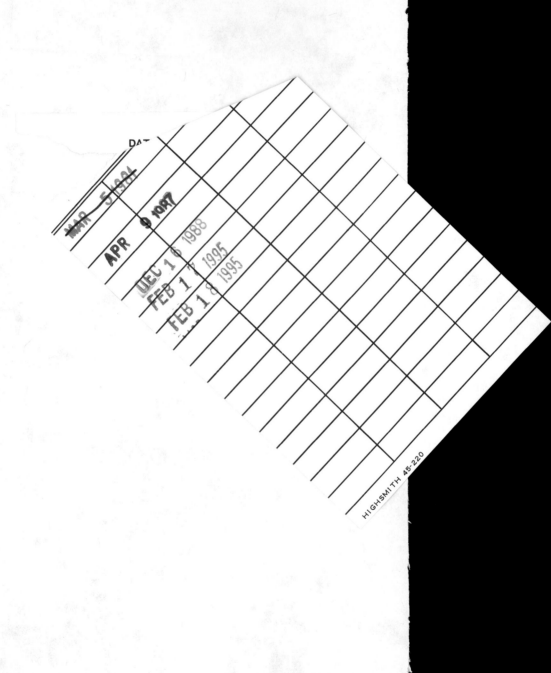